# Additional Praise for *Scaling Up*

"There is no one in the business of the business world like Verne Harnish.

"Unlike all too many authors and gurus who are obsessed by statistics, followers of the latest trends, and seekers of celebrity, Verne is firmly centered on the success and well-being of business leaders, who respect, trust, and benefit from the thinking, assistance, and advocacy of this passionate protagonist of our global business community.

"Verne is genuinely devoted to the business challenges and ambitions of his vast population of loyalists. A day doesn't pass without his instant response to requests for help. He has an uncanny ability to connect businesses with reliable resources who can make invaluable contributions to their success.

"Now, Verne has published a new book filled with timely insights about the benefits and problems associated with scalability. For everyone who is curious about barriers to growth; concerned about what's around the corner; or suffering from unrelenting 3 a.m. nightmares about their businesses' sustainability and that urgent need for an aggressive new growth strategy, this is a 'got-to-read-right-now' book from today's compulsive storyteller of business content, Verne Harnish."

— Robert H. Bloom, strategist and author of *The Inside Advantage* and *The New Experts*

"Scaling up is every entrepreneur's dream — and nightmare. Hypergrowth is terrifying, and it's most often success that kills great companies. This book goes way beyond advice, offering specific habits, processes, and outlines to ensure that growth is the beginning, not the end, of success. Nobody understands the day-to-day reality of hypergrowth like Verne Harnish, and his book is full of the tough love you'd want from an outstanding mentor: fully aware of the challenges but determined to overcome, not duck, them. With great structured thinking and not a word wasted, highly appreciative of the value of time, and immune to sentiment, this book will help anyone determined and smart enough to follow its advice."

— Margaret Heffernan, serial entrepreneur and author of *Willful Blindness, Women on Top,* and *A Bigger Prize*

"Delivers the practical lessons that most B-schools don't. If you want to grow *your* business faster, buy *Scaling Up*, turn to Chapter 14, and read 'The Power of One.' Not next week. Not tomorrow. Now."

— John Mullins, professor of entrepreneurship at London Business School, and author of *The Customer-Funded Business, The New Business Road Test*, and (with Randy Komisar) *Getting to Plan B*

"*Scaling Up* is a blueprint for building a growth company. With this book, Verne has pulled back the curtain on how the fastest-growing companies in the world fuel their growth. *Scaling Up* gives you an insider's view into the inner workings of the most successful companies on earth. A must-read for an ambitious entrepreneur."

— John Warrillow, founder of The Sellability Score and author of *The Automatic Customer: Creating a Subscription Business in Any Industry* and *Built to Sell: Creating a Business That Can Thrive Without You*

"I didn't think it possible to discuss Strategy and Cash in the same book — or People and Execution in the same book, for that matter — but *Scaling Up* deals with all four topics in a compelling way. Verne Harnish and team have found juicy examples and simple rules that will help any growing business avoid costly mistakes. A great read for entrepreneurs and anyone trying to be a personal engine for growth in any organization."

— Richard A. Moran, CEO of Accretive Solutions and author of *Navigating Tweets, Feats, and Deletes*

# SCALING UP

How a Few Companies Make It...
and Why the Rest Don't

Verne Harnish
and the team at Scaling Up

ForbesBooks

Published by Forbes Books
www.forbesbooks.com

Revised Edition
ISBN 978-0-9860195-9-3

Printed in the United States of America

12 11 10 9 8 7 6 5 4 3 2 1

## THE DEDICATION

To the leaders who scaleup companies — and their families and teams that support them. You are the engines of our economies and the source of our freedom.

# THE ACKNOWLEDGEMENTS
## Thank You!

First, we want to thank the thousands of CEOs and executives who have utilized our open-source tools and provided input on how to improve them and their application to scaling up organizations. Your contribution to the community of "scaleups" is greatly appreciated.

## Business Leaders

Several of these leaders and their companies are highlighted throughout the book. Thank you for openly sharing your stories and lessons learned so that we might all benefit, specifically: Rob Banks, Jeff Booth, Gene Browne, Dwight Cooper, Fred Crosetto, John DeHart, Gunjan Doshi, Barrett Ersek, Mark Fullerton, Ben Godsey, Sam Goodner, Vishal Gupta, Roger Hardy, McKeel Hagerty, Jack Harrington, Alan Higgins, Nelson Jacobson, Mike Jagger, Kees de Jong, Rick Kay, Clate Mask, Henry McGovern, Lois Melbourne, Sanjeev Mohanty, Simon Morrison, Scott Nash, James Perly, David Rich, Stephen Roche, Alan Rudy, Ken Sim, Naomi Simson, Carey Smith, Jerry South, Adam Sproule, John Stepleton, Scott Tannas, and Graham Weston.

Two entrepreneurs went way beyond the call of duty to review the galley copy and provide extensive, critical, and detailed feedback, which resulted in significant changes to the style, approach, format, and design of the book: Kevin Daum, serial entrepreneur, author, and brilliant columnist for *Inc.* Magazine; and Jimmy Calano, founder of CareerTrack, who gave Verne his start as an author and was one of the early investor in Gazelles (now Scaling Up). Everything you like about *Scaling Up*, credit them. Everything you don't, it's likely because we ignored their advice!

## Thought Leaders

We've always believed it takes a "village of gurus" to help a company scale up, and it's no different for Scaling Up and the content in this book. We would like to especially thank Jim Collins, the late W. Edwards Deming, Pat Lencioni, Tom Peters, Hermann Simon, and Jack Stack. Their pioneering contributions to the world of business have helped millions and shaped many of the ideas you find in this book. In addition, we would like to thank Greg Alexander, David Allen, John Assaraf, Laurie Bassi, Josh Bernoff, Bob Bloom, Travis Bradberry, Greg Brenneman, Mark Burton, Jim Cecil, Ram Charan, Robert Cialdini, Chip Conley, the late Stephen Covey, Stephen M.R. Covey, Aubrey Daniels, Peter Diamandis, Mohamed Fathelbab, Frances Frei, Seth Godin, Marshall Goldsmith, Mark Goulston, Vijay Govindarajan, Adam Grant, Brian Halligan, Brad Hams, Darren Hardy, Chip Heath, Margaret Heffernan, Sally Hogshead, Luke Hohmann, Tony Hsieh, Mark Johnson, Hubert Joly, Rick Kash, Eric Keiles, Dave Kerpen, Todd Klein, Jim Kouzes, Mike Lieberman, Giovanni Livera, Jim Loehr, David Marquet, Ron McMillan, James McQuivey, Ari Meisel, Youngme Moon, Geoffrey Moore, Richard Moran, Anne Morriss, John Mullins, Alexander Osterwalder, Bob Parsons, Daniel Pink, Joe Polish, Joe Pulizzi, Fred Reichheld, Rich Russakoff, Tom Sant, David Meerman Scott, Robin Sharma, Brian Souza, Michael Bungay Stanier, Jim Stengel, Jeff Thull, Bill Treasurer,

Lynne Twist, John Warrillow, Pat Williams, and Liz Wiseman — all of whom have contributed to our various Scaling Up Summits around the world and our continuing online course offerings.

## Marketing and Coaching Partners

Critical to spreading the use of our tools around the world are our marketing partners: Patrick Cheo, Southeast Asia; Daniel Marcos, Latin America; Kees de Jong, Europe; Christo Popov, Eastern Europe/Middle East/Africa; Raghu Potini, India; and Preston Kuo, China.

We also want to thank our growing association of 200+ coaching partners around the globe, led by John Ratliff and his team. Many of our Scaling Up Certified Coaches (and those completing their certification) read through an advance copy of this book and provided detailed feedback. These current partners include John Anderson, Andy Buyting, Rick Crossland, Mark Fenner, Hayley Erner, Ken Estridge, Bill Gallagher, Lluis Gras, Jeremy Han, Nicolas Hauff (and his son Christopher), Hazel Jackson, Cheryl Beth Kuchler, Matt Kuttler, Neale Lewis, Dale Meador, Jeff Moore, Bahaa Moukadam, Paul O'Kelly, Craig Overmyer, and Howard Shore.

## Key Collaborators

There are a handful of key collaborators without whom this book would not have become a reality: Patrick Thean, who worked closely with Verne to create the original version of the Growth Tools; Kevin Lawrence, who provided significant help in updating the tools and served as an early sounding board in shaping the "Execution" content; and Alan Miltz (and his team), who contributed much of the "Cash" content, which was sorely missing in the first draft. A special thank you to Sebastian Ross, peer coach and dear friend, who contributed extensively to the "People" content and met weekly to review and provide important feedback for the entire book.

## The Council and Team

Scaling Up's "council" provided important support, encouragement, and feedback throughout the pro- cess of creating the book. This team includes the CEOs of the various Scaling Up companies: John Ratliff, Daniel Marcos, Andy Bailey, and Doug Walner.

We would like to especially thank the team at Scaling Up's HQ, including Joanne Costello, Missy Giltner, Kathleen McKune, Donna Whitwell, Mike Davies, Cameron Harnish and Jean Santos. Missy provided overall project management for the original book, keeping us on deadline and driving all the extensive details (printing, distribution, warehousing) of getting a book selfpublished. And thank you to our outsourced technology team, led by Raghu Potini — with direct support from Amruth Mekala, Dayanand Chilveri, Purity Correia, and Praveen Salitra, who created and continually update the *scalingup.com* websites and distribute the "weekly insights."

No book gets completed without a direct team of writers, editors, and designers. Thank you to writing partner and editor Elaine Pofeldt, who helped extensively with this book and supports the *Fortune* magazine and Growth Guy syndicated columns; Wendy Zuckerman, who provided extensive copyediting for this book (any mistakes were because we ignored her advice!); Hank Gilman, former editor and champion at *Fortune*, who helped with the book title; and Jun-Hi Lutterjohann, who designed the book cover, Growth Tools, and graphics, and typeset the entire book. A special thank you to the team at Forbes Books including Adam Witty, Evan Schnittman, Beth LaGuardia, Dee Kerr, and John Witty.

## Family and Friends

Thank you to Stephen and Shelly Watkins, Derek and Rachel Benham, David Meerman and Yukari Scott, and Rajeev and Arpita Agarwal for their support (and homes) in providing hideouts for completing the book. And a special thank-you to Catalan friend and partner Cesar Martinell.

Last, thank you to Verne's family for their support and patience through the writing of this book.

# THE TABLE OF CONTENTS

# THE INTRODUCTION
## Tools for Scaling Up

---

*If you want to teach people a new way of thinking, don't bother trying to teach them. Instead, give them a tool, the use of which will lead to new ways of thinking.*

— R. Buckminster Fuller
Designer, inventor, futurist

---

"Purpose moves people to make the world a bit better for all," notes Naomi Simson, Co-Founder and Director of Big Red Group, the largest experience marketplace in Australia and New Zealand. "We have an ethos of valuing experiences over material goods."

With a purpose to "shift the way people experience life," her company offers over 10,000 experiences people can gift and enjoy. Her long-term goal is to "serve an experience, sustainably, every second somewhere on earth" by 2030, up from one every 2.5 minutes in 2017 when she reset the firm's Big Hairy Audacious Goal (BHAG).

Her journey with Scaling Up began in 2005, when her team attended Verne's two-day Rockefeller Habits workshop in Sydney. There she set her first BHAG -- to serve up 2 million experiences by 2015. This was quite a leap — 250x — from the 7500 experiences they had served up since the founding of the firm.

"Yet, we got their two years early and at the time we set it…it was sooooo improbable and hard to imagine," exclaims Naomi. "We proved it was possible."

Naomi's original purpose for launching RedBalloon in 2001, when she left corporate life to become a mum in 1996, was "to spend more time with her little ones Natalia (now 20) and Oscar (now 18)." Her desire was to play with the children during the day and run RedBalloon at night. 22 years later her firm is on course to generate a quarter billion in revenue and more importantly, continue to scale its impact of providing people with experiences that will be remembered for a lifetime.

Dutch entrepreneur Hester Anderiesen Le Riche is on a similar purpose-driven path. Founder of Tover, she wants to change the way the world looks at people with cognitive challenges. "How do we accomplish this?" explains Hester. "With serious games with a proven track record of positively influencing quality of life. Playing for a better existence. That's what we call 'purposeful play'."

Bootstrapping the business, the first seven years, Hester raised capital and has scaled revenue eight-fold in five years. Tover offers 100+ games in 14 countries. And working with our Dutch coaching partners, she has also raised her own game. Originally targeting a BHAG of one million players per day over the next decade, she has 30x'd her goal to serve 30 million players per day by 2030. She's upping her impact.

Don Wells, Chief Empowerment Officer for the San Diego-based non-profit Just in Time for Foster Youth (JIT), has his organization on-purpose as well: "To engage a caring community to help transition age foster youth achieve self-sufficiency and well-being." Currently serving 1600 foster youth annually between the ages of 18 and 26, his team originally set a BHAG to 10x their impact in the community to 16,000 youth annually in ten years.

Initially skeptical if the Scaling Up methodology would be helpful for a social venture, Don and his team attended a couple sessions with a Scaling Up coach. As Don describes, "it started to change our thinking of what was possible." As a result, the team stepped up their vision and presented to their board a credible plan to serve 100,000 youth annually by 2032.

Notes Don, "we came out of those sessions with a new resolve and the tools to make it happen." It resulted in a statement where JIT is committed to "Building a nationwide Reliable, Responsive, Real '100K Community' of life changing choices and transformative impact for young people impacted by foster care."

Don shares how "100K Community" is now the rallying cry for JIT over this next decade and he and his team are excited for the possibility to have a much greater impact in supporting foster youth who are aging out of the system.

*Diane Cox, JIT co-founder; Tasha Matthews, JIT participant; Don Wells, Chief Empowerment Officer; James Hidds-Monroe, JIT alum & staff member; and Belen Gomez, Don's "Daughter on Purpose"*

## Scaling Purpose and Profit

Naomi, Hester, and Don are three of over 80,000 organizations around the globe using the Scaling Up/Rockefeller Habits tools and techniques to scale their impact while increasing their revenues, their capital raises, and their cash (donations). Dozens are detailed in the following pages and hundreds of mini-case studies and articles are available at *www.scaleups.com*.

For all of us at Scaling Up — and our 200+ coaching partners on six continents — what gives us great joy is helping you and your team scale easier with less drama. Increasing your financial performance is critical: doubling your cash flow, tripling your industry average profitability, and dramatically increasing the valuation of the firm. All this helps you sleep better at night and makes it a lot more fun to scale.

Yet it's not just about the money. Scaleups (you!) are the unsung heroes of their local and global economies — generating most of the net new jobs and innovations in their respective communities. And directly, you are responsible for the livelihoods of millions of people. This is a responsibility we take seriously in supporting you and recognize the pressures this creates for you and your team especially during chaotic times — and it's expected to be chaotic the entirety of these "roaring 20s."

Creating a great culture where people can thrive; provide products and services that delight customers; and generate extraordinary returns for all this effort, is what brings us joy. And whether your purpose is to spend more time with your family or have a significant impact in your corner of the world, for over 40 years we've been helping organizations of all sizes and geographies scaleup successfully. These tools and techniques have stood the test of time so long as you and your team have a growth mindset and willingness to learn.

## Most Important Routine/Habit

Leaders are learners! When Larry Page, CEO of Google was asked how he learned to run a company, he responded "I read a lot." For instance, he read three books on how to name things. Bill Gates, for decades, maintained his famous "Think Week", devouring a record 112 books/articles/whitepapers during one session.

Mark Cuban, the outspoken owner of the Dallas Mavericks, reads 3 hours per day. His goal is to find just one idea he can use to give him and the over 150 companies in which he's invested an edge in the marketplace. Mark Zuckerberg's personal development priority is reading a book every two weeks, exceeding by two the number of books (24/year) *Topgrading* author Brad Smart found separated A-player executives from B and C players.

And Charlie Munger, reflecting on the 50-year record of investing by his partner Warren Buffett, credited "his (Warren's) first priority would be reservation of much time for quiet reading and thinking, particularly that which might advance his determined learning, no matter how old he became."

All these accomplished biz leaders know one thing — nothing interesting can come out of your thoughts that you don't put in first. Having a natural curiosity and thirst for learning separates the good from the great in our experience. Happy learning!

# THE OVERVIEW
## People, Strategy, Execution, Cash

---

**EXECUTIVE SUMMARY:** *A 20-minute overview providing busy executives with a summary of the practical tools and techniques for scaling up a business. Aligned around 4 Decisions every business leader must make — People, Strategy, Execution, and Cash — they also represent the four main sections of this book where more specific how-to information, along with mini-case studies and examples, are detailed.*

**WARNING:** *This overview contains a lot of lists to keep it concise — you'll be drinking from a fire hose! But it will prep you for the rest of the book where the ideas will be served up in more bite-sized pieces. You might also want to read the last, three-page-long chapter titled "Next Steps."*

---

Start up, Scale up, Sc@%w up …

… or Stall out (fail to scale)!

This sequence describes the life cycle of most businesses as they move up the S-shaped curve of growth. The key to scaling this curve:

1. Attracting and keeping the right *People*;

2. Creating a truly differentiated *Strategy*;

3. Driving flawless *Execution*; and

4. Having plenty of *Cash* to weather the storms.

Millions of people start new ventures, and of those that survive, 96% remain "mice." It's only a few — the "gazelles" or scaleups — that scale beyond $10 million, $100 million, or $1 billion in revenue, the path that Naomi Simson's RedBalloon (mentioned in "The Introduction") is on. This book gives you the tools to scale up 10x or more.

Eventually, many growing firms — gazelles — get sold, some to "elephants" (and a rare few grow up to become elephants themselves), often crushing the innovative culture of what was a thriving, growing company. Completing the cycle, many of

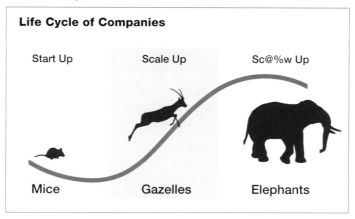

**Life Cycle of Companies**

Start Up — Scale Up — Sc@%w Up

Mice — Gazelles — Elephants

these big companies turn bad — often downright evil — and later become extinct or irrelevant at best. (Read Nassim Nicholas Taleb's breakthrough book *Antifragile: Things That Gain From Disorder* for ways to inoculate your family, company, and country from this tragic ending.)

Because of the sheer number of start-ups and small businesses, there is a huge market for the myriad number of books supporting these entrepreneurs — the two best being Michael E. Gerber's *The E-Myth Revisited* and Eric Ries' *The Lean Startup*. The large number of entrepreneurs also forms a significant enough voting bloc to garner attention from politicians.

In turn, the sheer size of the Fortune 500 companies provides a huge feeding trough for the thousands of business gurus and the 11,000 new business books they release each year. These large firms employ expensive lobbyists to do their bidding with governments, receiving all kinds of special favors.

Largely ignored, by gurus and governments, are the older, high-impact growth firms. Though they generate almost all of the innovation and job growth in economies, there are not enough of them to garner the favorable attention of politicians or book publishers. Verne and his team are focused on helping cities and countries create scaleup eco-systems to support the already robust startup eco-systems that exist.

## High-Impact Firms — Apple and Starbucks

In a study for the US Small Business Administration titled "High-Impact Firms: Gazelles Revisited" the authors note: "High-impact firms are relatively old, rare and contribute to the majority of overall economic growth. On average, they are **25 years old**, they represent between **2 and 3 percent** of all firms, and they account for almost all of the private sector employment and revenue growth in the economy."

To underpin this "older" idea, we looked at the trajectory of two well-known gazelles: Apple and Starbucks. Apple, which started in 1976, had only 9,600 employees when it released the iPod in 2001, its 25th anniversary. The rest is history. All the phenomenal growth of Apple in revenue and employment (154,000 in 2021) occurred after this historic milestone, resulting in the 2nd largest-market-cap company in the world at the time of this book's publication.

Starbucks followed an almost identical growth path, launching in 1971 and taking the first 20 years to perfect its business model and reach 100 locations. By its 25th anniversary, it was at 1,000 stores and ventured outside the US for the first time. Since then, it has rocketed to more than 32,000 stores in 80 countries and more than 383,000 employees.

To paraphrase Steve Jobs, "I'm always amazed how overnight successes take a helluva long time." If you've been in business less than 25 years, you still have time to make it big; if it has been more than 25 years, and you've not scaled up, it's never too late!

# Scaling Up

"How do we scale up the business?" is a question we've heard from countless leaders over the years, prompting the name and focus of this book. "How to survive the process" with your sanity and relationships intact is the second question.

## Dumbest in the Room

Senior leaders know they have succeeded in building an organization that can scale — and is fun to run — when they are the dumbest people in the room! In turn, if they have all the answers (or act like they do), it guarantees organizational silence, exacerbates blindness (the CEO is always the last to know anyway), and means the senior team ends up carrying the entire load of the company on their backs. The best leaders have the right questions, but turn to their employees, customers, advisors, and the crowd to mine the answers. Every business is more valuable to the degree that it does not depend on its top leader. For more on these topics, read Margaret Heffernan's book *Willful Blindness: Why We Ignore the Obvious at Our Peril* and Liz Wiseman's *Multipliers: How the Best Leaders Make Everyone Smarter*.

To scale up a business from a handful of employees to something significant (i.e., build a company that has a chance to both put a "dent in the universe" and dominate its industry), our tools and techniques focus on **three deliverables**:

- Reduce by 80% the time it takes the top senior team to lead the business (operational activities)
- Refocus the senior team on market-facing activities
- Realign everyone else (onto the same page) to drive execution and results

And when our tools are successfully implemented, organizations attain these **four outcomes**:
- At least double the rate of cash flow
- Triple the industry average profitability
- Increase the valuation of the firm relative to competitors
- Help the stakeholders — employees, customers, and shareholders — enjoy the climb

Yet there are **three barriers** to scaling up, which we'll discuss in the next chapter:

- **Leadership:** the inability to hire and develop enough leadership throughout the organization who have the capabilities to predict, delegate, and coach

- **Scalable infrastructure:** the lack of systems and structures (physical and organizational) to handle the complexities in communication and decisions that come with growth

- **Marketing:** the failure to scaleup an effective marketing function capable of attracting new customers, talent, advisors, and other key relationships to the business

## Scaling Up

Thus, to overcome these barriers your team must master, using our tools, **four fundamentals**:

- **In leading People**, take a page from parenting: Establish a handful of rules, repeat yourself a lot, and act consistently with those rules. This is the role and power of Core Values. If discovered and used effectively, these values guide all decisions (people and process) in the company.

- **In setting Strategy**, follow the definition from the great business strategist Gary Hamel. You don't have a real strategy if it doesn't pass two tests: First, what you're planning to do really matters to enough customers; and second, it differentiates you from your competition.

- **In driving Execution**, implement three key habits: Set a handful of *Priorities* (the fewer the better); gather quantitative and qualitative *Data* daily and review weekly to guide decisions; and establish an effective daily, weekly, monthly, quarterly, and annual meeting *Rhythm* to keep everyone in the loop. Those who pulse faster, scale faster.

- **In managing Cash**, don't run out of it! Pay as much attention to how every decision affects cash flow as you would to revenue and profitability.

With these fundamentals in mind, you're ready to scale.

## Flow Like a River

For many years, we've used a "climbing Mt. Everest" metaphor for scaling a company. Identify a summit, create a plan, and then persevere through a painful and grueling climb (represented by this image used in our workshops and the first edition of this book)!

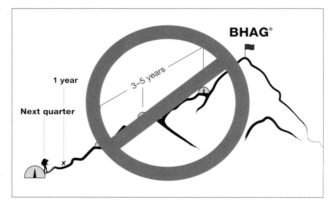

We feel it's time to let go of this worn-out analogy. In Verne's work with an organization he co-founded, Geoversity (Mother Nature's U), it's clear that nature moves the other direction — down the mountain!! It's the same direction civilization has preferred, to be near the oceans. As we'll discuss in "The Barriers" chapter, it's better to go with the flow — to catch the right wave and ride it — than fight the winds of the marketplace.

And like a river, as it flows from Everest to the ocean, the overarching rule is taking a path of least resistance rather than drudge/fight your way up a hill. We'll see in the

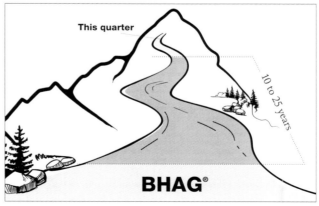

Strategy section that the ultimate "job to be done" by all our products and services is to make everything easier, not harder, for customers and employees. The same in growing a business. Our tools are designed to make it easier to scale, not harder — and without all the drama along the way (unlike most Everest climbing adventures and the movies that depict them!)

Thus, guided by a set of Core Values (rules of the river/sea) and Purpose (why make the journey in the first place), we set our sights on a Big Hairy Audacious Goal (BHAG) representing a far-off destination to be reached in 10 to 25 years. Then we set sail, determining waypoints along the route, a series of three- to five-year targets divided up into annual goals. These are further reduced to specific actionable steps the voyage takes over the next few weeks, adjusting tactics (tacking) as the market conditions dictate. Granted, there may be Class V rapids and storms along the way — and times you might have to walk your raft around obstacles/constraints — but at least you're headed in the right direction, down the mountain.

In the end, it's keeping everyone focused on the destination and then deciding the appropriate next course correction (quarterly Priority) — all along keeping in mind Bill Gates' admonition that "most people overestimate what they can do in one year and underestimate what they can do in ten years."

Everything in between this quarter and the next 10 to 25 years is a WAG: a wild-ankle guess! There are no straight lines in nature or business. As a winding river must follow the contours of the landscape on its way to the ocean, a business must navigate the undulations of the marketplace on the way to its BHAG. The key is keeping your eye on the prize and adjusting course accordingly.

*"Routine sets you free."*

And along the journey, there is a set of habits — routines — that will make the journey easier. "Routine sets you free" is a key driving principle behind our methodologies and tools. You may set a goal to lose weight, but unless you change some daily and weekly routines, it will never be accomplished. Goals without routines are wishes; routines without goals are aimless. The most successful business leaders have a clear vision and the disciplines (routines) to make it a reality.

## Wasted Debate

Nothing is more maddening than hearing teams debate whether a certain idea is applicable in a business-to-business or business-to-consumer engagement. In the end, we're all in the same business: people to people. None of us sell to companies; we deal with the people (consumers) inside these companies, who have the same motivations, challenges, and emotions as any other person.

The other needless delineation is between product and service companies. In the long run, most product companies add on services to increase profitability and most service companies productize their offerings to make them easier to sell. We recommend that you avoid these debates, and consider most of the examples in this book applicable to any organization in any industry.

# Scaling Up 4D Framework Getting to Results

A proven business growth method used by thousands of growing companies to achieve **_RESULTS_**.

**1** **Driver** (with Accelerators)

Coaching – Advisors, Consultants, Coaches
Learning – Continuous Business Education (CBE)
Technology – Management Accountability System

**2** **Demands** (Balance)

People (Reputation) – Employees, Customers, Shareholders
Process (Productivity) – Make/Buy, Sell, Recordkeeping

**3** **Disciplines** (Routines)

Priorities – The Main Thing
Data – Qualitative/Quantitative
Meeting Rhythms – Daily, Weekly, Monthly, Quarterly, Annual

**4** **Decisions** (Right Questions)

People – Happiness/Accountability
Strategy – Revenue/Growth
Execution – Profit/Time
Cash – Oxygen/Options

**!** **Results**

2x Cash Flow • 3x Profitability • 10x Valuation • More Time!

# 4D Framework

McKinsey has its 7-S Framework for large companies; we have our 4D Framework for growth firms. This framework evolved from the fundamentals, barriers, and goals described earlier and was based on this quote attributed to Albert Einstein: *"Everything should be made as simple as possible, but not simpler."* Scaling a business is a complex endeavor and requires robust — yet simple enough — tools and techniques to get the job done.

The framework includes these elements (see diagram on Page 10):

1. **Driver:** Leaders drive implementation of the Rockefeller Habits with their teams. Execution is much easier if they and their teams engage in coaching, embrace learning, and encourage the use of new technologies to accelerate implementation of our tools.

2. **Demands:** Leaders have to balance two often competing demands on the business — People and Process. This requires simultaneously maintaining a great reputation with the employees, customers, and shareholders (the People side of the business); and improving the productivity of how the firm makes/buys, sells, and tracks these transactions (the Process side of the business).

3. **Disciplines:** To effectively execute, there are three fundamental disciplines (routines): Set *Priorities*; gather quantitative and qualitative *Data*; and establish an effective meeting *Rhythm*. It's in these meetings, debating the data (the brutal facts!), where the priorities emerge.

4. **Decisions:** Ultimately, all of the above require some decisions. To scale the business requires getting four key decision sets — People, Strategy, Execution, and Cash — absolutely right, and there are right and wrong answers. Shortchange any one element and you're not maximizing your opportunity.

 **WARNING:** *Since* Mastering the Rockefeller Habits *was written, many bits and pieces of our 4D Framework and tools have been copied by others. In the process, several have oversimplified our work to the point that it might still be helpful — setting a few priorities and key performance indicators (KPIs) is better than nothing — but there is huge potential left on the table in terms of revenue and profit. "Simple, not simpler" is our aim, as Einstein warned.*

In turn, we know that it takes a "village of gurus" to help a company and that no one person has all the answers. Therefore, we'll be referencing many important books and ideas that fill in important gaps around leadership, sales, marketing, hiring, etc.

## Right Questions

Our last guiding principle in designing the 4D Framework:

*We have the answers, all the answers; it's the question we do not know.*

Most of the teams we work with are wicked smart. With enough perseverance and grit they'll find answers. Our concern is they might be working on the wrong question. Much of our work is helping leadership teams formulate the right questions. Once they get the questions right, the answers tend to appear.

Each of the 4 Decisions — People, Strategy, Execution, and Cash — is anchored by an overarching Key Question. And the accompanying Growth Tools (our label for the collection of one-page worksheets summarized next) are designed to focus teams on specific questions driving growth and performance for each of the 4 Decisions areas of the business.

*"We have the answers, all the answers; it's the question we do not know."*

So, to start implementing the 4D Framework, the first question is, *"Which of the 4 Decisions — People, Strategy, Execution, and Cash — needs the most attention next?"* Start there! We have a complimentary individual 4 Decisions Assessment available at *scalingup.com* to help you determine your starting point.

It's important to note that all four decisions are intertwined and connected. We've learned that the root constraint to scaling might be the decision before (see diagram) the one the senior team decides is the immediate constraint.

For instance, if the team feels the #1 constraint to scaling is Strategy, it could be that you don't have the right People (or anyone) working on Strategy. In turn, if Execution is the perceived constraint, then maybe you're trying to execute a flawed Strategy. Continuing around, Cash constraints could be due to sloppy Execution; and the lack of key People could be due to Cash constraints.

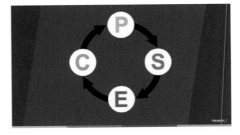

So, the first step is agreeing, as a team, the entry point to our 4D Framework. Once you agree, consider the underlying constraint might be the decision just ahead of it!!

Our methodology and tools are like crossword or Sudoku puzzles. Start where you can and work your way through. There is no specific sequence. However, we do have five initial "next steps" outlined in the last chapter.

The following overview of each decision will further help you choose where to start in scaling up the business.

# People

**KEY QUESTION:** *Are the stakeholders (employees, customers, shareholders) happy and engaged in the business; and would you "rehire" all of them?*

Do you have the "right people doing the right things right" inside the organization?

*"Right people doing the right things right."*

Do you feel the same about all the key relationships surrounding the business? Would you keep all your existing customers? Are you happy with your investors/bank? Are your vendors supporting you properly? Are your advisors — accountants, lawyers, consultants, and coaches — the best for the size of the organization and future plans? The toughest decisions to make are when the company has outgrown some of these relationships and you need to make changes.

It starts with your own relationship goals and priorities, then being clear who are the leaders accountable for the main functions and processes that drive the business.

*The tools (three-quarter-size copies are included in the introduction to the "People" section):*

**One-Page Personal Plan (OPPP):** Our personal and professional lives are intertwined — and best if aligned. This tool looks at four key decisions — Relationships, Achievements, Rituals, and Wealth — which mirror the four key decisions for the business: People, Strategy, Execution, and Cash. Having a strong and fulfilled personal life provides an important foundation for sustaining your efforts in the business.

**Function Accountability Chart (FACe):** Jim Collins, author of *Good to Great: Why Some Companies Make the Leap... And Others Don't*, emphasizes the importance of getting the right butts in the right seats at the top of the organization. After all, the bottleneck is

always at the top of the bottle! The FACe tool provides a list of seats (functions) that all organizations must fill.

> *"The bottleneck is always at the top of the bottle!"*

You want to delegate these functions to people who fit your culture and pass two tests:

1. They don't need to be managed.
2. They regularly wow the team with their insights and output.

Next designate one or two key performance indicators (KPIs) for each function, defining objectively what activities each senior leader needs to be focused on day-to-day. Last, decide on a handful of results/outcomes accountable to each function (i.e., who is accountable for revenue, gross margin, profit, cash, etc.). These outcomes normally represent line items on the financial statements.

When completed, this one-page accountability tool helps you diagnose where you have people and performance gaps on the leadership team.

**Process Accountability Chart (PACe):** Most work flows horizontally across the various functions. Functions are not isolated cells. When these functions aren't working well together, the firm can stall. These processes are also how both your customers and employees experience the business — they are key to providing great CX and EX, which will give you great SX (shareholder experience)!

This chart provides a place to delineate the four to nine processes that drive the business (i.e., the processes for developing and launching a new product; for attracting, hiring, and onboarding new employees; for billing and collecting, etc.).

Next, designate who is accountable for each process, which can be tricky since these processes cut across various functions and there might be some ego/control issues between the functional heads.

Last, decide on two or three KPIs that track the health of the process — the most important being the length of time, from start to finish, for a specific process. We'll discuss how a variety of organizations are utilizing the principles of Lean, a management practice invented by Toyota, to streamline and speed up their processes.

**"The Team" chapter:** There's a continual war for talent. We'll share guerilla marketing techniques for attracting a large number of qualified candidates and review the Topgrading methodology for interviewing and selection.

In retaining employees and keeping them engaged, we'll cover the five activities of great (vs. good) managers (we prefer the term "coaches" — more on this later):

- Help people play to their strengths.
- Don't demotivate; dehassle.
- Set clear expectations and give employees a clear line of sight.
- Give recognition and show appreciation.
- Hire fewer people, but pay them more (frontline employees, not top leaders!).

# Strategy

 **KEY QUESTION:** *Can you state your firm's strategy simply — and is it driving sustainable growth in revenue and gross margins?*

It's time to break apart a 50-year-old business term — *strategic planning* — and think about it in terms of two distinct activities: *strategic* thinking and execution *planning*. Each requires two very different teams and processes.

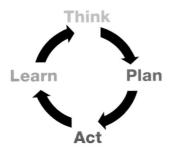

Strategic thinking requires a handful of senior leaders meeting weekly (it's not sufficient to do strategy work once a quarter or once a year) in what Jim Collins calls "the council." It's a meeting separate from the standard executive team meeting. Rather than getting mired in operational issues, the strategic thinking team is focused on discussing a few big strategic issues including those outlined in the SWT and 7 Strata tools summarized below.

Execution planning, in turn, requires a much larger team engaged in implementing the broader strategy. Setting specific annual and quarterly priorities, outcomes, and KPIs is best if middle management and frontline employees are involved. They are closer to the day-to-day operational issues of the company, and their participation in setting the plan creates better buy-in.

Add in both disciplined *action* and active *learning* activities and you have a simple Think, Plan, Act, Learn cycle of strategic planning.

*The tools (three-quarter-size copies are included in the introduction to the "Strategy" section):*

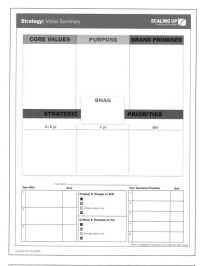

**Vision Summary:** If you want to get everyone on the "same page" you need the page! For companies just getting started implementing the Rockefeller Habits as well as firms with 50 employees or fewer, the Vision Summary provides a simplified One-Page Strategic Plan (OPSP) framework. And for larger firms taking advantage of the more detailed aspects of the OPSP, the Vision Summary provides a one-page format to communicate key aspects of the company's vision to employees, customers, investors, and the broader community.

> *"If you want everyone on the same page, then you need this page first."*

**SWT:** We've augmented the standard SWOT (strengths, weaknesses, opportunities, and threats) process with a tool called the SWT (strengths, weaknesses, and trends).

Whereas the SWOT process drives leaders to look inward at both their company and industry challenges, the SWT focuses on exploring broader external trends beyond their own industry or geography. It's a powerful tool to spot opportunities before the competition and prevent "inside/industry myopia."

**The 7 Strata of Strategy:** This tool represents the seven components (stratum) of a robust, yet simply stated, strategy. It's designed to provide the kind of differentiation and barriers that allow you to dominate your niche in the marketplace.

The seven components:

1. What word(s) do you own in the minds of your targeted customers (e.g., Google owns "search")?

2. Who are your core customers, what three Brand Promises are you making them (e.g., Southwest Airlines promises Low Fares, Lots of Flights, Lots of Fun), and how do you know you're keeping these promises (Kept Promise Indicators, a play on KPIs)?

3. What is your Brand Promise Guarantee (e.g., Oracle has been advertising the chance to win $10 million if its Exadata servers don't outperform the competition by a factor of five)?

4. What is your One-PHRASE Strategy that likely upsets customers (Apple's "closed system") but is key to making a ton of money and blocking your competition?

5. What are the three to five Activities that fit Harvard strategist Michael Porter's definition of the essence of differentiation (e.g., IKEA's furniture needs assembly)?

6. What is your X-Factor — a 10x to 100x underlying advantage over the competition — that completely wipes out any and all rivals?

7. What are your Profit per X (economic driver) and BHAG® for the company? These come straight from Jim Collins' hedgehog framework.

**One-Page Strategic Plan (OPSP):** The OPSP is our best-known and most widely used tool. It's designed to drive alignment, accountability, and focus.

The body of the plan consists of seven columns organized around seven basic questions you need to answer if you want to accomplish anything: *Who, What, When, Where, How, Why*, plus *Should/Shouldn't*. We've aligned these with standard strategic planning language like Core Values, Purpose, Annual Priorities, etc. — but anchor the plan with these simpler questions.

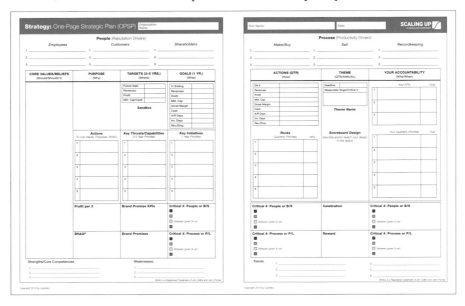

The first three columns of the OPSP represent the strategic thinking part of the plan supported by the work done on the 7 Strata; the last four columns represent the execution planning part of the plan. The OPSP has space along the bottom to summarize your SWT and along the top to list the key metrics monitoring your reputation (People) and productivity (Process).

# Execution

 **KEY QUESTION:** *Are all processes running without drama and driving industry-leading profitability?*

You know you have execution issues if three things exist:

*"Is the company generating three times industry average profitability?"*

1. There is needless drama in the organization (e.g., something shipped out late; the invoice was wrong; someone missed a meeting; etc.).

2. Everyone seems to be working more hours, spinning their wheels, or spending too much time fixing things that should have been done right the first time.

3. Most important, the company is generating less than three times industry average profitability.

 **WARNING:** *Companies can get by with sloppy execution if they have a killer strategy or highly dedicated people willing to work 18-hour days, eight days per week to cover up all the slop. Just recognize you're wasting a lot of profitability and time (i.e., you'll burn both cash and people in the process!)*

*The tools (three-quarter-size copies are included in the introduction to the "Execution" section):*

**Who, What, When (WWW):** Improve the impact of your weekly meetings by taking a few minutes at the end summarizing *Who* said they are going to do *What, When*. This isn't about micromanagement; this is about excellent management and being clear in both communication and accountability.

The key is setting a "when" that is no longer than the time between weekly (or monthly) meetings. And if you have a more substantial initiative, the key is breaking it into pieces (eat the elephant one bite at a time) that can be accomplished within a few weeks.

**Rockefeller Habits Checklist™:** There are 10 fundamental habits that support the successful execution of your strategy — habits that haven't changed for 100 years since John D. Rockefeller implemented them, becoming the wealthiest person ever and building what has morphed into one of the largest companies today: ExxonMobil.

These habits dramatically increase profitability and reduce the time it takes to lead the business. And like the checklists that are critical to the airline industry in making sure planes stay in the air, consider these 10 habits as a "preflight" checklist for keeping your company growing and ensuring that it doesn't stall out.

**WARNING:** *You'll drive everyone in the organization crazy if you implement all of these habits at one time. The key is focusing on one or two each quarter, giving everyone roughly 24 to 36 months to install these simple, yet powerful, routines. Then it's a process of continually refreshing them as the company scales up.*

The habits ("Routines that set you free!"):

1. ***The executive team is healthy and aligned.*** Here we pull a page from Patrick M. Lencioni's *The Five Dysfunctions of a Team: A Leadership Fable*, a book we recommend that all leaders peruse (it's a quick read). In essence, your executive team needs to have a level of trust that permits true debate and constructive conflict to occur. What prevents this in large companies is politics; what blocks it in growth firms is friendship. Members of the team must embrace its diversity (the more the better) and be willing to challenge each other in making decisions and exposing the brutal facts.

2. ***Everyone is aligned with the #1 thing that needs to be accomplished this quarter to move the company forward.*** As mentioned earlier, scaling a firm is about taking one significant step at a time and then checking data and adjusting accordingly. It is about setting a quarterly goal, providing the company with a badly needed finish line every 90 days, vs. just running and running and running. It also affords everyone an opportunity to celebrate or commiserate — and have some fun along the way. This is the power of setting a Quarterly Theme, which we'll discuss in depth later.

3. ***Communication rhythm is established and information moves through the organization accurately and quickly.*** The #1 challenge when two or more people are working together is communication (anyone married?). The key is an effective daily, weekly, monthly, quarterly, and annual Meeting Rhythm, which, when executed properly, actually saves everyone a tremendous amount of time. It's counterintuitive, we know. Specific agendas for each meeting will be detailed in the "Execution" section.

4. ***Every facet of the organization has a person assigned with accountability for ensuring goals are met.*** If communication is the #1 challenge, then nailing down accountabilities as the company scales is #2. This needs to be clear both vertically (across functions) and horizontally (across processes) throughout the organization. And it really gets messy when the organization moves to discrete business units.

5. ***Ongoing employee input is collected to identify obstacles and opportunities.*** A key component of the weekly qualitative data you need to guide the business must come from your employees, especially your sales channels and your frontline employees. They are closer to the action. We recommend that each senior leader formally talk to one employee each week and ask, "What should the company Start/Stop/Keep doing?" Pay particular attention to the "stops." These are the roadblocks you need to eliminate from the company to keep people motivated.

6. ***Reporting and analysis of customer feedback data is as frequent and accurate as financial data.*** The second key component of the weekly qualitative data that you need to guide the business must come from customers. We suggest that each senior leader formally ask customers questions that

are more about gathering market intel, especially about competitors, than discerning whether they like your particular product or service.

7. ***Core Values and Purpose are "alive" in the organization.*** These are the handful of rules (Core Values) that you'll use to guide all the HR systems in the company: hiring, feedback, rewards and recognition, handbook, etc. And the Purpose (a better word than "mission") provides the critical "why" behind everything you do (i.e., what difference is your company making in the world?).

8. ***Employees can articulate the following key components of the company's strategy accurately.*** You want all employees to align their actions with the strategy of the company. To do this, they need to know and understand the company's 10- to 25-year goal (BHAG®); who the core customers are; the three Brand Promises everyone needs to keep; and what the company does — and be able to explain it when asked (the elevator pitch).

9. ***All employees can answer quantitatively whether they had a good day or week*** (*Column 7 of the OPSP*). Is each employee or team clear on their priorities and KPIs for the week? And do they know how they did that week? People love to know the score; thus the attraction of video games, sports, fundraisers, competitions, etc.

10. ***The company's plans and performance are visible to everyone.*** We're big on sports analogies, and we strongly suggest stealing one idea from that industry: having huge scoreboards visible to everyone like the RedBalloon scoreboard highlighted in The Introduction. We'll share additional examples and photos of growth firms that do.

# Cash

**KEY QUESTION:** *Do you have consistent sources of cash, ideally generated internally, to fuel the growth of your business?*

Growth sucks cash. This is the first law of entrepreneurial gravity. And nothing ages a CEO and his or her team faster than being short of cash. In fact, Jim Collins and Morten T. Hansen, in their best-selling book *Great by Choice: Uncertainty, Chaos, and Luck — Why Some Thrive Despite Them All*, found that successful companies held three to 10 times more cash assets than average for their industries, and they did so from the time they started. (We highly recommend that you read this book, Collins' first that directly addresses growth firms.)

*"Growth sucks cash — the first law of entrepreneurial gravity."*

Yet many growth company leaders pay more attention to revenue and profit than they do to cash when it comes to structuring deals with suppliers, customers, employees (think bonus plans), or investors/banks. And when they receive their monthly financial statements, the cash flow statement is either nonexistent or ignored.

The quickest action you can take is to have your CFO give you a modified cash flow statement every day detailing the cash that came in during the last 24 hours, the cash that flowed out, and some idea of how cash is looking over the next 30 to 90 days. This will keep cash top-of-mind and give you a great feel for how cash is flowing through the business.

It's also critical to know your Cash Conversion Cycle (CCC). It's a technical term for how long it takes, after you spend a dollar/euro/yen on rent, utilities, payroll, inventory, marketing, etc., for it to make its way through your business model and back into your pocket. So that you can see how to calculate this, we recommend that you read a classic *Harvard Business Review* article titled "How Fast Can Your Company Afford to Grow?" by Neil C. Churchill and John W. Mullins.

*The tools (three-quarter-size copies are included in the introduction to the "Cash" section):*

**Cash Acceleration Strategies (CASh)** — Break down the CCC into four components, and brainstorm one of three ways to increase the cash flow in the business. We've had many clients double their operating cash flow immediately after working through this tool. It's also a great exercise to do with middle managers, to strengthen their understanding of how cash flows through the organization and to illustrate how everyone can make a positive contribution to improving the CCC.

The goal is to reverse the first law of entrepreneurial gravity and develop a viable business model in which the faster you grow, the more cash you generate — through larger deposits, faster collections, shorter sales and delivery cycles, etc. Then you've built a company that can self-fund its own growth.

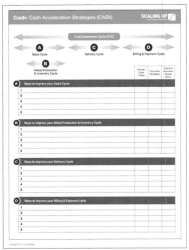

**The Power of One:** The 7 main financial levers available to managers to improve cash and returns in the business are:

1. **Price:** You can increase the price of your goods and services.

2. **Volume:** You can sell more units at the same price.

3. **Cost of goods sold/direct costs:** You can reduce the price you pay for your raw materials and direct labor.

4. **Operating expenses:** You can reduce your operating costs.

5. **Accounts receivable:** You can collect from your debtors faster.

6. **Inventory/WIP (work in progress):** You can reduce the amount of stock you have on hand.

7. **Accounts payable:** You can slow down the payment of creditors.

The tool calculates the benefit to cash if a 1% or one-day change is made to each of these levers.

# Final Recommendations

Downloadable documents of the various tools, in multiple languages, are available at *scalingup.com* at no charge. Feel free to modify them and to suggest changes. They remain an open-source set of tools, and they are constantly being improved by the community of growth company executives using them.

## Weekly Insights: Sign Up!

If you like the style and substance of the book, you can receive a very concise weekly email of best practices for leading a growing firm: ideas we pick up each week from executives like you.

Simply send an email to *verne@scalingup.com* and put "weekly insights" in the subject line. And please include a first and last name and your title, and tell us where your company is based. We'll add you to our expanding list of over 100,000 leaders of growing companies.

## Technology and Coaching Support

We've created several cloud-based tools to make implementation of the Rockefeller Habits 2.0 much easier and faster. The first is an online version of Verne's 2.5-day Scaling Up Master Class providing a convenient way to educate your team and create a common language around our tools and techniques. Visit *www.ScaleUpU.com*.

We've also created Scaling Up Scoreboard, an online and mobile-based app that hosts our one-page tools and helps you track all your cascading KPIs and Priorities in one easy location. Visit *www.ScalingUp.com/software* for more information and to start your trial today.

We also have certified coaching partners around the globe that can support you locally in implementing the Rockefeller Habits 2.0. No one has ever achieved peak performance without a coach. Visit *www.scalingup.com* to locate a coach near you.

## Relax With the Process

None of this is complicated (except strategy): It just requires some discipline and perseverance. Treat our tools as you would Sudoku or crossword puzzles. Fill in what you know as you go. Again, it's not necessary to work through the tools in any kind of sequence. Start where it makes the most sense for your organization. "Get it down; then get it right" is one of our mottos.

*"Get it down; then get it right."*

The key is lots of iterations: reviewing and updating our Growth Tools every quarter. Routine will set you free.

The rest of this book provides the practical how-to details behind our recommended processes and tools. Enjoy, and best of luck as you scale your business — and let us know how we can help.

# THE BARRIERS
## Leadership, Infrastructure, and Marketing

---

**EXECUTIVE SUMMARY:** *There are predictable evolutions and revolutions as an organization grows. These are dictated by the increasing complexity that comes with adding employees, customers, product lines, locations, etc. Handling a company's growth successfully requires three things: an increasing number of capable leaders; a scalable infrastructure; and an effective marketing function. If these factors are missing, you will face barriers to growth. Scaling up successfully requires leaders who possess aptitudes for prediction, delegation, and repetition.*

*I'm tired of sailing my little boat*
*Far inside of the harbor bar;*
*I want to be out where the big ships float —*
*Out on the deep where the Great Ones are! …*
*And should my frail craft prove too slight*
*For storms that sweep those wide seas o'er,*
*Better go down in the stirring fight*
*Than drowse to death by the sheltered shore!*

— Daisy Rinehart

---

Alan Rudy was a disillusioned CEO. "Wasn't I supposed to be making more money and having more fun, the bigger the company got?" wondered the founder of Express-Med, a mail-order medical supplies firm based in Ohio. "I was angry all of the time," remembers Rudy. "I had a long weekend planned to go skiing with my father and two brothers for the first time in 10 years, yet I bagged out at the last minute because the business needed me to hold things together."

To make matters worse, on March 30 of that year, Rudy's CFO showed him financials that estimated a first-quarter profit of $300,000, yet two days later, his CFO said that they had actually *lost* $350,000. "For several hours, I thought it was an elaborate April Fools' joke," he chuckles today. "I kept trying to be a good sport about it, yet it turned out to be true." Turmoil among his staffers capped it off. Associates had fistfights in the parking lot, and one employee slashed the tires of another because of something said at work. The endless firefighting meant Rudy was putting in 80-hour workweeks. Needless to say, "stress was a little high," says Rudy.

## Scaling Up

Yet within two years, Rudy had reversed the trends, addressing the barriers we'll outline in this chapter. Utilizing the tools and techniques you'll learn in this book, he scaled up his 7-year-old firm into a $65 million industry leader. More important, he says, "It was fun again, and we were making money." Rudy went on to sell the company for $40 million, completing his own entrepreneurial life cycle: start, scale, sell.

Drawing on the lessons he learned in scaling up Express-Med, Rudy launched an investment firm to unlock the growth and profitability of additional companies. Incubating multiple firms amplified the importance of getting the right people into leadership positions. Because Rudy is a driven leader who "can take over a huddle and tell everyone what to do," he had to make himself "push accountability down," so everyone at each company had a stake in helping the business to excel.

Besides mastering these leadership and delegation challenges, Rudy learned a crucial lesson from the marketplace: You have to get your strategy right. This is what he calls finding the "ping" in the business. (Imagine the sound of flicking a plastic cup, representing a weak strategy, vs. flicking a fine crystal goblet, indicative of a clear one.) Great execution won't get you anywhere if your strategy is wrong. Understanding this has paid off handsomely for Rudy at several of his investments, including Perceptionist.

## Perceptionist's "Ping"

Perceptionist started out as a call center, answering the phones for companies in 60 to 70 different industries. To uncover the Ohio-based firm's growth potential, Rudy spent three months on the road visiting customers. (CEO Lou Gerstner had the senior managers at IBM do something similar in an initiative code-named "Operation Bear Hug.") One of Perceptionist's clients began grousing about paying monthly rates equivalent to about $1 per minute to have calls answered, especially for misdials. Moreover, the customer waxed indignant about the problems of playing phone tag with clients who just wanted to make an appointment. In his frustration, the customer exclaimed to Rudy, "Forget the buck per minute; I'd pay you $25 to take over my calendar and book appointments!"

A light bulb went on. Rudy sold off accounts that needed only answering services (including ours at Scaling Up!) and shifted the company's direction to booking appointments for its clients. While everyone else in the industry was focused on achieving a certain profit per minute, Rudy focused on attaining a targeted profit per booked appointment. This turned around a situation in which Perceptionist had been struggling to compete with overseas rivals with rates equivalent to 50 cents a minute. Focusing on this new metric and a handful of targeted industries — core customers — that needed appointments booked (plumbing, HVAC, and maid service firms) helped the company bring in revenue averaging $5 a minute. This was more than four times the industry average.

In addition, complexity decreased. "Training costs went way down, since our new reps went from needing to learn the language of 60 different industries to [mastering] just a few," says Rudy. "In the past, we often could not take on a new customer because we did not have trained personnel," a huge People problem in scaling the business.

Rudy eventually sold his stake in the company back to the original owner, and he says it is now doing well. Meanwhile, he tripled the value of his investment in the firm.

## Grow Where You're Planted

Rudy has achieved some of his greatest successes with firms when following the old adage, "Grow where you're planted." In other words, stick to the businesses and markets you know best. For Rudy, this approach shortens the learning curve of entering a new industry, allowing him to better leverage the contacts and knowledge he already has to address the People, Strategy, Execution, and Cash aspects of each new business. (For more on this key point from the founders of Pizza Hut, BostonChicken, Celestial Seasonings, and California Closets, read Verne's *Fortune* article "Businesses Worth Repeating.")

In Rudy's case, growing where he was planted meant focusing on the medical supplies and pharmaceutical industries. When he bought a minority stake in MemberHealth, a pharmacy benefits management company that helps seniors get discounts on prescription drugs, it was bringing in $7 million in revenue. Rudy helped the 18-person team implement the Rockefeller Habits, coaching MemberHealth's founder Chuck Hallberg. At Rudy's suggestion, the company dived into the first habit, holding a daily huddle at 7:30 a.m. to keep everyone focused on execution. Eventually, Rudy took on the role of chairman, while Hallberg remained CEO. The company rocketed to $1.2 billion in revenue, with the duo selling it to Universal American Financial, a Nasdaq-traded company, for $630 million. It is now a division of CVS — a really big ship.

As a serial entrepreneur and investor, Rudy has experienced firsthand the importance of getting the right **People** in place and learning how to delegate; the power of a focused **Strategy** to reduce complexity and drive industry-leading performance; and the importance of bringing disciplined **Execution** to all these ventures through habits like the daily huddle. (He's a big fan, if you haven't already guessed.) And he's both invested and made significant **Cash** — while continuing to learn what is required to make the ride enjoyable along the way.

## The Growth Paradox — an Anchor, or Wind at Your Back

Like Rudy, who continues to go out beyond the harbor bar, you will find that leading a growth company is one of the more exhilarating things you can do in the world. And eventually sailing among the "big ships" can be an incredibly fulfilling and rewarding opportunity.

### Jack Harrington's Big Boat Experience

Raytheon acquired Virtual Technology Corporation (VTC) in 2006, and within 30 days, Jack Harrington, VTC's co-founder and CEO, was asked to run a $750 million, 2,000-person Raytheon division specializing in command, control, communications, computers, and intelligence (or C4I, in defense industry terms). Admittedly, this was a daunting move for the growth-oriented CEO, who was used to running the much smaller $30 million company. "I immediately called

Verne and said, 'Holy cow, Batman, I've got a $750 million business,'" he recalls. "He told me that I had all the skills and talent I needed and that I could do it. And in my heart, I wanted to see if I could take what I learned in growing a fast, entrepreneurial company and apply it to a larger business. I immediately brought in the Rockefeller Habits, starting with the morning huddles, and then quarterly strategic planning meetings using the One-Page Strategic Plan. It was really incredible to increase our alignment, strategic thinking, and debate."

Harrington was next asked to lead an even larger organization, ThalesRaytheonSystems, a joint venture equally owned by Raytheon Company and France-based Thales S.A. He notes that the same habits and meeting rhythms were responsible for creating a more collaborative culture across the French and American operations. Plus, the organization became much more aligned around the strategic vision of the company. What was once a divide-and-conquer approach to managing the business changed dramatically. "Everyone is building trust and relationships," he says. "It's tremendous, because you're not just getting together to discuss operations. You're discussing strategy and debating the market, and that really brings out incredible insight and power."

Yet for many business leaders, scaling the business is a nightmare. Does every employee you hire, every customer you acquire, and every expansion you drive actually make you tired? Are you working longer hours, although you'd thought there should be some economies of scale as the business grew? Does it feel like everyone is just piling onto an increasingly heavier anchor that you alone are dragging through the sand? This isn't what you signed up for. It's supposed to get easier as you scale, so what happened?

You're experiencing the growth paradox: the belief that as you scale the company — and increase your dream team, prospects, and resources — things should get easier, but they don't. Things actually get harder and more complicated.

Yet Harrington's experience in scaling VTC to $30 million and leading a growing 2,000-person division at Raytheon demonstrates that the techniques you're learning in this book do scale — and that they are as applicable to some of the largest companies around the globe as they are to growth firms.

So why do only a fraction of companies actually scale up, while others fail to scale? How do you counter the growth paradox? What did Harrington have to master at VTC that was transferable to his Raytheon experience?

In short, he had to conquer complexity (and so do you!).

## Complexity

Think back to when your company was just the founder and an assistant with a plan on the back of a napkin. This start-up situation represents two channels of communication (degrees of complexity), and anyone in a relationship knows that is hard enough. Add a third person (or customer or location or product), and the degree of complexity triples from two to six. Add a fourth, and it quadruples to 24.

Expanding from three to four people grows the team only 33%, yet complexity may increase 400%. And the complexity just keeps growing exponentially. It's why many business owners often long for the day when the company was just them and an assistant selling a single service.

This complexity generates three fundamental barriers to scaling up a venture:

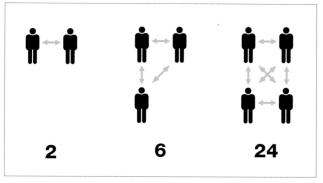

- **Leadership:** the inability to staff/grow enough leaders throughout the organization who have the capabilities to predict, delegate, and coach.

- **Scalable infrastructure:** the lack of systems and structures (physical and organizational) to handle the complexities in communication and decisions that come with growth

- **Marketing:** the failure to scaleup an effective marketing function to both attract new relationships (customers, talent, etc.) to the business and address the increased competitive pressures (and eroded margins) as you scale

When you remove these barriers, then that anchor you've been dragging turns into wind at your back. You can get your boat sailing ever faster. You can better navigate through the "Valleys of Death" — those points in the company's growth where you're bigger, but not quite big enough to have the next level of talent and systems needed to scale the venture. These are points where the business needs to leap from one whitecap to the next or risk falling into an abyss (see figure).

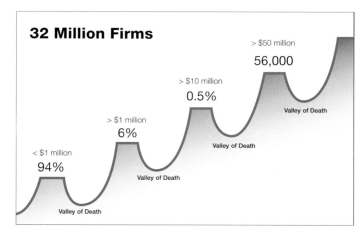

There are roughly 32 million firms in the US, of which 81% have no employees — they are solopreneurs. Only 6% reach more than $1 million in revenue. Of those firms, only about one out of 10, or 0.5% of *all* companies, ever make it to $10 million in revenue, and only 56,000 companies surpass $100 million. Finishing out the list, the top 500 public and private firms exceed $6 billion. Data indicate that there are similar ratios in other countries.

What defines the hills and valleys is related more to the number of employees than to revenue, since this is what drives the complexity equation mentioned above. If you figure roughly $100,000 revenue/employee for small firms and $500,000 revenue/employee for larger firms (yes, larger firms are more efficient on average); and you figure that one can lead seven to 10 others, you get some natural clusters:

## Scaling Up

- One to three employees (the majority of home-based businesses)
- Eight to 12 employees (a very efficient company with a leader and a bunch of helpers)
- 40 to 70 employees (a senior team of five to seven people, leading teams of seven to 10 — in a company where you still know everyone's name)
- 350 to 500 employees (seven leaders, with seven middle managers each, running teams of seven to 10 — actually a very efficient company)
- 2,500 to 3,500 employees (more multiples of seven to 10)

Any company with an employee count between these natural clusters is likely feeling a bit stuck. Everything seems to take longer to complete. Problems you thought you had solved earlier start creeping up again. And you're feeling this "big, but not big enough" syndrome — even in making minor decisions like what size photocopy machine you need next.

As an organization follows this growth path, it goes through a predictable series of evolutions and revolutions. For more on these natural cycles, read professor Larry E. Greiner's classic *Harvard Business Review* article titled "Evolution and Revolution as Organizations Grow," from July-August 1972 (updated in May 1998).

### Scott Tannas and His Valleys of Death

In 2011, Western Financial Group (WFG) — an Alberta-based financial services company with more than 2,000 employees — was acquired by Quebec-based Desjardins Group in a $440 million transaction. In the 15 years between WFG's IPO in 1996 and its return to being privately owned, the company's stock price rose 1,038%. Founder and Vice Chairman Scott Tannas remains committed to growing the company, and regularly shares with other entrepreneurs his insights on how to handle growth. "Verne talks about the Valleys of Death in how companies grow, and for those of us who have grown a big business, it's true," he says.

Drawing from his own experience scaling WFG during 20 years as CEO, Tannas shares that when a company grows from two to 10 employees, it arrives at a "Valley of Death" because processes have to change. You'll need to hire an assistant manager. "You can't run the business all by yourself, so you need to change the way you run it, and some guys can't get over it," says Tannas. After 25 employees, you face another set of challenges. For example, you need to hire someone to control money. At around 100 employees, "you need internal communications processes because you can't have a single staff meeting anymore," Tannas says. Company politics also come into play. "You have employees who think they know more than others," he notes. "All these different challenges come at different stages of growth that require you to change things.

If you don't, then you will either fall backward or you're doomed to stay a company of that size."

Hoping to tap into some of his business experience to grow the economy of his own country, Tannas was appointed a Senator in the Parliament of Canada and an investor in many scaleups.

The three barriers to leadership, infrastructure, and marketing that can prevent firms from dealing with complexity are obstacles that Rudy, Harrington, and Tannas negotiated when growing their companies. Let's examine each barrier in more detail.

# Leadership: Prediction, Delegation, and Repetition

As goes the leadership team, so goes the rest of the company. Whatever challenges exist within the organization can be traced to the cohesion of the executive team and its capabilities in prediction, delegation, and repetition.

## Prediction

Leaders don't have to be years ahead, just minutes ahead of the market, the competition, and those they lead. The key is frequent interaction with customers, competitors, and employees.

This is much easier when the company is small and the leadership team (or lonely entrepreneur) is personally handling all the sales, programming the software, and delivering the company's products and services directly. This becomes increasingly more difficult as the business scales up. Senior leaders become further isolated from customers and frontline employees, losing their gut feel for the business and the marketplace.

This is why Rudy spent three months on the road visiting Perceptionist's customers, discovering a new business model that tripled the value of his investment. In "The Data" chapter, we'll delineate specific routines, along with tips on harnessing the power of big data, to help leaders improve their ability to "see around corners" in the marketplace. Ultimately, our tools and techniques will free the senior team so they can spend 80% of the week engaged in market-facing activities.

## Delegation

Letting go and trusting others to do things well is one of the more challenging aspects of being a leader of a growing organization.

Most entrepreneurs prefer to operate alone. This is why most companies have just a handful of employees. We often exclaim (tongue in cheek) that many business owners would love their companies even more if they didn't have to deal with employees or customers! It's the idea — the dream — of their business that they love the most.

To get to 10 employees, founders must delegate activities in which they are weak. To get to 50 employees, they have to delegate functions in which they are strong! In many cases, the strength of the top leader becomes the weakness of the organization. For example, if the founder is the CEO and the main sales driver, either everyone ignores the big picture or revenue stalls. The leader needs to delegate one of these two functions if the company is to continue to scale up.

## Scaling Up

From 50 employees on up, the senior leaders must develop additional leaders throughout the organization who share the same values, passion, and knowledge of the business. This way they have enough talent to whom they can delegate the myriad number of activities and transactions necessary to grow the business.

Most MBA programs don't offer a single course or even a lecture on how to delegate, yet it is one of the most important skills a leader must develop. And many leaders confuse delegation with abdication. Abdication is blindly handing over a task to someone with no formal feedback mechanism. This is OK if it is not mission-critical, but all systems need a feedback loop, or they eventually drift out of control.

Successful delegation requires four components, assuming you have delegated a job to the right person or team:

1. Pinpoint what the person or team needs to accomplish *(Priorities — One-Page Strategic Plan)*.
2. Create a measurement system for monitoring progress *(Data — qualitative and quantitative key performance indicators)*.
3. Provide feedback to the team or person *(Meeting Rhythm)*.
4. Give appropriately timed recognition and reward (because we're dealing with people, not machines).

The Rockefeller Habits provide the methodologies for leaders to delegate properly.

 **NOTE:** *Beehives have only one leader. So why do companies need more? Some firms are experimenting with "bossless" organizations. In these companies, essentially everyone is a leader, able to act on his or her own. This requires a tremendous amount of training and development so all employees share the same DNA (values, purpose, knowledge, etc.) as the CEO. These "agile scaleups" (our preferred term) must also have technology-driven systems in place to handle several of the delegation activities listed earlier. Our favorite book on the topic is Ron Lovett's* Outrageous Empowerment: The Incredible Story of Giving Employees Their Brains Back. *The Rockefeller Habits, when fully implemented (and automated through technology), facilitate the decentralization of organizations, providing pheromone-like communication and feedback trails similar to those that guide the activities of ants and other communities without bosses.*

 **WARNING:** *Since computing technology has yet to reach the capability of "HAL" in* 2001: A Space Odyssey *(though it's getting closer), organizations that attempt the bossless experiment find they still need quasi-team leaders they call "champions" or some other related term.*

## Repetition

The leader's final job is "to keep the main thing the main thing" — to keep the organization on message and everyone heading in the same direction. L. David Marquet, author of *Turn the Ship Around!: A True Story of Turning Followers into Leaders*, led the US Navy's worst nuclear sub to first place in a year (without throwing anyone off the sub!). He had a picture hanging on the back of his stateroom door showing a man repeatedly asking his dog to sit, until the dog sits and the man exclaims, "Good dog!" This was a continual reminder to pick a message and then repeat it a lot until the organization responded.

Repetition encompasses consistency. Finish what you start. Mean what you say. And don't say one thing and do something else. Consistency is an important aspect of repetition.

We'll reinforce the power of repetition throughout the book. Specifically, we will look at:

1. **Core Values:** the handful of rules defining the culture, which are reinforced through your People (HR) systems on a daily basis
2. **Core Purpose:** the top leader's regular stump speech to keep everyone's heart engaged in the business
3. **Big Hairy Audacious Goal (BHAG®):** the 10- to 25-year goal that provides constant context for all of the decisions made throughout the organization
4. **Priorities/Themes:** a handful of three- to five-year, one-year, and quarterly priorities, which require repeated review on a daily and weekly basis to keep them top-of-mind

A key function of leadership is delivering frequent messaging and metrics to reinforce these key attributes of the company and culture.

## Scalable Infrastructure

As an organization grows, it becomes more complex. It's a force of nature. The lowly amoeba can do everything it needs with one cell. (The home-based business is similar.) However, as the number of cells increases, the organism begins to develop subsystems — for feeding, elimination, circulation, procreation, etc. In order to survive, each cell must be located close enough to a nutritional source and have sufficient surface area to absorb energy and eliminate waste. That's why a cell can get only so big.

The same is true for companies, only these subsystems (cells) represent the various functions, locations, and business units within the organization (organism). As these subsystems grow, they must continue to segment, or they become too big and insular and thus experience the problems we see with large bureaucracies. Just as living cells need to be near nutrients, companies need to be close to customers (in terms of locations, product groups, and customer segments). This drives how companies structure their organizations and establish accountabilities.

To keep things flowing, an organization needs a scalable infrastructure (similar to the blood supply and the nervous system). When you go from two employees to 10, you need better phone systems and more structured space. When your company reaches 50 employees, you still need space and phones, and you suddenly also require an accounting system that shows more precisely which projects, customers, or products are actually making money. Between 50 and 350 employees, your information-technology systems need to be upgraded and integrated. And above that, you must revamp them again, as the organization attempts to tie all systems into one comprehensive database. Otherwise, a simple change of address by a customer can unleash a series of expensive mistakes.

**NOTE:** *Don't decide the physical location of employees and teams haphazardly. Certain functions are best co-located together, which we'll discuss in the "People" section of the book. Even determining the location of restrooms, break rooms, and meeting rooms is important, especially when a company grows to occupy a second floor or more in a building. Serious communication issues surface when employees on different floors no longer bump into each other. The goal is to increase the cross-interaction (accidental collisions) of various individuals and functions.*

## Key Organizational Shift — Agile vs. Traditional

A revolutionary change is happening inside organizations. The traditional top-down organizational chart is crumbling and being replaced by a new one that's more fluid and agile. It's not by accident that the standard org chart, originally designed to help organize human might/muscle to build great walls and go to war, looks like the human skeletal system, with a head, shoulders, arms, legs, fingers, and toes. Our skeleton is quite an efficient and effective muscle machine.

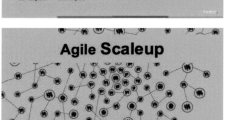

The challenge, as we've moved from organizing muscles to minds (more brain work than back work), is the organizational chart — it didn't morph with this transition. What is needed is an organizational design that looks more like the work we're doing — one that mimics our nodal networked brains. One that looks more like how ant colonies and bee-hives organize to find the food (our equivalent of customers!)

To scale, ant colonies don't need multiple layers of management — just two. There is the queen and then a whole bunch of three-ant ant teams, each with a team lead chosen at birth for its ability to socialize with the other team leads, sharing information.

That's all you need, as well. A senior team, team leaders, and team members. This is how Ron Lovett organized his 3,500+ private security guard firm he describes in his book *Outrageous Empowerment*. No area, district, or regional managers needed — just private security guards organized in special forces-like teams, each with a team lead. These team leads then met monthly to share knowledge (intel) across the various teams.

There are two key books, in addition to Lovett's, detailing this transition:

1) *Teeming (Version 2.0): How Nature's Oldest Teams Adapt and Thrive* by Tamsin Woolley-Barker

2) *Humanocracy: Creating Organizations as Amazing as the People Inside Them* by Gary Hamel and Michele Zanini

Hamel's book is full of examples of firms that have stripped out all of these layers, like Haier, the China-based whitegoods manufacturer. Other firms scaled without adding these layers, like Netherlands-based nursing firm Buurtzorg, which has more than 14,000 nurses and nurse assistants worldwide.

Woolley-Barker's book goes further and outlines five principles of superorganisms the biomimicry guru has identified. These principles power most of the unicorn companies, which have scaled much faster and more easily than other firms. The five:

- Cultivate collective intelligence
- Nurture swarm creativity
- Rely on distributed leadership
- Depend on reciprocity and sharing
- Compound regenerative growth

Read the three books mentioned above and put these principles to work in scaling your organization.

# Marketing

The #1 functional barrier to scaling up is the lack of an effecting marketing department, separate from sales (accounting is the second — discussed in the Cash Section). Marketing is critical to both attracting new relationships (customers, talent, advisors, investors, etc.) to the business and addressing the increased competitive pressures (and eroded margins) as you scale. To prevent margin erosion, marketing's role (with lots of customer input) is to determine the right *what* we should be selling to the best *who's*; and *how* best we should sell at the right *price*. And because marketing strategy equals strategy, the head of the organization is usually intimately involved in these decisions.

It's Regis McKenna, author of the classic *Relationship Marketing: Successful Strategies for The Age of the Customer*, who taught Steve Jobs, Andy Grove, and most of the Silicon Valley tech stars how to market in the 80's. It was McKenna and his firm that also guided Verne as he built his early global entrepreneurship organizations. McKenna's focus was twofold. First, the key to effective marketing is setting aside one hour per week to focus on marketing i.e. establish a marketing meeting (do you have one?). Second, to make a list of the top 25 (or 250 if you are a bigger firm) influencers — relationships — you need to get behind the venture to scale it up. Then spend time each week figuring out how to network your way to these people. With a compelling vision (elevator pitch), then convince these influencers to help.

The more influential the names you put on the piece of paper, the more potential you have to scale the business bigger and faster. Being young and dumb, as a student at Wichita State University (go Shockers!), Verne boldly included President Ronald Reagan, Steve Jobs, Michael Dell, and the owners of *Venture* and *Inc.* magazines on his list of 25. What's crazy, in just 36 months of working the list, one hour per week, the Association of Collegiate Entrepreneurs (ACE) became a global "overnight" success, hosting a major event in Los Angeles for over 1100 entrepreneurs including Jobs and Dell with full page ads for the organization donated by *Venture* and *Inc.* magazines — and a congratulatory telegram from President Reagan. So the first step is to stop and make your list!

The other major agenda item for the weekly marketing meeting is Dr. Philip Kotler's 4Ps of marketing — Product, Price, Place, and Promotion. Of the four, pricing tends to get the least attention yet is one of the most important decisions you'll make. Whereas we'll spend hours working on the cost side of the business; the pricing side is lucky to get an educated guess. To up your skills in this area we strongly recommend reading pricing guru Hermann Simon's book *Confessions of a Pricing Man: How Pricing Affects Everything*. His firm Simon-Kucher & Partners is the leading pricing consultancy in the world — you might consider engaging them.

We also encourage you to search for Olgivy's 4Es of Marketing. One of the largest ad agencies in the world, they have updated the 4Ps of marketing and have provided a complimentary online presentation and whitepaper on the 4Es — Experience, Exchange, Everyplace, and Evangelism. Spend time each week working on how to execute better the 4Es of the business.

Last, we encourage you to read Adele Revella's book *Buyer Personas: How to Gain Insight into your Customer's Expectations, Align your Marketing Strategies, and Win More Business*. Ultimately, marketing's job is to identify and attract the best (right) customers to the venture and arm the sales team (or those driving your online marketing activities) with a definitive list of prospects and plenty of information to help them make the sale. If not, sales teams (distributors) will chase any low hanging fruit they can find which is the quickest way to defocus the business and crush your margins.

# Market Dynamics

More broadly, the marketplace makes you look either smart or dumb. When it's going your way, it covers up a lot of mistakes. When fortunes reverse, all your weaknesses seem to be exposed. Bill Gross, founder of IdeaLab which has launched over 100 companies, looked at the key factors to the success of growing firms — including people (team), strategy (business model and idea), and cash (funding). What he determined is that market timing trumped them all. Too early or too late with your great idea and you miss the wave.

There's an additional cruel and counterintuitive market dynamic when you're growing a business. As the firm scales from $1 million to $10 million in revenue, the senior team tends to be focused externally on amassing new business. Yet this is precisely the time when a little more internal focus, to establish healthy organizational habits and a scalable infrastructure, would pay off in the long term. As the business scales past $10 million, organizational complexities tend to draw the attention of the senior team inward (leading to firefighting). This is precisely when the team needs to be focused more externally on the marketplace (by talking to customers, as Rudy does), given the increased competitive pressures that come with size.

There is also an important sequence of focus when it comes to your financial metrics. Between start-up and the first million or two in revenue, the key driver is *revenue* (sell like hell). The focus is on proving that a market exists for your services. As for cash, which many business owners might think is the first focus, the entrepreneur has to rely mainly on family and friends (or fools!).

It's between $1 million and $10 million that the team needs to focus on *cash*. Growth sucks cash, and since this is the first time the company will make a tenfold jump in size, the demands for cash will soar. In addition, at this stage of organizational development, the company is still trying to figure out its unique position in the marketplace, and these experiments (or mistakes) can be costly. This is when the cash model of the business needs to be worked out (e.g., "How is the business model going to generate sufficient cash for the company to keep growing?"). Will the business model generate its own cash internally; have sufficient lines of credit to sustain growth; and attract investors with deep-enough pockets to support it?

As the organization passes $10 million in revenue, new internal and external pressures come to the forefront. Externally, your organization is on more radar screens, alerting competitors to your threats. Customers are beginning to demand lower prices as they do more business with your company. At the same time, internal complexities increase, which cause costs to rise faster than revenue. All of this begins to squeeze an organization's *gross margin*. As gross margin slips a few points, the organization is starved of the extra money it needs in order to invest in infrastructure, like accounting systems and training. This creates a snowball effect of further expensive mistakes as the company passes the $25 million mark.

To prevent the erosion in your margins, it's critical that you maintain a clear value proposition in the market. At the same time, the company must continually streamline and automate internal processes to reduce costs. Organizations successful at doing both will see their gross margins increase during this stage of growth, giving them the extra cash they need to fund infrastructure, training, marketing, R&D, etc.

By the time it reaches $50 million in revenue, an organization should have enough experience and a strong-enough position in the market to predict profitability accurately. It's not that profit hasn't been important all along as the organization grows. It's just more critical, at this stage, that organizations generate *predictable* profit, since profit swings of a few percentage points either way represent millions of dollars.

Which brings us full circle to the main function of a business leader: to build a predictable revenue and profit engine in an unpredictable marketplace and world. The "20-Mile March" lesson from Jim Collins and Morten T. Hansen's book *Great by Choice: Uncertainty, Chaos, and Luck — Why Some Thrive Despite Them All* highlights how companies with steady growth year in and year out dramatically outperform firms that experience wild swings in revenue and profits.

The spoils of victory go to those who maintain a steady pace, day in and day out, in all kinds of weather and storms. And it's this predictability, driven by effective processes, that is ultimately the key to crafting an organization that attracts and keeps top talent; creates products and services that satisfy customer needs; and generates significant wealth.

In summary, growing a business is a dynamic process as the leadership team navigates the evolutions and revolutions of growth. And like the growth stages of a child, they are predictable and unavoidable. To deal with these challenges, the company must grow the capabilities of the *leadership* team throughout the organization; install scalable *infrastructure* to manage the increasing complexities that come with growth; and stay on top of the *market dynamics* that affect the business.

To do this, there are 4 Decisions that leaders must address: People, Strategy, Execution, and Cash. These are the same four that Rudy and his team continue to face as they scale up their latest venture. The rest of the book is organized around these 4 Decisions, providing you with tools, techniques, and best practices for making the critical judgment calls that drive growth.

# SCALING UP
## PEOPLE

# THE PEOPLE INTRODUCTION

 **KEY QUESTION:** *Are all stakeholders (employees, customers, shareholders) happy and engaged in the business; and would you "rehire" all of them?*

Business leaders need great people (A-Players) both inside the company and out — investors, suppliers, customers, partners, advisors — as well as a great support network at home. All of these people are critical to the business.

So how do you know you need to make changes on the people side of the business, and in your life, as you scale up the venture? Two questions:

1. *Are you happy?* We're not talking about some kind of monklike peace, even in misery. This is a more straightforward question. Do you enjoy coming to work? Or are you experiencing irreconcilable issues with business partners? Is there a specific executive not getting the job done? Is there a team member who disrupts everyone else? Is there a customer with too big a piece of your revenue? Is there a supplier not delivering? Is an investor or the bank making your life difficult? Are you having issues with a family member or friend?

2. *Would you enthusiastically rehire everyone, knowing what you know today?* This goes hand-in-hand with the questions above (except for family!) and includes not only employees but existing customers, suppliers, and other stakeholders in the business. It's a painful question that requires one to face the brutal facts and make changes. It's especially tough when the company has simply outgrown some earlier relationships.

If you fail to address these relationship issues head on, they will continue to drain your emotional energy, leaving little left to expend on the Strategy, Execution, and Cash aspects of the business. That's why we address People first in our 4 Decisions model.

 **ACTION:** *Is there a relationship that is draining you emotionally? If you need to deal with a contentious situation, we suggest you read* Crucial Conversations: Tools for Talking When Stakes Are High, *by Kerry Patterson, et al.*

## Section Overview

**The first chapter, The Leaders,** details three one-page People tools to help you think through your personal relationship goals; specific accountabilities for the company's functions and business units; and the various process accountabilities in your organization. Working through these will help you recognize and prioritize the People challenges in your business and your life.

**The second chapter, The Team,** shares techniques for attracting, hiring, and coaching talent. We'll emphasize the need for a strong marketing function to help recruit people, and the use of the Topgrading methodology for interviewing and selecting the A Players you need to grow the business.

**The third chapter, The Core,** bridges the People and Strategy decisions and examines the Core of the organization: its Values, Purpose, and Competencies. A strong Core is the foundation for an effective strategy. We'll share specific approaches for discovering each element, and discuss how to leverage this Core to drive a strong culture through the people (HR) systems — and prevent culture drift as the organization scales. A weakened culture will torpedo any strategy.

Three one-page People tools will be covered in this section:

1. **One-Page Personal Plan (OPPP):** provides a framework for people to plan their personal life

2. **Function Accountability Chart (FACe):** clarifies the people who are accountable for scaling the business

3. **Process Accountability Chart (PACe):** lists the processes, and people accountable, that keep the business running smoothly

 **NOTE:** *The "e" in the FACe and PACe acronyms represents the **e**nergy and **e**ntrepreneurial spirit that leaders must possess in order to scale up a business.*

*A special thank-you to Sebastian Ross, German tech entrepreneur and partner in Barcelona, for co-authoring this "People" section and serving as an ongoing collaborator on the book.*

## Everybody, Somebody, Anybody, And Nobody

This is a little story about four people named Everybody, Somebody, Anybody, and Nobody.

There was an important job to be done and Everybody was sure that Somebody would do it.

Anybody could have done it, but Nobody did it.

Somebody got angry about that because it was Everybody's job.

Everybody thought that Anybody could do it, but Nobody realized that Everybody wouldn't do it.

It ended up that Everybody blamed Somebody when Nobody did what Anybody could have done.

*Unknown author of condensed version of Charles Osgood's – A Poem About Responsibility.*

Name: _____          Date: _____

| | | Relationships | Achievements | Rituals | Wealth ($) |
|---|---|---|---|---|---|
| Faith | 10–25 Years (Aspirations) | | | | |
| Family | 1 Year (Activities) | | | | |
| Friends | 90 Days (Actions) | Start | Start | Start | Start |
| Fitness | | | | | |
| Finance | | Stop | Stop | Stop | Stop |

# People: Function Accountability Chart (FACe)

**SCALING UP**
A GAZELLES COMPANY

**1** Name the person accountable for each function

**2** Ask the four questions at the bottom of the page re: whose name(s) you listed for each function

**3** List Key Performance Indicators (KPIs) for each function

**4** Take your Profit and Loss (P/L), Balance Sheet (B/S), and Cash Flow accounting statements and assign a person to each line item, then derive appropriate Results/Outcomes for each function

| Functions | **1** Person Accountable | **3** Leading Indicators (Key Performance Indicators) | **4** Results/Outcomes (P/L or B/S Items) |
|---|---|---|---|
| Head of Company | | | |
| Marketing | | | |
| R&D/Innovation | | | |
| Sales | | | |
| Operations | | | |
| Treasury | | | |
| Controller | | | |
| Information Technology | | | |
| Human Resources | | | |
| Talent Development/Learning | | | |
| Customer Advocacy | | | |
| | | | |
| | | | |
| Heads of Business Units • _____ | | | |
| • _____ | | | |
| • _____ | | | |
| • _____ | | | |

**2** Identify: 1. More than 1 Person in a Seat; 2. Person in more than 1 seat; 3. Empty seats; 4. Enthusiastically Rehire?

Download a full-sized copy of this tool at *scalingup.com*

# People: Process Accountability Chart (PACe)

1. Identify 4 to 9 processes that drive your business.

2. Assign someone specific accountability for each process.

3. List Key Performance Indicators (KPIs) for each process (better, faster, cheaper).

| ② Person Accountable | ① Name of Process | ③ KPIs Better, Faster, Cheaper |
|---|---|---|
| | | |
| | | |
| | | |
| | | |
| | | |
| | | |
| | | |
| | | |
| | | |
| | | |

# THE LEADERS
## The FACe and PACe of the Company

---

**EXECUTIVE SUMMARY:** *"The bottleneck is always at the top of the bottle," notes management guru Peter Drucker. Challenges within the company normally point to issues with, or among, the leaders. To address them, this chapter will focus on the leadership team. We will share three tools that help leaders get clear on their personal goals; define senior leadership accountabilities, key performance indicators (KPIs), and outcomes; and delineate the four to nine processes that drive the company. We include a short primer on organizational theory to help you think through how to properly divide the company into functions, product/service lines, and divisions.*

 **HINT:** *Keep everyone as close to his or her respective customers as possible!*

---

Co-founders Stephen Roche and Simon Morrison realized that if they wanted to keep Shine Lawyers growing, they needed to bring up the next generation of leaders to drive the day-to-day so Roche and Morrison could focus on expansion. In addition to promoting Jodie Willey and Lisa Flynn into senior legal management roles, they brought on a new executive team to assist the 700-person law firm, with 40 locations across Australia, in its next stage of growth.

A decision to take the Rockefeller Habits-driven firm public, making it one of the first three law firms in the world to hold an IPO, spurred even more shifts in the organizational chart. Morrison moved to managing director and Chief Executive Officer, while Roche now consults and has written two books promoting the purpose of Shine Lawyers. They also recruited new board members with key IPO experience.

"We now have a great team of talented young people who will take the business to new heights," says Morrison.

As a company scales up, the toughest decisions involve people and their changing roles in the organization, especially within the leadership team. Loyalties, egos, and personal friendships make these decisions even more difficult when the company faces a situation in which it has outgrown some of its early leaders.

In this chapter, we'll explore these senior leadership dynamics of a growing company, and the functions and processes needed to scale up the business. But first, a quick primer on organizational design.

## The Organization: A Growing Organism

Remember the days when the start-up team was crammed into a single office like clowns squeezed into a Volkswagen? Now the company has 150 employees, or 1,500, and you find it infinitely more difficult to know how to divide up teams and set clear accountabilities. Worse, both customers and employees seem confused about how to navigate your organization.

We can take a clue from nature to solve these problems. Human organisms are made up of billions of cells vs. just a few specialized ones for a good reason: A single cell can only get so big and stay healthy. Once it reaches a certain size, the outer membrane won't have enough surface area to bring in nutrients and eliminate waste to support the cell. The cell will start to die from the inside out (like big bureaucracies!).

This means that the cell must divide. So, too, must your company or it won't be able to function in a healthy way. And just as no cell can be too far from the blood supply, no team can be too far removed from the action of the marketplace — or so big that it becomes unwieldy and unresponsive (think of Amazon's "two-pizza rule" — no team should be so big that it can't be fed with two pizzas).

This is the main principle underpinning effective organizational design. Divide big teams into smaller ones aligned around projects, product lines, customer segments, geographical locations, etc., based on the idea of getting everyone in the organization into small teams and as close to his or her respective customers as possible. This is a way to increase the surface area of the company, giving the maximum number of employees a chance to interact with the marketplace.

Each cell within the organization must have someone clearly accountable for it. This doesn't mean the person is boss and/or gets to make all the decisions. In fact, it's important to delineate the differences between accountability, responsibility, and authority.

## Accountability, Responsibility, and Authority

Though spelled differently, these business terms are often haphazardly interchanged. Here are our definitions:

*Accountability*: This belongs to the ONE person who has the "ability to count" — who is tracking the progress and giving voice (screaming loudly) when issues arise within a defined task, team, function, or division. It doesn't mean he or she makes all the decisions (or even any decisions) — which is why people often talk about leaderless teams. However, someone must still be accountable. The rule: If more than one person is accountable, then no one is accountable, and that's when things fall through the cracks.

*Responsibility*: This falls to anyone with the "ability to respond" proactively to support the team. It includes all the people who touch a particular process or issue.

*Authority*: This belongs to the person or team with the final decision-making power.

As an example, Scaling Up's CFO has *accountability* for cash — she literally "counts" and reports it to the team daily. And she's accountable for alerting the team if she senses any potential issues now or later in the year. In turn, Verne, as CEO, maintains the

*"If more than one person is accountable, then no one is accountable."*

*authority* over cash, signing off on major expenditures and investments. And everyone in the company has *responsibility* for making sure that cash is spent wisely and that deals/contracts are structured so they help generate vs. absorb cash as Scaling Up continues to grow.

But don't accountability and authority need to be roughly equal — as in "I need sufficient authority if I'm going to be held accountable?" For frontline staff, yes. At a Ritz-Carlton hotel, where the philosophy is that any employee who receives a complaint from a guest "owns" that complaint (accountability), first-line employees such as desk clerks, bellhops, and housekeepers are empowered (authority) to spend up to $2,000 to handle any customer complaints. Managers can spend up to $5,000 without additional authorization. A full 250 to 300 hours of first-year training make this possible.

As one moves up the organization into more middle and senior leadership positions, it's assumed that this balance of accountability and authority holds. However, those who have advanced up the ranks find that they've taken on increasingly more accountability for things they have less and less real control over — until they reach the top and find they are liable (often legally) for anything that goes wrong in an organization that is expanding beyond their day-to-day reach. This is why leaders get paid the big bucks — to bridge this ever-increasing gap between accountability and authority, using their skills of communication, persuasion, education, visioning, etc.

Getting accountabilities clear throughout the organization is crucial. To assist, we have three one-page People tools to help you think through your personal relationship goals; assign specific accountabilities for the company's functions and business units; and delineate the various process accountabilities in your organization. Working through these will help you identify and prioritize the People challenges on which you need to focus next in scaling up the organization.

## One-Page Personal Plan (OPPP)

People often joke that the best moments of owning a boat were the day they bought the boat and the day they sold it.

There are similar punctuation marks in our lives — the day we're born and the day we pass away. As busy executives, if we're not careful, we can find that our personal lives end up as neglected as those vessels forever docked in the harbor (or parked in storage!). Thus, we're big believers in establishing personal priorities and aligning them with your professional goals.

Just as there are 4 Decisions you make to build a thriving company — People, Strategy, Execution, and Cash — there are parallel areas in your personal life — Relationships, Achievements, Rituals, and Wealth. We encourage each leader of a company to complete a One-Page Personal Plan (OPPP). As with all the one-page tools we'll detail in this book, you can

find a three-quarter-sized copy of the OPPP in the section introduction, or download a full-sized copy at *scalingup.com*.

To complete the OPPP, start by filling in the Name and Date spaces at the top. Next, let's walk through the four columns of the OPPP.

## Column 1 — Relationships

In the end, what matters most in life are the depth of your relationships with friends and family; and the sheer number of people you've helped along the way. These represent true measures of wealth. Financial wealth, then, is seen as a resource for fostering your relationships. For an inspirational story about an entrepreneur who used his wealth to help millions, read Conor O'Clery's *The Billionaire Who Wasn't: How Chuck Feeney Secretly Made and Gave Away a Fortune* (you'll also pick up some important tips on scaling up a global business).

 **NOTE:** *The list of 5Fs located down the left-hand side of the OPPP — Faith, Family, Friends, Fitness, and Finance — is contributed by James Hansberger. He found, through his decades as a wealth advisor, that what mattered most to those near the end of their life were these 5Fs, in the order they are listed. They serve as a gentle reminder as you set priorities in the OPPP.*

Starting at the top of column 1, list the key groups of people with whom you want a lasting relationship (10 to 25 years). In business, you have a tremendous opportunity to help your employees and customers — so consider adding them categorically to the list. In your personal life, important relationships include family and friends.

Also list the various communities in which you're involved. Ted Leonsis, a Greek-American sports team owner, venture capital investor, filmmaker, and philanthropist, is author of *The Business of Happiness: 6 Secrets to Extraordinary Success in Life and Work*. He notes in his book a strong correlation between happiness and the number of diverse communities in which you are active.

The next step is to look at the groups listed and pick a few key relationships on which to focus your attention for the next 12 months and the next 90 days. Verne took a year to focus on deepening his relationship with his 6-year-old son, Quinn; and one quarter with his sister, who needed support with some health issues.

At the same time, there may be some people in your personal or professional life who are destructive — literally draining the life out of you — and/or distract you from your higher goals. There's a space on the form where you can note relationships you want to end gracefully.

## Column 2 — Achievements

Many CEOs find that even after reaching critical milestones for growing their company, they still feel they haven't made a real difference in the world. The achievements section of the OPPP can pave the way to a more meaningful life. Think about the major ways you'd like to make an impact through your work *beyond* reaching monetary goals — perhaps by mentoring others or setting up a nonprofit organization — and set objectives in these key areas.

In your personal life, you'll want to think about how you can make a real difference with the key people in your life. For instance, you might aim to have a blissful marriage, instead of just *staying* married, as many people do. Signing on to facilitate the five-year strategic plan for his children's school was an achievement Verne enjoyed prioritizing while writing this book.

The key is focusing on short-, medium-, and long-term achievements relative to the people listed in the relationship column. This might include stopping the pursuit of achievements that are taking you away from the relationships that matter most.

## Column 3 — Rituals

Establishing regular routines in your life will help you achieve your larger goals. Examples of rituals might include planning a weekly date night with your spouse and booking some alone time with each child once a week. For distant family members, you might schedule a regular routine of biannual gatherings.

You might also establish rituals with people whose presence in your life supports your bigger goals. Meeting regularly with a workout buddy; spending time with close friends; participating in a business forum of like-minded leaders; and having a peer coach (a friend who holds you accountable each day — a recommendation by über-executive coach Marshall Goldsmith) are some examples.

The key is getting these rituals scheduled into your weekly and annual calendar as far out as possible. If not, another year goes by — and then ten — and you've missed out on opportunities to deepen relationships with people you know and love.

And just as there are destructive people with whom you need to end your relationship, there might be some bad habits or behaviors you wish to stop — particularly those that have proved harmful to those around you.

## Column 4 — Wealth

Rather than viewing financial wealth as an end in itself (as a wise guru once told Verne, "All assets become liabilities!"), see it as a resource for supporting the rest of your personal plan. Besides determining how much money you want to set aside for retirement, set goals for the amount of money you want to donate to causes and communities that matter to you over the next several years. Decide how much money you need to support activities with your family and friends, investing in experiences in the coming 12 months that create lasting memories. And note any wealth-producing assets or cash-draining liabilities you need to address in the coming months.

> *"All assets become liabilities!"*

Overall, focus on how your wealth will flow through you in the service of others, rather than hoarding it. This seems to attract more wealth — the natural law of reciprocity. Lynne Twist's insightful book titled *The Soul of Money: Transforming Your Relationship With Money and Life* expounds upon this idea.

We hope you find the OPPP a useful planning tool for your life. Let's now turn our focus to the company.

# Function Accountability Chart (FACe)

The second one-page People tool — the Function Account-ability Chart (FACe) — focuses on making sure you have the right butts in the right seats at the top of the organization (i.e., the "right people doing the right things right").

An organization is simply an amplifier of what's happening at the senior level of the company, which is one of the reasons our coaching partners do a quick employee survey as they start working with an organization.. If the survey reveals that the IT people are upset with marketing, there is likely an issue between those two functional leaders at the top.

The chart lists a common set of functions that must exist in ALL companies. Even start-ups have all these functions, only it's the founder(s) doing everything! In scaling the business, the idea is to figure out which function on the chart to delegate next.

Like Shine Lawyers' Morrison and Roche, who continue to promote and recruit new leadership as the business scales, you want to delegate the functions listed on the FACe tool to leaders who pass two tests (including culture fit):

1. They don't need to be managed.
2. They regularly wow the team with their insights and output.

The chart asks you to list one or two key performance indicators (KPIs) for each function. These KPIs represent the measurable activities each functional leader needs to perform on a day-to-day basis. The last column on the chart captures the outcomes expected for each function (i.e., who is accountable for revenue, gross margin, profit, cash, etc.). These outcomes normally represent line items on the financial statements.

When completed, this one-page accountability tool helps you diagnose where you have people and performance gaps on the leadership team.

As a general rule, you can move people up or over into these functional positions at any time. How-ever, if you need to bring someone in from the *outside* to fill a senior leadership position, you should do this only once every six to nine months. It takes this length of time to find the right person, get him comfortable in the position, and transfer the DNA of the organization into his psyche. In turn, the new executive will need this amount of time to positively impact the organization enough to pay back his salary.

Now you can afford to bring in another leader. The rule is to take it slow when bringing outsiders into senior leadership roles. The exception is when the company is venture-backed and/or growing 100% a year and needs to bring on three or four key executives within a short period of time.

**WARNING:** *Whatever is the strength of a leader often becomes the weakness of the organization (e.g., if the founder is strong in marketing, the business may eventually find it's weak in this function- al area). Why? Because leaders have a tendency to hold on too tight, strangling the efforts of those around them. Or the leaders figure they can "watch over the details," bringing in someone too junior to oversee the function vs. bringing on the powerhouse they really need. Instead, leaders must make a counterintuitive decision and find people who exceed their own capabilities in their area of strength, to prevent the company from stalling.*

Please read through the following instructions for completing the FACe tool. It often illuminates immediate changes that might need to be made at the top of the organization.

## Completing Your Function Accountability Chart (FACe)

### STEP **1**

The first column lists the functions every business must support and provides a few blanks so you can add those unique to your business. There is also space to note discrete business units. Notice we don't list titles (CEO, COO, etc.). The idea is to focus on the jobs that need to get done.

1. Start by having each member of the executive team fill in the first blank column by adding the initials of the person they think is accountable for each function or business unit. It's accept- able if a function is outsourced (i.e., to an outsourced CFO or marketing consultant). If it's outsourced to a firm, list the main person accountable from the contracted company.

2. We've provided a couple of blank lines for you to add functions that might be unique to your industry or business (for example, a chief technical officer or a quality control person). There is also space to list the names of various business units. For Scaling Up, these would include our coaching, online, social initiatives, and technology divisions.

    **NOTE:** *When looking at business units farther down the first column, even though you might not have formal business units, you might organize discrete teams around customer groups, product lines, or locations. You can consider these quasi-business units.*

3. Compare lists to see if there's agreement among the members of the leadership team. There often isn't, even when it comes to who is the head of the company!

### STEP **2**

Once the team has agreed on the people accountable for each function, consider the four questions summarized at the bottom of the form:

1. *Do you have more than one person accountable for a function?* The founder might be sharing ac- countability for sales with another executive, or partners in a professional services firm might all be listed next to "head of company." The rule is that only one person should be accountable; otherwise, there will be confusion. Having more than one name in a box is a red flag.

2. *Does someone's name show up in more boxes than everyone else's?* We recognize that in growth companies, leaders may wear multiple hats, but if one executive's name shows up three or four times compared to everyone else's one or two, that leader is either going to die young (a little dramatic) or one of the functions he or she owns will not be supported sufficiently. This is another red flag.

### The FACe of Perly Fullerton

When James Perly and Mark Fullerton worked through the Function Accountability Chart (FACe) for their Ontario-based consultancy, Perly Fullerton, a problem immediately jumped out at them: There were six people in the room, but only three names were being put in the boxes. "The problem was that everyone was coming to us for everything," says Perly. "Even though we hired new people, we just never got rid of any of our senior responsibilities."

Although it was a long process, now everybody knows exactly who's accountable, including Perly and Fullerton. "Our roles became really clear in our own minds based on what suits us best for our personalities," says Perly. "Mark is more of a go-getter with lots of energy, so he's the chief operating officer because he drives things forward. I take on more of a visionary role [as president], focusing on strategy."

3. *Do you have any boxes with no names in them?* This often happens when someone says, "Hey, who's accountable for marketing?" and the response is, "All of us!" "All of us" really means "none of us," and the box should be left blank. This doesn't necessarily require you to hire someone. Let's take the customer advocacy box as an example. You may have seven or eight people who are overseeing various groups of customers. It's natural to conclude that this accountability is covered. The rule of accountability means one person must ultimately take ownership, however, so the person to whom these people report has overall accountability. But if that leader isn't doing anything active to monitor levels of customer delight and follow up, then this function will underperform. Rather than hire an additional person, you might choose one of the customer service reps to hold overall accountability, rotating this role among the reps every six months. Again, this doesn't mean that any of these people is the boss; it means they are to monitor the situation, ensure that customer-satisfaction feedback is gathered and reported to the leadership team at the weekly meeting, and alert the team if there are issues.

### Dell's Empty Boxes

A company is never so big or sophisticated that it doesn't sometimes encounter "empty boxes" on its organizational chart. When Michael Dell took back the reins of computer company Dell Inc. in January 2007, he lamented that the chief marketing officer (CMO) position had been empty for two years even though Kevin Rollins had more than 20 executives on the executive leadership team. And indicative of Dell's customer service problems, there was no one leading the customer advocacy function. So Dell immediately hired Mark Jarvis from Oracle to be the CMO and moved over Dick Hunter from manufacturing to lead the customer service function. That was the beginning of a turnaround and repositioning of Dell that led to Michael taking the company private again in 2013 and back public again in 2018.

4. *Are you enthusiastic about the person you have in each box?* If the leader isn't getting the job done, then a change may need to be made. Maybe this leader is in the wrong seat or in too many seats. Maybe there are performance issues. Maybe a person is talented but doesn't fit the culture (this often happens when a "big company" executive is brought into a growing firm).

 **ACTION:** *Discuss these four questions and decide where there are glaring gaps in the leadership team.*

 **WARNING:** *CEOs often avoid these decisions because they involve executives who have become dear friends. We recognize that this is a touchy subject, but it must be faced if the organization is to grow. One option is for some of the early team members to help launch a new product or division. They are usually more comfortable in a start-up situation or working on a smaller team. And several of the early leaders might be relieved to have the burden of an increasingly important and complex function taken off their shoulders. You won't know until you have these crucial conversations.*

## STEP ❸

The second blank column is for listing one to three KPIs for each of the listed functions. These are intended to be leading indicators, measuring the daily and weekly activities of a particular leader and meant to drive superior results. For help in selecting KPIs appropriate for your industry and/or function, visit *KPILibrary.com*. For more general KPIs, we recommend the book *Key Performance Indicators: The 75 Measures Every Manager Needs to Know,* by Bernard Marr.

 **WARNING:** *A common mistake is simply noting down KPIs that are representative of the daily and weekly activities of the person listed for a particular function. It's critical to zero-base your KPI decisions. Do this by covering up the names listed in the "Person Accountable" column (metaphorically or physically) and then decide on KPIs for each function that align with the business model of the company. Then consider if the person in the job function has the skills and aptitude to deliver on those KPIs. A mismatch might indicate a potential problem.*

### "Head of Company" KPI

What is the most important KPI for the head of the company? Many might suggest vision, but how do you measure that? Others might suggest more tangible measures, like return on investment or profit, but these are outcomes more suitable for the last column on the FACe tool. Again, the idea of a leading indicator is to measure the specific actions that lead to results. In the case of the head of the company, it's simply the ratio of all the other boxes on the FACe tool that are right (i.e., the main job of the head of the company is to make sure she has the right people doing the right things right). And when many founders/CEOs realize this, they often bring in someone else to head the company so they can focus on R&D or marketing or customer advocacy. That's why we emphasize separating titles from functions.

The late W. Edwards Deming, who led the quality revolution around the world, believed that the fundamental job of a leader is prediction. The right KPIs, along with sufficient market intelligence (discussed in "The Data" chapter), help executives navigate what are expected to be turbulent markets throughout the foreseeable future.

 **ACTION:** *In the third column of the FACe, note one or two KPIs — leading indicators — for each function and business unit.*

## STEP 4

For the fourth column of the FACe — "Results/Outcomes" — pull out a recent detailed Profit and Loss (P&L) and Balance Sheet (B/S) statement and assign a person accountable for each line item. Then discuss the same four questions we asked earlier about the people listed for the functions (summarized at the bottom of the FACe tool):

1. *Do you have more than one person accountable for any line item (like revenue)?*

2. *Does someone's name show up next to more line items than anyone else's?*

3. *Do you have a line item with no name next to it (is someone watching telecommunication expense)?*

4. *Are you enthusiastic about the person you have accountable for each line item?*

Again, don't confuse accountability for authority — recall the earlier cash example within Scaling Up. And, as with the functions, spread the workload evenly among the leadership team, with just one person ultimately accountable for each line item.

It was Jack Stack, founder and CEO of SRC Holdings Corporation and author of the classic book *The Great Game of Business: The Only Sensible Way to Run a Company*, who argued that the Phoenician monks left out a critical column on the first accounting statements they created in the late 1400s: the "Who" column. There should be a person clearly accountable for each line item, even if it's a middle or lower manager, when considering a highly detailed P&L and B/S.

This exercise has led to some of the most important accountability discussions we've ever facilitated in companies. Who is accountable for overall revenue? Who is protecting gross margins from overly zealous pricing concessions? Is anyone watching telecommunications expenses? And for those enamored of formal organizational charts (we're not — in growing firms, they tend to be outdated by the time they are printed), consider rotating the P&L clockwise 90 degrees and aligning each executive with one of the major line items (CFO owning profit to the left; COO owning gross margin in the middle; VP of sales owning revenue to the right; etc.). Then you have team leaders owning the next layer of line items and employees owning the last detailed line items. Finish by listing the head of the company at the top of this rotated P&L and you have a useful accountability chart from a results standpoint.

 **ACTION:** *This is a great exercise for the CFO or person in charge of accounting to lead. Go through your financial statements and decide who is accountable for each line item. Then pick the most important line items for each of the functions listed on your FACe tool and transfer the answers to the "Results/ Outcomes" column.*

**NOTE:** *Most organizations, at some point in time, develop detailed job descriptions for all the key roles in a company … a huge project. We are not big fans of job descriptions and prefer Topgrading's Job Scorecards, which you'll learn about in the next chapter.*

Jim Collins, in his book *How the Mighty Fall, And Why Some Companies Never Give In*, shares a key insight he's discovered when working with executive teams. When he initially asks them to introduce themselves, he finds that executives with good companies tend to share their titles, whereas executives at strong and great companies share what their accountabilities are in a very measurable fashion, e.g., "I am accountable for driving revenue into this company."

A concise FACe, with single points of accountability and relevant KPIs and outcomes, aligns with Collins' insight about the leaders of great companies.

## Strategist/Orchestrator vs. Visionary/Integrator

The late Steve Jobs and Tim Cook have been held up as a perfect example of a well-functioning #1 and #2 — a CEO and President/COO — what we call a Strategist and an Orchestrator.

Some have suggested other language like Visionary and Integrator. For one, we hope no CEO runs around referring to themselves as a visionary — that's either a little creepy or egotistical or both. Setting vision is important, but it's just one aspect of what Harvard professor Michael Porter suggests is the #1 job of a CEO, which is set strategy. Strategy encompasses so much more and represents a much more complete role of the top leader.

In turn, if you Google the image of "integrator" it pulls up images of integrated circuits. We integrate things, we orchestrate people. Consider how a conductor leads a symphony. It's with respect, care, and deference. She can't force her lead on the orchestra. Instead, she must appreciate and blend the gifts that each unique musician and instrument contributes to bringing the music alive.

Take a moment and search for Ben Zander "Music Offers Valuable Lessons for Leadership" video. The iconic music director of the Boston Philharmonic Orchestra, Zander has been teaching leadership lessons to global leaders from around the world for decades. As Zander notes, the term "symphony" means to let all voices be heard.

Continuing the analogy, Beethoven would be the Strategist — he wrote the score. Zander would be the Orchestrator, who brings that musical score to life through a talented group of A-Player musicians. He sets the rhythm, coaches each individual team member, and blends all this into something beautiful.

Language matters. How you refer to things/people matters. Give it careful thought before wholesale adopting inaccurate or inappropriate labels for anything or anyone inside the organization.

# Organizational Structure — Beyond Functions

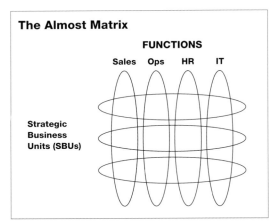

**The Almost Matrix**

**FUNCTIONS**

Sales  Ops  HR  IT

**Strategic Business Units (SBUs)**

The first natural organizational split is by function. When the business gets above 50 employees, the organization needs to start aligning teams around projects, product groups, industry segments, and geographical regions. This is the beginning of what is commonly called a matrix organization (see diagram).

The pressure to create these new business units usually comes from customers. They complain that they don't know whom to call to get help. They get the runaround when they finally reach someone. And they feel overwhelmed by the crush of communications that come from multiple business units. Internally, employees may not know from whom they should take direction.

Unless you get accountabilities straight, productivity and innovation will slow, and you'll waste a lot of time oscillating between centralizing and decentralizing various shared functions among the business units.

To navigate this organizational transition, the functional heads, who have been used to driving the business, need to adapt. They need to become more like coaches/advisors to the business unit leaders, rather than acting as their "bosses." In turn, the heads of the business units need to lead as if they are individual CEOs. You don't want weak "yes-people" heading up your business units.

This transition is hardest for the traditional functional leaders — especially for those who were around in the earlier start-up phase. Used to making unilateral decisions, many will have to switch their style from telling to selling as they spend more time outside the organization garnering best practices and then sharing what they've learned among the business unit leaders. And respect for the functional leaders' decisions will have to be earned, not blankly accepted simply because of their position.

Because of these needed transitions, it's often best to have some of the original functional leaders head business units — maybe head up expansion to a new country or lead the launch of a product line — so they can maintain direct operational control. New functional heads are then recruited who have specific domain expertise (sales, marketing, HR, etc.) and will be more collaborative in working with the business unit leaders.

## Who Is Boss in a Matrix Organization?

A matrix organization is also a challenge for employees since they feel like they have multiple bosses. Employees might be serving several business units, in addition to having a functional head overseeing all their activities.

The key is being clear who decides whether an employee gets a raise or a promotion. The mistake is leaving this decision solely to the functional heads. Instead, take the situation where Tom is providing marketing support to several product lines. The functional head of marketing for the company must see his or her role as a trainer/coach to Tom and make it clear that his performance is assessed based on feedback from the heads of the business units Tom serves — and not on what the functional head alone thinks. This way, Tom remains responsive first and foremost to the business units.

Matrix organizations are tricky, and you should seek expert guidance (we can help). Otherwise, companies can waste a lot of time debating about the centralized or decentralized structure, with endless fights over overhead allocations and accountabilities.

Once you have established clear accountabilities, you'll know very soon if you've gotten it right. Customers will be happy, and everyone on your team will be clear on his or her role in serving customers. If you notice patterns of negative feedback from customers — or see internal signs that your "cells" are not healthy — it's time to revisit the question of organizational structure.

Remember, your company is a living organism that needs to survive in an environment that's always changing. To thrive, it has to be able to adapt. Charles Darwin it's not the survival of the fitness but of the most adaptable.

## Process Accountability Chart (PACe)

The third one-page People tool — the Process Accountability Chart (PACe) — lists who is accountable for each of the four to nine processes that drive the business and how each process will be measured to guarantee it's running smoothly.

Example processes include: developing and launching a product; generating leads and closing sales; attracting, hiring, and onboarding new employees; and billing and collecting payments. Almost all these processes cut across the various functions, requiring a coordination of activities that gets more complicated as the organization scales up.

To keep these processes streamlined, we strongly recommend that companies implement the principles of Lean, a management practice invented by Toyota that is as applicable to service businesses as to manufacturing companies. (It's no accident that Eric Ries called his book *The Lean Startup*.)

Lean is an approach to process design focused on eliminating time wasted on activities that don't add value for customers. Using Lean practices, John Stepleton of Research Data Design (RDD) realized a 28% productivity improvement in his call centers within a week; Mike Jagger saved $60,000 in IT costs from his first Lean session at Provident Security; and Ken Sim, co-founder of the award-winning franchise Nurse Next Door, was able to handle a 100% increase in business in 2008 without adding any headquarters staff.

We are so bullish on Lean that we're confident that the first company in any industry to fully embrace this methodology will dominate. And for those thinking that Lean is synonymous with the overly complicated and expensive Six Sigma approach to quality improvement, you can relax. Lean, though it requires a real change in mindset, uses a few very simple tools to drive dramatic improvements.

Following are four more detailed examples of how the middle-market company leaders just mentioned applied Lean to their processes. We'll then follow with specific how-tos for using the PACe one-pager.

### Power of Lean

John Stepleton — who built 500-person research company RDD, listed three times on the Inc. 500 — was the first CEO to turn us on to Lean as a powerful tool for middle-market service firms. He applied it so successfully that his former firm was recognized by the Northwest Shingo Prize for its innovative implementation of the Lean principles.

If you're not sure that Lean is right for your business, Stepleton emphasizes, "I implemented Lean into my call center business, where I had $10/hour employees engaged in continuous improvement programs, that realized productivity improvements of 28% in time periods as short as one week."

One of the keys to Lean is objectively modeling and measuring productivity and then using simple visual systems to eliminate costly mistakes. In Stepleton's case, his team color-coded research forms to make sure the appropriate number of subjects was called for each campaign.

Booth engaged Guy Parsons, early partner with Jim Womack at the Lean Institute, to help him with his initiatives. Booth also produced a five-minute video interview of Parsons as a way to explain to his team and others how they are using Lean. You can visit *scalingup.com* to view the video.

### Eliminating Waste

"Lean describes waste as anything that happens in a company that a customer would not want to pay for," explains Mike Jagger, CEO of Vancouver, Canada-based Provident Security. "So our first initiative was to divide all of our costs into two columns: things that add value to our clients and things that don't.

"For instance, we have a huge IT investment that we require for our monitoring business, which adds client value," continues Jagger. "However, our clients don't care who hosts our email... so we cancelled our scheduled server upgrade for our exchange servers and migrated the entire company to Gmail."

First-year savings on hardware, software, management, and support were just under $60,000. "We have another great tool now to help us look at the business in a very different way," Jagger says, with regard to Lean.

### Bored Billing Accountant

Ken Sim sent us a partial list of dramatic outcomes from Nurse Next Door's first year of implementing Lean, including growing the business by 100% the following year with eight fewer people in the head office. That's a huge net gain in productivity.

**NOTE:** *Sim emphasizes that there were eight fewer people because of natural attrition. "We will never let go of a person because of Lean," exclaims Sim. "Otherwise, Lean will die as an initiative. No one is going to implement stuff that will end up costing them their job."*

Case in point: Nurse Next Door's payroll and billing accountant, Noreen, was working evenings and weekends before implementing Lean. A year later, with twice the payroll, she was accomplishing the job in half the time. When she mentioned in a huddle that she had nothing to do because of her success, the leadership team suggested she take some time off as an example and incentive for everyone else in the office to pursue Lean initiatives. Nurse Next Door is now teaching these Lean techniques to its franchise partners, so they can work on growing their businesses vs. doing payroll all day.

Parsons, like Sim, warns that Lean is not about reducing headcount. It's about reducing waste. Redirect the time and energy your people get back from eliminating wasted efforts, devoting them to serving customers, making sales, and growing the business.

Nurse Next Door's additional gains from Lean include doubling the current volume of its call center without adding headcount, while reducing fees to franchise partners; eliminating process steps to ease franchise partners' work flow and make more money; reducing inventory levels to almost zero so franchise partners require much less capital to start and run their businesses; and streamlining the process for adding new franchise partners.

Adds Sim: "It used to be a challenge to add one new franchise partner each quarter. Now we add two per month and can add up to five per month without breaking a sweat! More important, our Lean initiatives are a major reason (but not the only one) that we and our franchise partners have been able to thrive during a terrible economic period."

## Completing Your Process Accountability Chart (PACe)

### STEP ❶

Gather your executive team together (it's smart to include some team leaders further down in the organization) and name the four to nine key processes driving the business. Several of the processes — like "How do we bill and collect from customers?" — will be similar for most companies. However, there will be a few that are specific to your firm or industry. In our experience, this chart takes a couple of 90-minute sessions to complete.

Here are the seven processes for Barcelona-based Softonic, the world's leading Web portal for downloading free, safe software:

- Recruitment
- Product development
- Sales to cash
- Innovation

- People development
- Customer satisfaction
- Content creation and publication

 **ACTION:** *Discuss and agree on the four to nine key processes in your organization.*

## STEP ❷

Next, assign accountability for each process to a specific person. This can be a more difficult decision than initially perceived. Since processes cut across various functions, there might be some turf battles between the functions. In this case, remind everyone that assigning someone accountability for a process doesn't mean that he is the new boss of everyone who touches the process, nor does he necessarily have increased decision-making authority. His job is to monitor the process (time, cost, quality), let the team know if there are any issues, and lead a regular meeting to fix or improve that particular process. Ideally, this person will have some cross-functional experience.

The person to whom all these process leaders report is usually the head of operations (a COO type). Operations people are generally systems-focused. You want a head of operations who is obsessed with process mapping and improvement — or better yet, experienced in implementing Lean.

 **ACTION:** *For each key process you've identified, decide who within the organization will be accountable. These people are then accountable to the head of operations.*

## STEP ❸

Identify a few KPIs to track each process. As with the FACe tool, the Process Accountability Chart (PACe) requires that each process have indicators (time, cost, or quality) that will signify its health.

One of the most important KPIs for processes is time — in either number of days (to deliver) or number of hours (to produce). It applies to almost every industry, as customers normally want things better, faster, and cheaper, whether we're talking about a product or service. Although time is not the only KPI, it does drive efficiency in your business and customer satisfaction and is the key measurement in the Lean process of designing and streamlining processes.

 **ACTION:** *List one to three KPIs for each process to measure its speed, quality, and cost.*

Following are a few resources that can help you improve the PACe of the organization.

## Mapping the Process

Once you have completed your PACe, gather someone from every function that touches a specific process, including a few customers who are affected by the process (if possible). Using colored Post-it Notes to represent each function (sales is green, accounting is blue, etc.), map out the steps and decision points as the process currently flows. Then step back and begin streamlining the process, eliminating wasteful steps and removing obstacles.

For instance, think about how a certain piece of paper (physical or electronic) moves from a website, to an email inbox, to an order fulfillment desk in the warehouse, including emailed confirmations and order tracking systems for the customer. You'll be surprised at the number of steps and people required for a simple process.

Along the way, set specific KPIs at critical steps and decision points, so the process can be monitored continuously. The beauty of identifying and documenting the processes in your business is that it provides you with an excellent how-to manual for new employees or existing ones who are off track.

It's important to revisit and examine one process every 90 days as part of your quarterly planning process. Like hallway closets and garages, these processes get junked up and need to be recleaned periodically. With four to nine processes, each will get examined roughly every 12 to 24 months, which is sufficient to keep your company running drama-free.

 **ACTION:** *Assemble the appropriate people for each key process, and list, debate, and decide the steps and decision points for that process.*

 **NOTE:** *As mentioned earlier in the PACe section of this chapter, we highly recommend using the tools from Lean to both map and improve your processes. Take a look at Paul Akers' "2 Second Lean" videos on YouTube, including how to set up a "lean desk."*

## Time to Reduce "Division of Labor"

The industrial age pulled us off our homesteads and lined us up in factories to produce stuff — with dozens of people touching a process (or piece of paper) along the way — institutionalizing the idea of "division of labor." We were expected to repeat the same activity, often mindless work, over and over for years.

Division of labor, over time, extended to all aspects of scaling a business. With the advent of technology, much of this is starting to change. In short, you want to figure out how to have the fewest people handling as much of the total process as possible. Fewer handoffs means fewer chances to slow the process or create errors.

Motorcycle manufacturer Harley Davidson embraced this change a decade ago when it razed 41 buildings on 232 acres and replaced them with one streamlined facility. Rather than a motorcycle frame crawling along a standard assembly line, teams of five or six people now assemble an entire custom motorcycle (one of 1,200 variations). The factory's 62 job classifications were slashed to five and cut in half the number of salaried staffers. Today, frontline employees initiate process improvements daily.

The same approach is just as necessary in services work as manufacturing. Dozens of people touch the process of securing a mortgage, making it a frustrating and time-consuming experience for everyone. The same holds true with various accounting and customer service processes. Relying on more automation and cross training, so a smaller team can tackle more of an entire process, will make work more interesting and easier. See where this might be applicable in your firm.

## Checklists

Once you've identified and mapped your processes, you can then bring them to life every day through checklists. Checklists are valuable for key parts of your four to nine processes and help ensure that the right things happen.

In his book *The Checklist Manifesto: How to Get Things Right*, Dr. Atul Gawande shares how his research on improving success in surgeries came down to a simple surgery checklist. Among Gawande's findings: "[Checklists help] with memory recall and clearly set out the minimum necessary steps in a process. ... In this one hospital, the checklist had prevented forty-three infections and eight deaths and saved two million dollars in costs. ... [Checklists] provide a kind of cognitive net. They catch mental flaws inherent in all of us — flaws of memory and attention and thoroughness. ... I have yet to get through a week in surgery without the checklist's leading us to catch something we would have missed."

Apple stores draw more people in one single quarter than visit Disney's four major theme parks in one year. How does Apple do it? One reason is that it is known for delivering fantastic customer service. An article appearing in *The Wall Street Journal* shared some insight on Apple's checklist of simple and easy-to-remember steps of service training, the initial letters of which spell out APPLE:

- **A**pproach customers with a personalized warm welcome.
- **P**robe politely to understand all the customers' needs.
- **P**resent a solution for the customers to take home.
- **L**isten for and resolve any issues or concerns.
- **E**nd with a fond farewell and an invitation to return.

We'll discuss the power of checklists more in the "Execution" section of the book. In the meantime, if you're experiencing some drama, maybe a simple checklist will help.

To conclude, the strength of your People comes from the right leadership doing the right things right (FACe); and the right systems and processes supporting these people to keep the business flowing (PACe). With the combination of the right FACe and the right PACe, you have the key people and process ingredients for a great company.

# 4

# THE TEAM
## Attacting, Hiring, and Coaching

---

**EXECUTIVE SUMMARY:** *Attracting and hiring A Players, at all levels of the organization, is as critical as landing the right customers. This requires a robust employee referral program, active support from the marketing function, and the use of Topgrading methodology in the interviewing and selection process. With all three, detailed in this chapter, your company will have a huge pool of candidates from which to choose enough "strange" people (who fit your differentiated strategy and culture) to scale up the business.*

*Once you've hired your team members, it takes great managers/coaches to keep them happy and engaged. We identify five critical activities that distinguish great managers and the routines they use to educate their people — and we suggest that the term "manager" be replaced with the word "coach," which more accurately describes the role. We'll also share hard evidence that investments in training and coaching (vs. R&D and capital expenditures) provide you with the best returns available to your business.*

 **NOTE:** *The cost of a bad hire is 15x his or her annual salary, according to Topgrading, so it's important to get the recruiting and selection process right.*

---

When Scott Nash needed a CFO for MOM's Organic Market, simply asking a recruiter to scour the country for a financial whiz who knew the grocery industry wasn't going to cut it. Nash founded MOM's in 1987, at age 22, as a home delivery and mail order company based in his mother's garage in Maryland. It has a unique culture, built around the company's Purpose: *to protect and restore the environment*. Now a chain of 22 stores with 1000+ employees, MOM's is willing to walk away from potential sales to stick with its core commitment. For instance, it bans the sale of plastic water bottles in its stores. So MOM's challenge was recruiting a top-notch CFO willing to embrace the spirit of the company's Purpose while navigating the financial trade-offs required to "live" it.

Gene Browne, who founded Galway-based The City Bin Co. in 1997, was facing a similar challenge recruiting people to work on the back of his garbage trucks and then keeping them. Though his business was recognized as one of the Best Managed Companies in Ireland by Deloitte for four consecutive years and won Deloitte's Gold Standard Award, CEO Browne still couldn't easily attract and hold on to employees to sling garbage cans. It's a dirty and physically demanding job requiring an early start in the morning.

Follow along as we share how Nash, Browne, and other leaders recruit and hire tough-to-find talent.

## Will, Values, Results, Skill

It's important to hire the best A Player you can find for each position in your company based on four criteria (in this order!):

- **Will** — a desire to excel, act with courage, persevere, learn, and innovate
- **Values** — the test for culture fit — do they align with your core values
- **Results** — in the end can they deliver on your KPIs/outcomes
- **Skills** — the least important since most skill-sets need updating every 5 years

Doing so builds an internal momentum and strength that pays dividends for years. You hire the right people and life is great; you hire the wrong people (fit) and life is miserable.

Based on these four criteria, create a Job Scorecard (vs. the standard job description). A Job Scorecard details a person's purpose for the job, the desired outcomes of this individual's work, and the competencies — technical and cultural — required to execute it. This tool is part of Topgrading, a methodology for hiring A Players, co-created by Brad and Geoff Smart. We consider it the best interviewing and selection system available. It has a proven track record of helping leaders hire the right person more than 90% of the time vs. the 25% to 60% success rates achieved with "feel-good" conversations, testing, or standard behavior-based interviewing approaches. And considering the costs of making a bad hire, it pays to get this process right.

An A Player, by the Smarts' definition, is someone in the top 10% of the available talent pool who is willing to accept your specific offer. Read that definition again.

### — Sample Job Scorecard —

**Position:** Inside Sales Representative
**Location:** Chicago, IL

**Mission:**
The core mission of the Inside Sales Representative is to increase revenue from new and existing customers. Inside Sales Representatives will be expected to make cold calls in addition to following up on leads from marketing activities. Customer contact is mainly via telephone and e-mail. Inside Sales Representatives sell advertisements in a specialized medical trade publication and sponsorships for an annual conference.

**Accountabilities**

| | Metric | Rating (A, B, C) | Comments |
|---|---|---|---|
| Generate revenue | • $15,000 monthly within 3 months<br>• $40,000 monthly within 12 months | | |
| Average sale size | $4,000+ within 12 months | | |
| Customer volume | • Closes sales with at least 4 customers monthly within 3 months<br>• Closes sales with at least 10 customers monthly within 12 months | | |
| Activity (tracked by completion of daily activity sheets) | • 50 cold calls per day<br>• 5 scheduled sales presentation phone appointments per day<br>• At least 10 proposals sent per week | | |
| Documentation | Completes all necessary documentation on time | | |

**Key Competencies**

- Integrity
- Results-Oriented
- Excellence
- Customer Focus
- Resourcefulness

- Listening
- Energy/Drive
- Work Ethic
- Goal Setting

They are not implying that you have to pay beyond what your business model can sustain. They do mean that you need to attract the largest and most capable talent pool excited about the job and willing to accept your compensation package (e.g., McDonald's has the same chances of hiring A Players as Goldman Sachs), and have the tools to select the best people from this group of prospects. The Job Scorecard is the starting point.

A central element of a Job Scorecard is the handful of specific and measurable outcomes that a potential hire needs to accomplish over the coming one to three years. While a job description tends to list what people will be doing (e.g., coaching sales reps, building client relationships), a

Job Scorecard describes the outcomes you want from such activities ($8 million in revenue, seven new S&P 500 clients, a 100% contract renewal rate among the customers the trash collector serves). This is a critical distinction between the job description (hope you've not wasted time creating these) and the Topgrading Job Scorecard.

Being specific about outcomes allows you to directly evaluate each candidate's capacity to actually deliver these results. Can you really see the person you're interviewing taking your top line from $20 million to $35 million over the next three years? Is there anything in her history of results that supports this conclusion? (For more practical insights about building Job Scorecards, read Bluewire Media's excellent blog on the topic.)

Another central element is the list of candidate competencies that align with your culture and strategy. As experienced leaders discover, it's more important to hire for this kind of fit than for specific skills, so long as a person has the capacity to learn and grow (though it's best if you can find someone who's a match in both cultural values and skill set). The rapidly changing requirements of most professions require a constant updating of skills, anyway. On the other hand, cultures are like immune systems and will spit out very capable people who don't align with its norms (Core Values).

In addition to seeking culture fit, it is critical to hire people who can deliver on the Brand Promises and activities underpinning your strategy (see "The 7 Strata of Strategy" chapter). The City Bin Co. looks for garbage collectors who possess the competencies to deliver on its customer service promise. Southwest Airlines needs flight attendants who can deliver on its Brand Promise of "Lots of Fun."

These central elements of the Job Scorecard — the outcomes and competencies — drive the recruiting, interviewing, and selection process.

## The Best Hires

Good managers play checkers while great managers play chess, according to researchers Marcus Buckingham and Curt Coffman, authors of *First, Break All the Rules: What the World's Greatest Managers Do Differently*. In checkers, the pieces all move in the same way, whereas in chess, the pieces move differently, allowing you to bring different strengths to the game.

In scaling up the people side of your business, it's crucial that you start playing chess sooner rather than later. Think of "The A-Team" of action television fame — a ragtag group of renegades bringing their individual and unique talents, personalities, and strengths together to act on the side of good!

You, too, need a team of absolute specialists — chess pieces — to achieve your ambitious goals. In our experience, the learning curve for well-rounded generalists (checker pieces) is simply too long and too steep in today's fast and complex world. This is why we encourage leaders to look for "idiot savants" (i.e., people who are extremely talented at one particular thing and possibly quite bad at others). As Geoff Smart points out, "You would not let your family-practice doctor perform open-heart surgery on you." Teams need to be well-rounded, but their individual members don't have to be. Leaders don't always grasp this, which explains why the traditional "feel-good" interview has such a high failure rate. We have a tendency to hire people most like ourselves and end up with a company of look-alikes vs. tapping the diversity of talent, backgrounds, and personalities needed to drive the fruitful debate, innovation, and differentiation that powers growth.

Daniel M. Cable goes one step further and suggests you hire people who are downright strange. Author of *Change to Strange: Create a Great Organization by Building a Strange Workforce* (a book that we strongly suggest you read), Cable notes, "If your competitive advantage depends on your people creating something valuable and distinctive, then your workforce can't be normal." Therefore, if you want to have a differentiated strategy, you can't hire, compensate, and have the same HR systems supporting the same people as your competition.

 **NOTE:** *You need a "strange" culture and a "strange" strategy to differentiate your firm in the marketplace. This is why it's so critical to discern the real Core Values underpinning your culture; and create the elements of an industry-dominating strategy. (How to do both is detailed in the "Strategy" section of this book.) With these values and strategic attributes, you can then generate Job Scorecards, as described above, and use them to identify the right "strange" people to hire.*

## First Source of Talent

According to Geoff Smart's extensive research on hiring A-Players, the best source of talent is referrals from your existing employees. The exception is recruiting senior leaders, where you want to tap into your broader network of influencers and contacts and/or use a headhunting firm.

The key to scaling up employee referrals is offering a substantial enough recruiting bonus — something closer to $5,000 vs. the $500 average we see most mid-market firms offer. And to encourage the team to support the new recruits, we suggest you pay 10% of the bonus when the referral is hired; another 40% when the recruit has been there six months; and the final 50% on the one- (or two-) year anniversary.

If attracting talent is a key constraint to your growth, the CEO must make hiring A-Players a priority. At ProService in Hawaii, you'll notice in this photo that CEO Ben Godsey is leading one of the various teams responsible for recruiting candidates for hire. And it's obvious from the design of the scoreboard that recruiting bonuses are a key component of the company's strategy for encouraging referrals.

## Recruiting Is a (Guerilla) Marketing Function

The best source of talent is referrals. However, this might not provide enough candidates quickly enough, so you will need clever ways to attract a sufficient applicant pool of specialists who fit your culture. Research strongly suggests that you need a minimum of 20 applicants per position (frontline to senior) if you want to dramatically increase your odds of hiring A Players. Sadly, because of the stress that comes with growth, many leaders simply hire whoever comes along and can fog the mirror (e.g., "You're breathing. You're hired!").

This is why marketing is such a critical function to scaling up a business. The marketing team must be as actively involved in recruiting a steady stream of potential employees as it is in attracting potential customers, yet most organizations fail miserably in this area. They think the perfect candidates will fall from the sky. The best candidates are probably working somewhere else and need a reason to consider your organization. And because budgets are always tight in growing firms, you must find clever marketing approaches to attract the specific kind of "strange" talent you're seeking.

One of the classic recruiting campaigns was launched by Google in its early years. A single billboard (placed near Yahoo's headquarters — "Fish where there are fish"), with no mention of the company, simply displayed a sophisticated math riddle. The mere intrigue of the billboard generated millions of dollars of free publicity as the technorati went nuts over the question of who placed the ad. This, in turn, exposed the ad to tens of thousands of potential hires.

The actual solution to the puzzle led to a series of websites with additional equations to solve. Eventually, Google identified itself as the author of the billboard and said: "One thing we learned while building Google is that it's easier to find what you're looking for if it comes looking for you. What we're looking for are the best engineers in the world. And here you are."

This kind of guerilla marketing is within any company's reach. Atlassian, an Australian software company, hired 15 developers after it toured 15 European cities with a flashy bus that bore this message in large letters: "Europe, we're coming to steal your geeks" — generating loads of free publicity as news agencies reported on the unusual bus tour. Employment Group, a Michigan staffing firm, invited the local business journal to cover its quarterly meetings themed around various rock bands. This landed the company several fun articles and resulted in a score of unsolicited quality résumés. It is easy to stand out if you use whatever approach fits your culture and you show some originality.

## MOM's Goes Fishing

To find the ideal CFO candidate for MOM's Organic Market, rather than advertise on job boards or in the local *Washington Post*, CEO Nash cast a line where those most likely interested in his company's Purpose tend to hang out. He placed an ad for a CFO on Treehugger.com, a green-living and environmental news site. The ad asked questions chosen to help the company attract a financial pro who fit into the culture of MOM's: Do you want to work for a David, rather than a Goliath? Are you an entrepreneur in a CPA's body? Would you rather come to work in jeans? (To read a copy of the full ad, go to *scalingup.com*.)

Bingo! MOM's received 40 résumés in a week from a group of great candidates who clearly understood and appreciated the company's Purpose. Ultimately, Nash hired Kelly Moler, who had the requisite talent and shared the team's green values. Over the next 13 years she helped the profitable company navigate the challenges of growing to $230 million in annual revenue (2019) amid competition from giant players like Whole Foods.

MOM's has taken a similar approach to attract candidates in a variety of other positions, from grocery baggers to executive-level jobs. For instance, on the "Join us" page on its website, a recent advertisement said:

*You:*
- *are really interested in electric vehicles*
- *appreciate a good debate, even with your boss*
- *figure out how to fix it instead of who's to blame*
- *paid for your own stuff when you were a teenager*
- *have pulled recyclables out of the trash*

*We:*
- *work to protect and restore the environment*
- *like real food*
- *aren't afraid to make mistakes*
- *care more about your intelligence and values than your experience*

The ads have helped the company save time and money on attracting and retaining talent. "Ten years ago or so, before we did a lot of this stuff, people were churning in and out," recalls Nash. The typical candidate, he says, "was someone who wanted a paycheck. MOM's was a stepping-stone for people to go someplace better." Since MOM's tailored its recruitment strategy to its core culture, he says, "retention rates have just skyrocketed. It seems to be easier to hire people and find people." The ad, he notes, "is an example of how we give our company culture and value a high priority."

Appletree Answers, whose success in tackling employee turnover we'll discuss in "The Core" chapter, typically receives 500 to 600 applicants for every open call-center position it has — attributable to its reputation as a great place to work. Austin-based Rackspace Hosting, a longtime Rockefeller Habits practitioner, received 52,000 applicants for 569 openings in 2013, blowing away the recommended 20:1 ratio — again, driven by a stellar reputation. Rackspace has made *Fortune's* list of the 100 Best Companies to Work For five times.

 **NOTE:** *Given that even Harvard's record-low acceptance rate for the Class of 2026 was 3.19% (1,954 admissions out of 61,220 applicants), it's been noted that it's harder to get a job at Rackspace than to get accepted into an Ivy League school!*

Making it onto Best Places to Work lists, even local ones in your region or city, is a clear sign of an attractive workplace that will draw applicants to your company. A book written by the CEO (something we strongly recommend); a regular column in the local biz journal; a popular blog; and/or regular LinkedIn Influencer posts are great recruiting (and marketing) tools and ways to grab attention in an industry.

The City Bin Co.'s Gene Browne was winning similar workplace awards and garnering excellent local attention, yet he needed to get creative in attracting the right people to work on the back of his garbage trucks. Hearing Dan Cable, author of *Change to Strange*, speak at a Young Presidents' Organization program at London Business School, Browne wondered:

1. How can we expect our employees to be extraordinary and differentiate the company if we use the same hiring and onboarding methods as competitors?

2. What characteristics describe our ideal workforce that our competitors could not or would not use to describe theirs?

For Browne to try to differentiate his waste collection company through service is tricky, since the people working on the back of the trucks are the ones who can make or break a service experience. Yet shortly after Dan's lecture, something "strange" happened. A young man named Gary Manogue applied for a back-of-the-truck job because (a) he saw it as a chance to do part of his daily workout while also being paid and (b) the early start and finish times suited his lifestyle. Gary was a competitive kickboxer and had ambitions to win a world title fight. He needed to train as many hours a day as possible. In December 2013, Gary became the world super welterweight kickboxing champion. In a pre-fight interview, the *Galway Advertiser* noted:

> "This is Manogue's first seven-round fight and he has prepared with a fitness regime that involves an eight-kilometre run every morning, work-out in the gym in the evening, and in between working for The City Bin Co. 'Running after bins keeps me pretty fit too,' he says."

Based on this chance situation, The City Bin Co. has since developed a hiring campaign aimed at unemployed young men (no shortage of these in Ireland) who are big into fitness, asking, "Would you like to be paid for your daily workout?" The company is advertising in local gyms and letting word-of-mouth do the rest. These young men do not perceive the job in the same way as the typical young person who is handing out CVs looking for a job.

Like MOM's and The City Bin Co., many growth companies realize that to achieve their goals, they need the right people on the bus. But in many industries, these folks aren't just waiting at the bus stop. And you won't find them solely by advertising on job boards. The key to finding them, as Nash, Browne, and others have discovered, is by creating a recruitment strategy that reflects your Core Values and Purpose and then using your marketing skills to reach the right potential pool of talent.

### Unique "Fishing Holes" to Find Talent

Michael Dell recruited laid-off Kodak employees for many of his early team members — and later turned to MIT's Sloan School (engineers with MBAs) for the leaders he needed to run his factories. These were two of his regular "fishing holes" for talent. What are your unique fishing holes?

What you want to avoid is recruiting from within your own industry. Poaching from competitors means you not only have to train your new hires but also "untrain" them first. And you probably can't pay them much more than they were making if you're in the same industry.

One client, in the retail carpet business, turned to a similar (but not the same) industry — shoe retailing — to source her top salespeople. Their retail selling skills ported over beautifully yet they brought with them no biases about how to sell carpet. And because they had the potential to make twice as much selling carpet than shoes, they were enthusiastic recruits.

Another client discovered his alma mater's athletic department had a separate placement office. Given that the first requirement for hiring is "will," these student athletes have already demonstrated their willingness to learn, play as a team, and persevere in the face of defeat.

Once you start successfully recruiting from a single source (adjacent industry, firm, university, etc.), those employees will help you attract others from the same source, creating a virtuous vs. vicious recruiting cycle.

## The Topgrading Interview

Once you have attracted a large number of qualified candidates, which significantly increases your chances of finding A Players, a rock-solid evaluation process (not your gut feeling) is needed to bring the numbers down from 20 to 10, then to three, and finally to the one top candidate who will deliver 150% of your Job Scorecard.

At MOM's, the online job application asks questions such as "What companies do you admire?" to get a sense of a candidate's values. "That gets us to a place where we know what is important to them," says Nash. The company also asks why applicants are interested in MOM's. "Some people say they want to work for MOM's because we're in a booming industry. They want job security and some money. That's okay, but it has nothing to do with our values."

These gatekeeper questions, along with various online tests we recommend — Assess Systems' wide range of pre-employment tests and OMG's Sales Assessments among them — are very helpful in narrowing your long list to the final five or 10 candidates.

At this point, it's time to interview. And as mentioned above, the process we recommend is Topgrading. For an excellent overview, read Geoff Smart and Randy Street's book *Who: The A Method for Hiring*; to learn the details of the process, read Bradford D. Smart's book *Topgrading: The Proven Hiring and Promoting Method That Turbocharges Company Performance*. We also recommend that at companies doing regular hiring, at least one person become a Certified Master Practitioner through an online course at *scalingup.com* that includes several hours of video instruction by Brad Smart; interaction with other practitioners; and one-on-one coaching with one of Smart's certified trainers.

The Topgrading methodology starts with a PreScreen Snapshot (PSSS), a SaaS offering from Topgrading. All candidates can be easily directed to this online tool where, in 10 minutes, a candidate shares detailed information on their last two jobs. PSSS then provides you a visual "snapshot" of the candidate and guides you in choosing who to interview.

Notes Nyisha Moore, Director of Human Resources, Automation X, "Using the PreScreen Snapshot, I save about 16 hours for every time I fill an open position and I get much better candidates."

All Scaling Up coaching partners can share with you a free trial of this online tool.

Next, Topgrading provides a screening interview to further narrow your list from 10 to the top three candidates.. This interview consists of five powerful screening interview questions. They work for any position for which you're hiring and can be addressed in 30 to 45 minutes over the phone or in a short meeting.

Once you're down to the top three candidates, it's time for the Chronological In-Depth Structured (CIDS) interview — a thorough three- to four-hour interview covering a candidate's entire career history, with the objective of discovering behavioral and performance patterns that are likely to repeat themselves at your workplace. When hiring, bear in mind that past performance is the best indicator of future performance.

The length of this interview offers several benefits:

1. A Players like a vigorous process and are leery of companies that make it too easy.

2. "Professional" interviewees can't keep up the façade for hours.

3. Meanwhile, those who are not initially comfortable will have time to relax and open up.

4. Besides, what's three to four hours now vs. thousands of hours of headaches if you hire the wrong person?

 **NOTE:** *A three- to four-hour interview is appropriate for a middle or senior leader; one to two hours might be more suitable for entry-level or less experienced candidates with limited work history.*

While Topgrading was initially designed for senior executives at General Electric, it works at all levels. Speed Wire, a cabling contractor headquartered on Long Island, grew from 25 employees to 325 (mainly technicians) in one year, relying on Topgrading to make sure all its hires were A Players. Kevin Donnelly, founder of Speed Wire (now a MasTec company), was thrilled with the results. "We can't believe the caliber of people it has helped us hire. We couldn't have done it without Topgrading," he says.

At MOM's, Nash will lead the three- to four-hour Topgrading interviews with candidates for major positions, like successful CFO candidate Kelly Moler, while MOM's managers will do abbreviated interviews with other employees. "It's the most effective method I've come across," says Nash. The company will go through each candidate's entire work history, as recommended, and ask questions about whom they reported to at each job — including the spelling of that boss's name, to show that the company is serious about checking references. A typical follow-on question is, "What will so-and-so say about you?" "It's a real truth serum," says Nash. (This process is called TORC — Threat of Reference Check — in the Topgrading methodology. It works!) Interviewers will also ask candidates to discuss a time that they had to deal with a difficult boss or when someone said something painful to them. "We're looking for people who receive candor well," says Nash.

## Check for Culture Fit

As emphasized earlier, MOM's has customized the interview to its values. Nash believes that people who had to earn money for themselves as teenagers tend to be well-grounded, so the questions might include: "What did you spend money on as a teenager? How did you get that money?" (Hint to future candidates: You will not impress the team at MOM's by saying your parents gave you a $100-a-week allowance.) An interviewer might also ask questions like: "Do you discuss religion and politics with people? When was your last passionate debate? Who was it with? And what was it about? How did it turn out?" "If the answer to the last question was, 'I'll never respect that person again,' we know the person isn't open to different ideas," says Nash.

Checking for culture fit in the interview process can be handled in a variety of ways. At Southwest Airlines, for example, if people don't get the team's omnipresent jokes, it's clear that the airline is not the right place for them. Commerce Bank first screens for people smiling while waiting to be interviewed. At online apparel retailer Zappos, administrative assistants always handle part of the interviewing and testing, even for C-suite candidates. If a candidate seems irritated at being interviewed by lower-level employees, he probably lacks one of Zappos' Core Values, which is being humble.

## Test-Drive Potential Employees

Though it's not always possible, the best way to select the right people is to have candidates work with you for several weeks. For frontline hires, temp-to-perm placement firms are popular because they allow you to test-drive candidates. For leadership hires, see if they can work with you in the evenings on a consulting basis. The founders of Google appointed Eric Schmidt chairman of the board of directors four months before making him CEO.

Zappos requires all new hires, no matter what the position (executive, programmer, marketer), go through a four-week training program that includes extensive time working in its call center serving customers. During this trial period, they offer these newbies a $3,000 bonus (besides their salary for the month) if they quit, guaranteeing that only those who really want to work at Zappos stay. Since acquiring Zappos, Amazon has adopted something similar for fulfillment-center workers called Pay to Quit. In an employee's first year of work, the offer is $2,000. It goes up by $1,000 every year after that until it hits $5,000. The idea, writes Amazon's former CEO Jeff Bezos in his 2014 letter to shareholders, is "to encourage folks to take a moment and think about what they really want. In the long run, an employee staying somewhere they don't want to be isn't healthy for the employee or the company."

Next, we'll look at the leadership and people systems that Nash, Browne, and other leaders use to keep and grow this talent.

# Keep Your Talent Engaged With One Question

People join companies. They leave managers. Therefore, to keep your team happy and engaged, you need one thing above all else: great managers/coaches — not free lunches or yoga classes! As Gallup notes, "Managers account for at least 70% of variance in employee engagement scores." And great managers/coaches are not just born; they are continually advancing their skills and those of their employees.

As the business scales to more than 100 employees, reaching a critical point at which everyone doesn't know everyone else's name, it becomes crucial for the leadership team to build a capable team of team leads/coaches. As mentioned earlier in the book, failure to develop sufficient leadership is one of the three biggest barriers to growth.

So what does a great manager/coach do to keep a company's team happy and engaged? To answer this question, Google applied its data analytics capability, led by a "people analytics team," to bring the same level of rigor to People-decisions that it does to engineering challenges. What the data showed is that periodic one-on-one coaching (rather than superior technical knowledge) ranked as the #1 key to being a successful leader.

Similarly, Gallup found that employees don't want an "administrative-like" manager — that's why we have technology (like Align/Scoreboard!). Instead, they want coached. And at the risk of oversimplifying, Gallup CEO Jim Clifton suggested it revolved around asking every employee one question each week "*what is your goal and the barrier(s) to achieving it?*" Both answers provide coachable/teachable moments. First, is their goal (sprint) this week aligned with the company's goals; and second, how might they navigate the latest barrier(s) to achieving it?

This is why the daily huddle, which we'll detail in "The Meetings" chapter, is so powerful. In essence, every employee is being asked the equivalent of this question every day! After several days their team leader will see a pattern of priorities and "stucks" which provides the content for a coaching conversation each week or two.

More specifically, great managers must focus these coaching sessions with their "direct supports" (a better term than "direct reports") on five topics representing the five main activities of successful managers/coaches. In reverse order of importance:

5. Hire fewer people, but pay them more.

4. Give recognition, and show appreciation.

3. Set clear expectations, and give employees a clear line of sight.

2. Don't demotivate; "dehassle."

1. Help people play to their strengths.

Let's look at each of these activities in detail.

## 5. Hire less; higher pay.

Daniel H. Pink, in his best-selling book *Drive: The Surprising Truth About What Motivates Us*, shows why compensation is a lot less effective as a motivational tool than we thought. Extrinsic motivators ("carrots and sticks") have been overrated and become less effective in a world that needs more and more well-educated, right-brain knowledge workers. And people will sacrifice certain perks to work with a firm with a worthy Purpose that's making a difference.

Does that make compensation irrelevant? Of course not! If companies aren't competitive, it becomes challenging for them to attract and keep the best talent. When MOM's finds great people, at every level, it pays them more than the industry average. For instance, the company's minimum wage is $15 an hour, higher than that in its home state of Maryland, which is $12.50 an hour as this book went to press.

The key to affording higher wages (we're talking frontline employees, not senior leadership) is a lower total wage cost as a percent of revenue. You have to remain competitive, and the best companies know that one great person can replace three good ones. Through rigorous selection (i.e., Topgrading), they get the absolute best talent in the door, pay employees above-market rates, and then invest heavily in training and development to make them more productive.

Take storage-product retailer The Container Store, which has been named to the *Fortune's* list of Best Companies to Work For 14 years in a row (and counting!). Its Foundational Principle #1 is "1 Equals 3" — one great person equals three good people in terms of business productivity. "We have to be selective when interviewing potential employees because of the Brand Promise we've made to our customers to provide exceptional customer service," notes the company's website. As a result, the Texas-based chain hires only about 3% of all who apply. In turn, the company says, it pays salespeople as much as 50% to 100% more than the retail industry average, and provides 263 hours of training to all first-year full-time employees, compared to an industry average of seven hours. To paraphrase what the co-founders said when they launched their innovative retail concept, "Do we want a whole bunch of low-paid dumb folk; or would we rather have a whole lot fewer, better-paid smart folk?"

Costco pays its employees roughly 70% more per hour than Sam's Club, yet needs almost 40% fewer employees per dollar of revenue. And with a 6% employee turnover after one year vs. 21% for Sam's, Costco saves a tremendous amount on recruiting, training, and development. In general, competing on low labor and training costs is a slippery road and usually not sustainable.

And if you think this pattern holds only for low-wage jobs: Goldman Sachs pays its employees an average compensation package almost twice as big as the competition's, yet it has fewer than half the number of employees on a per-revenue basis and almost three times the profit per employee. Again, fewer people, paid more, with higher productivity.

How you structure the compensation — variable vs. fixed — should fit your culture. If your culture emphasizes rugged individualism, like Nordstrom, you might want to have a high-commission/bonus-based compensation plan driven by internal competition among employees. Given the culture of teamwork at The Container Store and its emphasis on customer service, paying store employees a straight (and high) hourly wage without commissions makes sense. Look to your Core Values, your business model, and your Brand Promise, and let them instruct you in the design of your compensation plan. Don't copy somebody else's system.

*"Don't copy somebody else's compensation system."*

Last, when it comes to the key people who absolutely drive performance, great managers/coaches simply do whatever it takes to keep them on board, including offering a customized compensation package. If one person wants less base and more incentive-based pay, so be it. If another wants more time off, let it happen. "Fairness" does not mean "sameness." You need to be creative and flexible in order to keep your top talent happy, from a compensation-package perspective.

Wages are one of your biggest expenses and should be used strategically to differentiate your firm from the competition, as in the examples above (and the Outback Steakhouse "X-Factor" example in "The 7 Strata of Strategy" chapter). Purchasing a compensation comparison study and paying people the same as everyone else will relegate the company to the heap of average firms.

 **NOTE:** *For more insights into setting up compensation plans, read* Scaling Up Compensation: 5 Design Principles for Turning Your Largest Expense into a Strategic Advantage *by Verne Harnish and Sebastian Ross. At just over 100 pages, it's a very quick read with dozens of practical examples of mid-market organization's compensation schemes. "Get it right and out of sight" is a key goal of the right compensation system.*

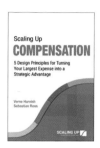

## 4. Give recognition and show appreciation.

"The deepest principle of human nature is the craving to be appreciated," wrote William James, the father of American psychology. It is impossible to be motivated and do great work if you don't feel that somebody cares and appreciates what you do.

Studies have shown that for people to be happy and productive at work, they need to experience positive interactions (appreciation, praise) vs. negative (reprimands, criticism) with their manager/coach in a ratio of at least 3:1. (Watch out: For a marriage to work, you actually need a 5:1 ratio!!) So make it a simple habit to thank people each and every day — and that includes using the word generously in emails to your team.

The way people want to receive recognition varies greatly: public vs. private, material vs. immaterial, from peers vs. from superiors, etc. Great managers/coaches test different approaches and observe reactions until they find the triggers that work best with each of their people. At MOM's Organic Market, managers will sometimes publicly recognize employees who have performed well, but CEO Scott Nash has often found that one-on-one comments are most effective.

To get ideas on how to create a culture of recognition and appreciation, see Chip Conley's excellent book *Peak: How Great Companies Get Their Mojo from Maslow*, Chapter 5.

## 3. Set clear expectations and provide a line of sight.

Great managers/coaches explain how their people's work contributes to the greater objectives of the company and then help them align their individual priorities with those of the firm. This is what Jack Stack, author of the book *The Great Game of Business: The Only Sensible Way to Run a Company*, calls "line of sight," an important concept to create engagement and a sense of purpose. Can your employees explain how what they're doing helps deliver on your company's purpose, strategy, and Brand Promise?

Once people understand their role and contribution, great managers/coaches set clear and consistent expectations about the outcomes of their team's work. By defining the *what* and not the *how*, great managers/coaches give employees the autonomy to find their own way of achieving these goals. Feeling the liberty to figure things out for themselves and apply their own style is very important for people, since autonomy is one of three main drivers of human motivation, as Dan Pink explains in *Drive*.

Many managers/coaches struggle with defining adequate and measurable targets for their people. Scaling Up's execution planning methodology and the One-Page Strategic Plan (OPSP), detailed in the "Strategy" and "Execution" sections of the book, will help. Specifically, column 7 of the OPSP provides space to define for each quarter:

1. **KPIs** — Two to three key performance indicators that objectively signal people on whether they had a productive day or week. At MOM's, says Nash, the company will explain what these measures are — for instance, there might be a particular sales goal for a section of the store — and then tell a manager: "Here's the goal. You have to figure out how to get there, either on your own or with others' help." Nash adds, "If they don't meet KPIs, we sit down with them right away and get a plan."

2. **Priorities** — A handful for the next quarter needed to achieve the Critical Number and improve on a KPI.

3. **Critical Number** — The main bottleneck that each employee or team must fix during the quarter.

Defining these individual outcomes in the context of the OPSP assures alignment with the company's strategy and its long- and short-term goals.

## 2. Stop demotivating; start "dehassling."

The best managers/coaches are less concerned about motivating their people and more concerned about NOT demotivating them. They consider it their job to prevent the hassles that block their team's performance. Such demotivators are usually related to issues with people or processes.

The #1 demotivator for talented people is having to put up with bozos, as Steve Jobs would call them. Nothing is more frustrating for A Players than having to work with B and C Players who slow them down and suck their energy. In that sense, "The best thing you can do for employees — a perk better than foosball or free sushi — is hire only 'A' players to work alongside them. Excellent colleagues trump everything else," explains Patty McCord, former chief talent officer at Netflix, in a recent *Harvard Business Review* article.

Fixing people issues for your team can also mean "firing" a client. Unreasonable clients who mistreat your employees and disrupt your business can become an important energy drain. Firing such clients can gain the manager/coach huge respect internally. The negative financial impact is usually counteracted by the immediate rise in the spirits and productivity of your team.

On the process side, do your people have the appropriate tools and resources they need to get the job accomplished? Are there lame policies and procedures frustrating your team? Do you need to bring in a Lean expert to help your people design new processes or streamline existing ones? Where might they be spinning their wheels because of unnecessary delays? Focus on ways to make your team's job(s) easier — a great definition of an effective manager/coach.

To reinforce this servant leadership approach, Fathom, a digital marketing agency from Cleveland and an exemplary Rockefeller Habits practitioner, started using "direct supports" (as in: the manager supports his people) instead of "direct reports" (as in: the people report to the manager) when referencing a manager's team. We like this twist and hope it spreads.

## 1. Help people play to their strengths.

What ultimately sets great managers/coaches apart from the merely good ones is that they help their people play to their strengths. To understand how to do this requires a refined definition of what constitutes a strength. A strength isn't just something you're good at; it's only a strength if it literally gives you strength, gives you energy (think about the fitness fanatics whom The City Bin Co. is hiring to work on the back of its garbage trucks!). In turn, a weakness, is something that, though you may be good at it, drains the life out of you.

Thus, a key function of great managers/coaches is helping individual employees refocus and prune their jobs over time so they focus more on activities that give them strength and less on activities that make them weak. Though there will always be parts of anyone's job that are draining, the companies that do better at minimizing these will have a more energized team.

Coming back to the chess vs. checkers analogy used earlier, Bobby Fischer, the great chess champion, once said, "Winning in this game is all a matter of understanding how to capitalize on the strengths of each piece and timing their moves just right."

Lois Melbourne, CEO of Texas-based Aquire (a subsidiary of PeopleFluent), has taken a page from strengths guru Marcus Buckingham. Instead of hiring more (and extremely difficult-to-find) programmers to keep up with the rapid growth of her HR software firm, she's focused on making her existing programmers happier and more energized.

To do this, Buckingham suggests taking a couple of weeks and documenting all those activities you either love or loathe. This is precisely what Melbourne has her programmers do regularly, noting all of the activities that drain their energy and keep these techies away from their primary strength: programming. She then eliminates those activities no one should have to do (they creep into every job) and then uses the remaining list to create a Job Scorecard for a new position — to be filled by a new chess piece that loves to do what others hate. Result: happier, more productive, and loyal programmers.

Whenever you have a department scream for more help, rather than throw more of the same people at the situation, try Buckingham's approach. And before starting the "love and loathe" exercise, have your team take the inexpensive online StrengthsFinder assessment offered by Gallup (*gallupstrengthscenter.com*). You will get insightful reports that will serve as conversation-starters and will help your people achieve self-awareness about their strengths.

Finding employees' strengths and focusing workers on those assets is the most powerful people-management tool we can suggest. And it goes hand in hand with dehassling a person's job. Embracing strengths-based management practices will bring you more fulfilled, happier, and engaged employees who will lift themselves and your organization to new levels of energy and performance.

 **CRITICAL:** *Don't forget to apply this to yourself. Focus on eliminating or delegating tasks that drain you. In Verne's case, he found someone who loves to build PowerPoint presentations, something that wears him out; and he continues to partner with various CEOs to run the Scaling Up family of companies. This gives him more time to teach, which truly energizes him.*

## Are You a Manager or a Leader?

Ask a *good* manager about his team and he will speak in generalities, saying that they are hard-working, responsible, fun, etc. Ask a *great* manager the same question and she will describe each of her team members with specific details about their personality, strengths, and achievements. Again, think about the "A-Team" action television analogy from the last chapter.

If you struggle with appreciating the differences in your team, you might be more of a leader than a manager. Managing is about differences; leading is about sameness. Great managers/coaches discover what is different about people and capitalize on it. Great leaders discover what is universal, build a common vision for a better future around it, and then rally people behind it. (Marcus Buckingham, this time in his book *The One Thing You Need to Know ... About Great Managing, Great Leading, and Sustained Individual Success*, explains this difference between managing and leading.)

Companies can cope with a charismatic leader (who struggles with managing) until they get to about 50 employees. But as soon as you approach 100 or more people, you have to put in place a team of manager/coaches capable of adopting the five habits outlined above. Scaling up a business requires both visionary leadership and great managers.

## Grow Your Talent

In 2010, Gene Browne, co-founder and CEO of The City Bin Co. in Galway, Ireland, decided to invest heavily in executive education. The company set up an internal learning academy named "Garbage University." It provides three hours of training every two weeks from September to May, in sync with the academic year. Each year, Garbage University has a particular focus that shapes the topics that the executive team discusses. And the

entire decade between 2020 and 2030 is focused on helping every City Bin employee achieve their lifelong education goals.

At MOM's Organic Market, in addition to executive education, produce managers will typically read four to five books together every year. Recent titles on their list include business books such as Liz Wiseman's *Multipliers: How the Best Leaders Make Everyone Smarter* and Patrick M. Lencioni's *The Five Dysfunctions of a Team: A Leadership Fable*. Other titles help them absorb knowledge that's specific to their field. One typical pick: Maria Rodale's *Organic Manifesto*. "We've read a lot of books on the organic industry," says Jon Croft, training director at the metro Washington-based company.

In order to keep your company competitive and your people loyal, you must grow them through education and coaching. And this investment in people is the biggest single predictor of a company's ability to beat its direct competitors and the overall market, based on exhaustive research done by Laurie Bassi, co-author of *Good Company: Business Success in the Worthiness Era*. Jack Welch, former CEO of General Electric, couldn't agree more. He declared that the ROI of GE's famous internal business school, Crotonville, was "infinite."

## Onboarding — Getting the First Impression Right

One of the biggest opportunities to grow and align your people is when they first start working for you. Their initial weeks on the job represent a unique chance to create connection and deeply ingrain a company's DNA into new people. Yet few companies make proper use of this opportunity. Instead, the first days on the job often feel more like *waterboarding* than *onboarding*: no desk, no computer, no phone, the new boss is traveling, and the first assignment is shadowing an unenthusiastic colleague for two weeks.

Famous sales coach and dear friend Jack Daly suggests, "Why don't you throw people a party when they start, instead of when they leave?" Sydney-based software firm Atlassian sends each new employee, whatever his or her position, to a resort spa the weekend before the start date as a way to celebrate the new job. The spouse or a guest gets to go along — making both new employees and their spouses raving Atlassian fans.

Why not have balloons suspended from her chair (Appletree Answers has a Herman Miller Aeron chair for each call center worker); a signed welcome card; and a celebration lunch with cake? Or, as Daly did for every new employee he hired, send a gift basket to his house/spouse, timed to be awaiting his arrival home after the first day on the job. Onboarding needs to be a celebration, not paperwork. It should create emotional connections between the new recruit and a maximum number of team members.

## Formal Orientation

To inculcate a new employee (bring her into the culture) properly, structure a formal orientation process. It's most effective when organized around doing real work while emphasizing the company's Values and Purpose. Zappos' four-week orientation has all new recruits work the call center phones as a way to understand the intense focus that the Las Vegas-based online apparel retailer places on customer service from the ground up.

Boston-based global services company Sapient had one of our favorite orientation processes, launched back when co-founder J. Stuart Moore was running the company. It was a five-day "boot camp" designed by a former second-grade schoolteacher working at the company. She approached Moore when the organization passed the 70-employee mark and warned that the culture was starting to "leak" (this always happens when a company reaches about this number of employees). She designed the boot camp so all new recruits would spend a week working on a list of nagging internal projects that no one else wanted to tackle (good to have newbies!). And as they worked on these projects, one Core Value was reinforced each day, so by the end of the week, everyone understood in a real way the cultural and strategic approach Sapient preferred on all projects.

Teams at this rapidly growing firm had been screaming that they needed more people in the field immediately. But they found that new recruits who went through the boot camp could hit the ground running at near 100% field-ready alignment, whereas before the orientation process was introduced, they had normally needed a frustrating six-month ramp-up period. Everyone became huge fans of the process as Sapient scaled up to 2,500 people.

At Blinds.com, a Houston-based online retailer of window blinds and shades with 250 employees, orientation includes a scavenger hunt — an excuse to meet and greet the new colleagues and answer their questions about the company and its culture. Founder and CEO Jay Steinfeld then personally drives new recruits to a run-down alleyway in Houston where the company had its first office back in 1996. There, he shares the history and Core Values of the company (which was acquired by The Home Depot in January 2014). The involvement of senior management in the onboarding process is critical.

As Harvard professor Frances Frei and organization builder Anne Morriss remind leaders in their breakthrough strategy book *Uncommon Service: How to Win by Putting Customers at the Core of Your Business*, onboarding is like the imprinting that happens to birds immediately after hatching. (Remember the mother hen vs. the farmer's boot?) People are exceptionally positive, receptive, and willing to learn in this phase, and they experience deep attachment to whatever you expose them to. So be careful about the kind of induction program you put in front of your "hatchlings." Dumping a 200-page binder of company policies on their desks is probably not sending the right message.

## All Growth Companies Are Training Companies

At its 20th anniversary celebration, Poland-based AmRest Holdings' co-founder and chairman, Henry McGovern, looked back at how the restaurant holding company grew from its first Pizza Hut in Wroclaw to more than 18,000 employees with restaurant locations throughout Eastern Europe, Russia, the US, and China. "We're more a training company than a restaurant company!" he said.

Most professions and trades understand this. Commercial pilots, thankfully, are required to hone their skills 60 hours per year in continuing education; doctors need to put in 45 to 60; embalmers and truck drivers must complete more than a dozen hours annually. Yet business professionals piloting their companies aren't required to obtain a single hour. We're hoping to change this. We require our

Scaling Up Certified Coaches to commit to 45 hours of annual professional education to keep their certification. And our more progressive clients, monitored by their CFOs, are starting to require a specific number of hours of ongoing education at all levels of the organization (we suggest 12 hours for the frontline; 24 hours for team leads; and 45 to 60 hours for senior leaders as a starting point).

Worried about spending all that money on training only to watch your people go elsewhere? The research definitively shows that training and development increases loyalty. Besides, what's the alternative? Do you really want your people not to be the best-trained for the jobs they have to do?

And how much should you spend on training? It obviously depends, but 2% to 3% of your payroll is a good benchmark. Who should you spend it on? Senior leaders, middle managers, frontline employees? They all need training, but focus first on your middle management. In most growth companies, they have the hardest jobs and are critical to employee engagement and retention, yet get the least preparation for it.

## Online Learning

Longstanding clients like AmRest and City Bin are taking advantage of online education as well. MOM's Organic Market frequently convenes members of its leadership team to watch webcasts on topics that will help them develop professionally and personally. It shows the videos every six to eight weeks in operations or other meetings. "It is a learning event incorporated into a meeting that has already been planned," says Croft, the training director.

The company watches the 45- to 75-minute online seminars as a group and then has a regional general manager lead a 30- to 60-minute "reflective dialogue" on the program, says Croft. At one meeting in March 2014, managers in the produce area and a group of employees interested in becoming managers watched Malcolm Gladwell's video seminar *Outliers: Why People Are Successful,* available on demand at *scalingup.com.*

"The general idea is to expose these emerging leaders, if you will, to different thoughts about how we grow ourselves and how we grow a business, and how we grow a unit within the business," explains Croft.

MOM's actively encourages employees to apply what they have learned to their work. At the end of each discussion, employees are asked, "What is the one takeaway that you are going to commit yourself to working on?" Very recently, MOM's expanded its program to hourly workers; it has been airing an online video on *The Happiness Advantage* by Shawn Achor for hourly workers at some of its stores on Sunday nights.

"Scott felt very passionately that we should figure out a way to incorporate more of our staff into these opportunities," says Croft. The training director, who has been leading the sessions with the hourly team, says the discussions have been "as good as — if not better and more energizing, passionate, and exciting than — any of the ones I've led in the past year."

Beyond providing a learning opportunity, *The Happiness Advantage* video has helped reinforce the company's values. "As a company, we care deeply about being whole people," Croft says. "We care deeply about having a wellness in our lives that includes our work lives, but also every other aspect of our lives. We would like for all of us to figure out how to use *The Happiness Advantage* in our work, but it's really so much more than that. It's the ripple effect we can have on others."

As mentioned in the beginning of this section, MOM's also strongly encourages employees to set aside time for professional reading and has organized a vetting committee to find intriguing books for its leadership team to discuss. To make sure employees truly learn from each book, Croft might prepare a sheet asking managers to focus on takeaways on which they plan to act, and the five key points they want everyone at MOM's to know.

With some books, the company will ask a member of the team to make a formal presentation on a specific chapter. "For *Multipliers*, we did some of the exercises Liz suggested in the book," Croft says. "The managers got a lot out of that book. I think the process really helped solidify that."

One book that has been a hit among Croft's team is *The Weekly Coaching Conversation: A Business Fable About Taking Your Game and Your Team to the Next Level* by Brian Souza.

"Managers absolutely love that book and the conversations around that book," Croft says.

Another that sparked passionate feedback was *Lean In: Women, Work, and the Will to Lead,* by Facebook's Sheryl Sandberg. A discussion among the leadership team that Croft expected would last two hours stretched to four, with the head of HR at MOM's furiously taking notes on potential changes to make the company more family-friendly. As a result, CFO Kelly Moler decided to form a committee to work on such initiatives. "We are going to take a good look at our policies and procedures," says Croft.

Meanwhile, Croft has planned another discussion of *Lean In,* including both women and men on the staff at the store level. "I believe there is a need to have that conversation not just with one gender or another," he says.

All this learning is obviously paying off: MOM's continues its rapid growth while achieving four times industry average profitability in an industry not known for spending a lot on training and development.

## Growing People Through Coaching

As Google's people analytics team discovered, one-on-one coaching is the #1 factor linked to employee engagement.. Again, this is why we've been quietly lobbying to get rid of the term "manager" and replace it with "coach" (e.g., sales coach vs. sales manager).

The best framework for coaching is Ken Blanchard and Paul Hersey's concept of Situational Leadership. It guides leaders in how to mix the right amount of direction and support, depending on the competency and confidence of the person being coached.

Based on this model, managers/coaches can move employees through a development cycle that reduces step by step the need for direction and support until a task can be fully delegated. The style chosen in each phase needs to be based on the task at hand. While one task might require specific how-to instructions, another might call for only some encouragement or nothing at all. Read the short management fable *Leadership and the One Minute Manager: Increasing Effectiveness Through Situational Leadership,* by Ken Blanchard, Patricia Zigarmi, and Drea Zigarmi, to gain more insight into this powerful coaching framework.

The other key resource is Michael Bungay Stanier's breakthrough book *The Coaching Habit: Say Less, Ask More & Change the Way You Lead Forever*. Have all your team leaders master the content in these two quick read books — and focus on the one Gallup question "what is your goal and the barrier(s) to achieving it" and you'll have a highly engaged team.

With this in mind, we finish this chapter with a plea: People are not resources that you consume. So rethink the name of the department that takes care of them. Call it Talent Development, Human Relations, People Support, or Head of People Experiences — whatever term fits your culture — choose to call this function anything but Human Resources.

In the last chapter of the People section we'll detail "The Core" which needs to be at the heart of all people systems in the organization.

# 5

# THE CORE
## Values, Purpose, and Competencies

---

**EXECUTIVE SUMMARY:** *Successful athletes know the power of having a strong core, no matter what the sport. Growth firms require a similar core to maintain a strong culture. This chapter will discuss the practical role of Core Values, Purpose, and Competencies when scaling up a business. It will explain how to articulate the Core so it's more than just a list posted on the wall. We will outline eight ways to use your Core to drive the people (HR) systems in the company, using the case study of Appletree Answers.*

---

John Ratliff knows the importance of articulating and communicating a company's Core: its Values, Purpose, and Competencies. Ratliff is the founder and former CEO of 650-employee Appletree Answers, an answering service and call-center provider based in Delaware. He made 24 acquisitions to build the company (which he sold to Stericycle Communication Solutions), and it has nearly as many geographical locations. Besides leading locations thousands of miles apart, Ratliff's leadership team had to integrate apprehensive groups of employees into the culture after they suddenly found themselves under new management. Toward the end of the chapter, we'll look at Appletree's approach to keeping its Core and culture strong.

Successful athletes need a strong core — or midsection — to provide overall stability, power, and control. The same is true for growth firms. Without a strong core, the organization risks instability from cultural challenges, loss of focus, disengagement, and lack of heart as it scales up. It will experience the proverbial wheels flying off as the business speeds down the highway. And just as a strong center is based on having stronger lower-back muscles, oblique muscles, and abdominal muscles, there are three equivalent muscles at the center of the organization: Values, Purpose, and Competencies.

This Core provides the link between People and Strategy in our 4 Decisions model. Once the company gets larger than organization scales beyond 50 to 70 employees — the number at which the senior leaders no longer know everyone's name and start seeing "culture drift" — it is critical to codify the Core, articulate it, and reinforce it on an ongoing basis.

These three foundational attributes of the company anchor the left side of the One-Page Strategic Plan (OPSP), fortuitously forming the letter "C" for Core (the shaded area in the diagram). They represent the heart and soul of the organization.

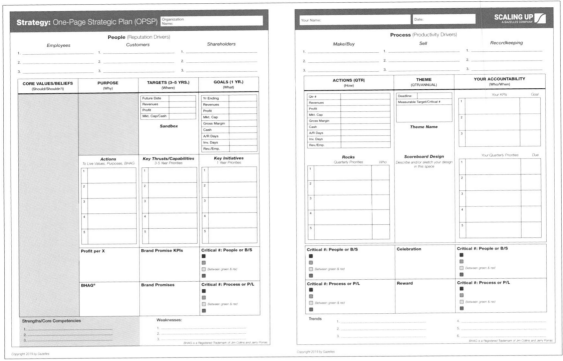

Let's take a look at each component of the Core, how it's determined, and practical tips for using each to anchor the focus and culture of the business.

# The Core Values

Hatim Tyabji built VeriFone from $31 million to $600 million in 11 years, dominating the global market in clearing credit card transactions. His key leadership tool, he says, was a small nine-page "blue book," translated into eight languages, which outlined the values at the heart of VeriFone's culture. When Tyabji took over as CEO, he discerned the rules that had made VeriFone successful up to that point, created the book, and then "essentially spent the next 11 years repeating myself," he notes. He led the turnaround of Best Buy as chairman (retired 2015, replaced by Hubert Joly) and in 2013 welcomed back founder Richard Schulze as chairman emeritus, clearly a nod to keeping the company rooted in its beginnings and its four Core Values.

Core Values are the rules and boundaries that define the company's culture and personality, and provide a final "Should/Shouldn't" test for all the behaviors and decisions by everyone in the firm. It's especially important that top managers lead by example, making sure their behaviors and decisions align with the Values.

When Values fully permeate the company, the leadership team can avoid being sucked into many of the day-to-day operational issues. The rule becomes, "If you think you need to ask me permission for something, just consult the Core Values!" This gives leadership the confidence to delegate important tasks. They can trust that employees will know the right things to do when faced with a decision or an ethical dilemma.

Similar values and boundaries play a parallel role in parenting. The key is having a handful of rules, repeating yourself a lot, and hoping that your family's values sink in by the time your children strike out on their own.

## The Organization's Personality

What are your Core Values? As we discussed in "The Leaders" chapter, your company is a living, breathing organism with a distinct personality. It expresses that personality through its Values.

Think of your company as a child. If it is less than 5 years old, its Values are still being formed. The Values you listed when you started the firm may take a few years to fully take shape. Years later, these will be baked in, just as someone's personality at age 50 is a more hardened version of who he or she was at age 5. Our behaviors, aspirations, knowledge, vocations, and interests may change, but not our foundational personality.

Attempting to change a firm's base personality (Values) will send the organization into endless therapy, the same if a parent tries this with their child. (Why do you think change management gurus make the big bucks but almost always fail?) J. Stuart Moore, co-founder of Boston-based global services company Sapient, shares that his biggest mistake was modifying the company's five Core Values to accommodate a major acquisition. He blames that change for the subsequent challenges Sapient faced. He resolved them only when the company went back to its initial list.

This speaks to why the term "merger" should be eliminated from the business vocabulary. There is no such thing. There are only acquisitions. The rare few companies that succeed in scaling up by making them, as Ratliff did at Appletree, have a process for quickly inculcating the acquired employees into the acquirer's existing culture (more on this later).

Creating such a process requires a company to accurately discover and define its own Core, starting with its Values.

## Discovering the Right Words

Companies can spend tens of thousands of dollars and many months laboring through employee surveys and endless meetings to figure out their Values, only to end up with a generic list of platitudes — like "honesty, integrity, teamwork, and customer service" — that misses the uniqueness and power of the existing culture.

Discerning the Core Values is a DISCOVERY process, not the creation of a wish list of nice-to-haves. Using an approach similar to that of archaeologists examining the artifacts of an ancient culture, our coaching partners help firms identify similar artifacts within their own company cultures and establish a starting set of Values.

 **WARNING:** *Once you have this starting list, do not carve it in stone, as one of our early clients did. (That client's CEO literally had small engraved stones sitting on everyone's desks a week after the*

*exercise.) Let the Values bake for a year, testing their validity at the next several quarterly planning sessions. Ask the leadership team, "Are there plenty of examples where we lived these Values?" If there are, you likely are talking about a Core Value. If there*

*"Discerning the Core Values is a discovery process."*

*are not, then it might have been a wish-list item or a Core Value that has weakened significantly. When Verne's team did something similar for Scaling Up, we discovered one Value that wasn't core, found we had missed one (we had lots of stories, but no Value representing them), and reworded a few to match the actual language we used as we told stories supporting that Value.*

To give you the flavor of the Core Values of a growth company, here are Scaling Up's:

- Create ecstatic customers
- Honor intellectual creatives
- Everyone an entrepreneur
- Practice what we preach
- Relentless transparency

For additional examples, read the *Harvard Business Review* article titled "Building Your Company's Vision," by James C. Collins and Jerry I. Porras. You'll notice that all the Values listed are phrases, not single words. And they are not all feel-good Values. One of Disney's Core Values is "Preservation and control of the Disney magic," which accurately describes one of the most controlling cultures you'll ever experience. Values are neither good nor bad. They just are! The key is to articulate them accurately.

To communicate these Values throughout the organization, do a search for "Atlassian's core values" and you'll land on a page detailing their five core values. Notice how it opens with a video featuring employees describing each value. Below that video is the list of values with each anchored by a unique visual symbol and listed as a phrase, not a single word — and then a paragraph describing the deeper meaning of that phrase. It's worth noting this landing page is part of their recruiting process.

Ezypay, Australia's largest direct-debit service provider, has taken this a step further and created an avatar and a supporting video for each Core Value. The avatars show up everywhere — in Quarterly Themes, on the walls of the company's situation room, in documents, etc.

Let us know if we can help you properly discover the right Core Values. Discerning the wrong list will only confuse the organization and relegate it to endless therapy!

## Our values

They guide what we do, why we create, and who we hire.

**Open company, no bullshit**

Openness is root level for us. Information is open internally by default and sharing is a first principle. And we understand that speaking your mind requires equal parts brains (what to say), thoughtfulness (when to say it), and caring (how it's said).

**Build with heart and balance**

"Measure twice, cut once." Whether you're building a birdhouse or a business, this is good advice. Passion and urgency infuse everything we do, alongside the wisdom to consider options fully and with care. Then we make the cut, and we get to work.

**Don't #@!% the customer**

Customers are our lifeblood. Without happy customers, we're doomed. So considering the customer perspective – collectively, not just a handful – comes first.

**Play, as a team**

We spend a huge amount of our time at work. So the more that time doesn't feel like "work," the better. We can be serious, without taking ourselves too seriously. We strive to put what's right for the team first – whether in a meeting room or on a football pitch.

**Be the change you seek**

All Atlassians should have the courage and resourcefulness to spark change – to make better our products, our people, our place. Continuous improvement is a shared responsibility. Action is an independent one.

**Like what we stand for? Make this your everyday.**

Our team's great, but we've got room for one more if you're interested.

Learn more

# The Core Purpose

If the Core Values are the soul of the organization, the core Purpose (some call it "mission") gives it heart. The Purpose answers the ageless question "Why?" Why does what we do matter, and what difference are we making in the world? Why would our customers or the world miss us if we weren't around?

Without a Purpose more heartfelt than that of making money (there are plenty of other places on the OPSP to represent this goal), employees will pour their enthusiasm and energy into something else. Research finds that if you ignite and capture their hearts, not just their heads, they will give you 40% more discretionary effort.

*"A powerful Purpose tends to revolve around a single word or idea."*

We find that a powerful Purpose tends to revolve around a single word or idea:

- 3M: *Science. Applied to Life.*
- Disney: *Happiness*
- Wal-Mart: *Robin Hood*

Even Starbucks' heritage was built on the idea of being an escape — a *third place* — between work and home.

When the international school that Verne's children attended wrestled with the question of Purpose, rather than settle for a rather lengthy and boring statement that sounded like every other school's, it grabbed hold of the idea of *engagement*: to create an environment where students, teachers, parents, and the community are so engaged (something you can feel and see) that learning becomes a lifelong pursuit. What it takes to create this kind of passion then drove the rest of the strategic plan for the school.

This central word or idea is then expanded into a phrase or two, but is most easily remembered and acted upon when it has a single word or idea at its core. To discern this Purpose, gather a team together and start with the question, "What do we do?" (You might answer: "We're a school." "We sell overpriced coffee." "We host a CRM system.") Then ask "Why?" several times (a technique known as the five whys). Why does this matter, or what difference can we make? Keep asking until you get to your version of "Save the world," and then back up one step.

At Scaling Up, we are an executive education, coaching, and technology company supporting scaleups. So why does this matter? Because scaleups are the job and innovation engines of our local and global economies. We could make a lot more (and easier) money consulting for the Global 500, several of which use our tools, but that's not where our hearts are. Our purpose is "transforming the world by empowering scaleups." Scaleups are the unsung heroes creating solutions to some of the world's most significant challenges. By empowering everyone in these firms we empower the world. Empowering is our word — our purpose — and we're excited to serve.

"Building Your Company's Vision," the *HBR* article referenced above, also lists several Purposes for well-known companies. Also check out Peter Diamandis' "Massively Transformative Purpose."

**WARNING:** *Most teams, when asked to determine a Purpose, often describe Brand Promises instead. (The Brand Promise concept is covered in the next section.) When asking the five whys, a staffing company might conclude, "We help our clients hire the best talent and save them valuable time in the process." These might be two accurate Brand Promises — Best Talent and Save Time — but the Purpose goes deeper than just describing the attributes of your product or service. For Michigan-based staffing firm EmploymentGroup, for example, the deeper Purpose is "Helping people succeed."*

Out of this single idea should emerge a "stump speech" that the CEO shares repeatedly, reminding everyone of the big picture and "why we do what we do." When CEO Howard Schultz famously shut down Starbucks for a global day of training, it wasn't as much about how to make a better latte as about recentering and reminding everyone of the real Purpose of the company: to be a third place for people to stop in and purchase an affordable luxury after a stressful day. Offering a place to relax in a comfortable setting, Starbucks plays a role similar to what the local pub once did.

## Mission, Vision, Values

"Mission, vision, values" likely became a popular moniker of strategic planning because it has a nice ring to it. Our use of related terminology and definitions differs. To clarify:

**Mission:** We prefer the term "Purpose," which is more heartfelt. "Mission" is more of a military term and usually connotes something shorter in duration (e.g., the kind of short-term assignments found in the popular *Mission: Impossible* television and movie series).

**Vision:** This is what we cover in the OPSP, from Core Values to the Quarterly Theme and everything in between. If you feel compelled to create a vision statement, you can extract pieces from the OPSP — Values, Purpose, the Big Hairy Audacious Goal (BHAG®), Brand Promises, etc. — and craft them into a soon-to-be forgotten paragraph. (Sorry for the sarcasm, but we're not big fans of vision statements.) It's better to keep these elements of your vision separate in people's minds, so they can remember them more easily. The Vision Summary tool, described in "The One-Page Strategic Plan" chapter, will provide your team with an easy-to-remember summary of your vision.

**Values:** On this term, we have consensus.

Pick whatever language you prefer — Mission vs. Purpose, for instance — and use the terms consistently.

# The Core Competencies

Understanding a company's inherent strengths is essential. Gary Hamel and the late C.K. Praha-lad labeled them Core Competencies in their groundbreaking May 1990 *Harvard Business Review* article titled "The Core Competence of the Corporation." Purchase a copy online and have the strategic thinking team read it; then discuss and determine your company's Core Competencies. (See "The 7 Strata of Strategy" chapter for more on this important meeting rhythm.)

A Core Competency has three attributes, according to Prahalad and Hamel:

1. It is not easy for competitors to imitate.

2. It can be reused widely for many products and markets.

3. It must contribute to the benefits the end customer experiences and the value of the product or service to customers.

*"Don't define Core Competencies too narrowly."*

Don't define Core Competencies too narrowly. Take BIC, the Paris-based company founded in 1945. It is known for the disposable BIC pen. Had BIC seen its Core Competency as simply making cheap pens, it wouldn't be the $2 billion firm it is today. BIC more accurately describes its strength as "making disposable plastic anything," which led it into lighters, razors, and other stationery products.

It's equally important for a company to understand what it is inherently *incapable* of doing, or its core weaknesses. 3M has never been effective at selling direct to consumers, so it has developed a core strength of working effectively with distribution partners. In turn, it has divested itself of certain product lines that the market has forced into direct channels.

As we'll discuss later in the "Strategy" section, your organization's Core Competencies provide boundaries for determining what product and service offerings you should pursue. They are also foundational in helping you determine how to differentiate the company in the marketplace. Once you articulate your Values, Purpose, and Competencies, put them to work in creating an engaged and focused team.

## Bringing Your Core Alive

It was during an off-site meeting to prepare for the fourth quarter of 2008 that Appletree Answers decided to tackle turnover among frontline employees at its call centers. While churn among nonexempt employees was only 3%, turnover was 110% for the employees who answered the phones for clients. "Clearly, we were doing something right for one group but not the other," says Ratliff, the founder.

Ratliff was well-aware that the company's 13 acquisitions to date made it difficult to achieve a cohesive culture. He knew that this lack of cohesion was contributing to the turnover. But he didn't realize that because he and his leadership team were painfully out of touch with the frontline employees' concerns, they were adding to the problem.

### The Dream On Initiative

Just how little he knew about the lives of the frontline employees became very clear after Lisa Phillips, the company's director of operations, asked how the company could become more like a Make-A-Wish Foundation for employees. Her question was in line with Appletree's Core Value "Take care of each other."

After having a small group of employees flesh out the idea, the company launched the Dream On initiative, which it advertised on its intranet and on posters. It asked employees to submit a request tied to one thing they would like to happen in their personal lives. There were no restrictions placed. A secret committee would review the requests.

As the responses trickled in, Ratliff got a crash course in the daily realities that his frontline employees faced. "It was nothing short of shocking," he says. "We started to really get an insight into the challenges of our employees and the situations they had inherited."

Many team members were grappling with health problems or coping with the challenges of caring for elderly parents — factors that affected their ability to juggle their jobs with their lives outside of work. Others were suffering financial problems, having had a period of unemployment before joining Appletree, and they needed a few thousand dollars to get caught up. Seventeen employees simply wished they could own a car to make it easier to get to work.

"I was surprised by the car situation — how a change in a bus route can force our employees to change jobs, or how a previous employer may have changed job hours, which no longer matched public transportation schedules," Ratliff says.

Some of the stories were heart-wrenching. To help employees turn them around, the company decided to provide grants and other resources through the program. One employee was living in the family car with her husband and child, after her mate had lost his job. The company helped the family secure a lease and put up deposit money, also providing furniture and gift cards to help them get set up in their new home.

"We meant to do this privately, but the employee let a lot of people know, and soon it was on our intranet," says Ratliff. "That dramatically increased submissions."

Over time, Appletree Answers used American Express points to send a couple on their honeymoon; flew a mother to see her daughter in the Navy over Christmas; and fulfilled the dream of an employee to take a first family vacation with her disabled daughter.

"What CEOs don't realize is the access you have that other people don't, and how you can create opportunities for people you never would have thought of," says Ratliff.

The program had a profound effect on turnover, given that call centers are usually run like the sweatshops of the Information Age. Not long after Ratliff and his team launched the Dream On initiative, turnover dropped to 20%. While the initiative cost money, it paid a 20 times return on investment in terms of reduced turnover costs in less than a year.

"The overall sense of belonging, of being part of something bigger than themselves or their individual sites, and part of a community, has been one of the biggest changes I've seen in employees," says Ratliff. "I felt more connected to our entire group, and the company became much more human to people."

As Ratliff grew the business, ultimately acquiring 24 companies in less than nine years, his leadership team determined a distinct set of seven Core Values:

- Integrity matters
- Think like a customer
- Spirited fun
- Be quick, but don't hurry (borrowed from legendary basketball coach John Wooden)

- Employees are critical
- Small details are huge
- Take care of each other

They also articulated a Purpose: "Enhancing the lives of customers and employees, one interaction at a time." The key word was "interaction." Appletree handled 25 million inbound calls a year, generating millions of interactions between customers, employees, and supervisors. Ratliff wanted the team to realize they had a conscious choice to enhance or diminish those interactions for everyone involved.

"The Purpose really created a common language," Ratliff says. "Growth companies are good at getting a lot of things done. The worst thing you can do is get a massive amount of the wrong things done. If you have clearly articulated Core Values and a Purpose that are part of your everyday experience, it helps direct that massive action around the right activities."

Appletree had a well-honed process for instilling these Values and Purpose in the employees of each acquired company from the very first day. The idea was to give new and existing employees a reference point to help them make decisions, even when their manager was not available to advise them.

"Appletree's strategy for getting a brand-new group of employees rapidly engaged into our culture was one of our main Core Competencies," said Ratliff. "We actually tracked site-level profitability. By immediately improving the engagement levels of these new employees, we were able to see a 10-point increase in EBITDA." This engagement took place because employees experienced a company where everyone, especially the leadership team, was living the stated Values and Purpose.

### Dell's Shock Absorber

When his company reached 50 employees, Michael Dell recognized the need to hire someone to manage the People side of his growing business and serve as a shock absorber between him and the rest of the organization. He recruited Barbara Kreisman from Motorola University. She helped him scale the company to 40,000 people before leaving Dell. (She is currently associate dean of the Daniels College of Business at the University of Denver.)

The HR department is normally one of the last functions to develop fully in a growing company. It normally begins as a part-time responsibility of the founder's assistant, who is told to "keep the employees happy" so the CEO can stay focused on the customers and the market in the early days of the business! As the function matures, random lists creep into the organization — a criteria list for hiring, a list of rewards to hand out, and a list of topics for the handbook. Someone typically downloads generic forms from the Web and executes global search-and-replaces to insert the company's name. It's this growing hodgepodge of HR activities that need to be brought back into alignment.

A leader must go beyond merely posting a company's Values and Purpose on the wall and handing out plastic laminated cards. The key is for you to align ALL of your HR (People) systems and processes around one list of your Values and Purpose.

## Scaling Up

Here are eight ways to use this list to reinforce your culture on a regular basis.

## Storytelling

Everybody enjoys a good story, and most great leaders have taught through parable or storytelling. Stories provide the explanation for Core Values that might seem unusual or cryptic on their own. Identify some "legends" and current stories that represent each Value.

To collect great stories about Appletree's Core Values, Ratliff and his team initiated a Core Values Hall of Fame event, held every quarter. Employees were encouraged to look for colleagues whose actions embodied a Core Value and to submit a written story about this. "It was more rewarding for the person who wrote the story than for the person who was recognized when we told the story," Ratliff says.

Some of the stories were dramatic, conveying the meaning of the Core Values better than a corporate HR department ever could. One particular story vividly illustrates the Value "Take care of each other." An employee got a call at 3 a.m. from a woman living upstairs from her parents, who ran a disaster restoration company that Appletree Answers served.

"I'm upstairs. Can you get my dad? It's really important," the caller said, and then the line went dead. The employee could easily have treated this as a prank but instead tracked down the caller's father. Her father went upstairs and found out she was having a heart attack. (She is fine now.)

That story was one of the winners in Appletree's quarterly contest, showing how the value of taking care of each other could go beyond the walls of the company.

Under Ratliff's leadership, Appletree gradually built a rich collection of employee-created content by hiring a documentary videographer. The videographer helped teams of employees create a 90-second video around each of the Core Values. "It wasn't the corporate marketing crap you always get," says Ratliff.

The videographer also created humorous videos around the company's Quarterly Themes (more on this in "The Priority" chapter), which helped transmit the company's Values in a different way. (No one says your discussions of Core Values need to be boring!) In one wacky 2010 series, employees from various offices put together talent shows around the theme of "The Summer of Love" and posted them on YouTube. The idea was to encourage employees to relax after a tough quarter.

## Recruitment and Selection

Design your interview questions and assessments to test how candidates align with your Core Values (more on this in "The Team" chapter). Then rate candidates in terms of their perceived alignment with each Core Value. Your goal, after all, is to hire for culture fit. This also applies when you are making acquisitions and deciding which employees to keep on board.

Shape your hiring processes around your Core Values. At Appletree, the online application form asked would-be hires to elaborate on a Core Value. Later, those who made it to the interview stage were asked to talk more about why a Value resonated with them. Interviewers looked for people who genuinely lit up when they talked about a Core Value and weren't just spouting a canned answer. "If we saw feigned interest or an indifferent attitude, we knew it was not going to be a strong culture fit," says Ratliff.

Hiring this way helps reduce turnover. "It's amazing how much more effective you can be at hiring when you select people who are excited about your culture before they come to work for you," Ratliff says.

## Onboarding Process

Many growth firms lack proper onboarding for new employees. Everyone seems too busy to organize it, and there's a mentality that new recruits are needed on the job from day one. However, a proper onboarding process makes new hires feel welcome and integrates them more quickly into the culture. The key is designing the process around the teaching of your Values and Purpose. (We prefer the term "onboarding" vs. "orientation." It's more than just showing people where the printers and bathrooms are.)

This is what Appletree did whenever it made an acquisition. On the very first day that employees in a newly acquired branch switched over to Appletree's payroll, employees from other locations would arrive to welcome their fellow associates. Appletree's team would share stories and videos created by employees to introduce the company's Values and Purpose.

*"Hire for culture fit."*

"We basically said, 'You don't have to live these in your personal life, but if you want to be part of the family we've created at work, these are the Values we've all agreed to work under. This is our shared language and commitment to each other,' " says Ratliff.

It is worth noting that Appletree renamed its HR Department the Employee Experience Department. "The #1 goal of HR was to create better employee experiences, and we wanted them to focus on that," says Ratliff.

See "The Leaders" chapter for more onboarding ideas.

## Performance Appraisals and Handbooks

Core Values should provide the framework on which you hang your performance appraisal system. With a little creativity, any performance measure can be made to link with a Core Value. In addition, organize your employee handbook into sections around each Core Value.

*"Organize your employee handbook into sections around each Core Value."*

Ratliff and his leadership team at Appletree made it clear that learning the Core Values wasn't just a feel-good exercise. Employees' performance was scored on how well they acted on the Core Values. For instance, employees would be graded on how well they thought like a customer.

"Anytime you have a discussion with an employee about performance, it's much easier if you have a Core Value you can tie it back to," Ratliff says.

Removing gray areas helped to make performance evaluations more productive, preventing rhetorical debate between team leaders and team members about what aspects of performance were important, he adds.

"When you both have agreed in advance to the rules of the game," says Ratliff, "it gives you a lot of leverage in your discussion with employees around performance."

It also made it easier for team leaders to give constructive feedback. "No one could say, 'I made mistakes because I was up against a deadline,'" says Ratliff. "We'd ask, 'How does that marry with, Be quick, but don't hurry?'"

## Recognition and Rewards

Organize your recognition and reward categories around your Core Values. You will gain a new source of corporate stories and legends each time a reward or recognition is given to highlight a Value.

In conducting its quarterly Core Values Hall of Fame, Appletree selected a winner for each of its seven Values, based on the stories employees submitted about them. Each winner received a T-shirt imprinted with the corresponding Core Value.

## Newsletters

Why struggle to come up with a catchy title for a newsletter when some word or phrase from your Core Values will do beautifully? Highlight one Core Value in each issue, incorporating stories (yes, more stories) about people putting these Core Values to work for the betterment of the company. Add a list of birthdays and anniversaries, and you have a useful newsletter.

If your company doesn't have a newsletter, get creative. Appletree spread the best stories employees submitted about co-workers living the Core Values by publishing them to a portal on the company's website. Appletree also sent every office a plaque printed with each of the inaugural seven stories to hang on the wall. As employees came up with new stories that better embodied the company's Core Values, the company updated the website and the plaques.

## Themes

Use your Core Values to bring attention to your corporate improvement efforts. Milliken, the textile manufacturer, takes one of its six Core Values and makes it the theme for the quarter, asking all employees to focus on ways to improve the company around the theme. The worldwide Ritz-Carlton chain goes to the other extreme and highlights one "rule" every day. In either case, establish a rhythm that keeps the Core Values top-of-mind by repeating them.

## Everyday Reinforcement (The Most Important Step)

Having team leaders who are engaged, every day, in reinforcing the company's Values and Purpose through their decision-making is the most important routine of the eight.

Ratliff made sure that frontline employees saw that they weren't the only ones who were expected to act on the company's Core Values. The leadership team very openly used its Values to make decisions about taking on new business and continuing to work with existing clients.

"One of our Core Values is 'Employees are critical,'" Ratliff notes. "If we had a customer who was abusive to employees, we'd have a conversation with them. If the customer would continue to be abusive, we would fire the customer."

The company's Core Value of "Integrity matters" also played a role in vetting new customers. "We often turned down companies that were on the fringe of integrity," says Ratliff. "A lot of companies would want to use us to shield them from angry customers they treated poorly. Some got into trouble and had a PR nightmare and wanted to come to us, so we would take all the angry customer calls. We wouldn't do that if we thought the reason the customers were mad was the company didn't act with integrity on the issue."

Your Core Values shouldn't be a marketing initiative, says Ratliff. At Appletree, he says: "We would talk about the Core Values all day, every day. They were part of our DNA."

Your Core Values will probably be different than Appletree's, but they should be just as much a part of daily life at your company.

### Carrots and Sticks — Tie to Values and Purpose

Leaders basically have two tools — carrots and sticks — and hopefully, they use more carrots than sticks or they are badly in need of a course subtitled "Anger Management"!

Every time you praise or reprimand someone, tie it back to a Core Value or Purpose. "The reason I'm excited about this new chat window on the website is it's exactly what will help us create 'ecstatic customers.'" Or "The reason I'm blowing a gasket is this is the opposite of what we mean by 'honor intellectual creatives.'"

*"Every time you praise or reprimand someone, tie it back to a Core Value or Purpose."*

We've found that managers and CEOs can repeat Core Values endlessly without it seeming ridiculous, as long as the Core Values they're using are relevant and meaningful to their employees and they make connections to real situations. When you make a decision, relate it to a Value. When a customer issue arises, compare the situation to the ideal represented by the Value. Small as these actions may sound, they probably do more than any of the aforementioned strategies to bring Core Values alive in your organization.

## Results?

In the end, does all this "soft" stuff matter or is it just a bunch of feel good consulting tricks to keep everyone distracted? As mentioned earlier, at Appletree Answers, Ratliff and his team were able to drive employee turnover down from an industry annual average of 200% to below 20%. In turn, they were able to drive profit up from an industry average 4% to 21%. And when it came time to sell, the firm commanded a 14 times multiple sales price vs. the industry's typical three times multiple. So, yes, getting the Core right and using it to drive the business makes great business sense besides creating a great place to work.

The Core also serves as a foundational piece to setting strategy, as we'll discuss in the next section.

# SCALING UP
# STRATEGY

# THE STRATEGY INTRODUCTION

**? KEY QUESTION:** *Can you state your firm's strategy simply — and is it driving sustainable growth in revenue and gross margins?*

Pizza delivered in 30 minutes or less, or it's free. That simply stated strategy made Tom Monaghan, founder of Domino's Pizza, a billionaire. (He is now in the process of giving it all away.) A half-century later, Domino's adjusted its strategy to focus more on quality and slowed service slightly — and growth returned, with the stock tripling in price in just 36 months since the change.

Articulating a similarly clear and differentiated strategy, supported by a strong core culture that can deliver on the brand's promises, is the key for any company wanting to scale up.

So how do you know when you have an industry-dominating, competitor-crushing strategy? Sustainable top-line revenue growth and increasing gross margin dollars (the true top line for many firms, as we'll discuss in "The Cash" chapter) are the two key financial indicators. Customers beating a path to your door, dragging along everyone they know, is another! In turn, if you don't have a killer strategy, your company will face continuous price pressures as the market commoditizes your products and services.

The other way to know if you have a strategy? Do you say "no" 20 times more than you say "yes" — no to the increasing number of opportunities coming your way; no to the wrong customers for your business model; no to nineteen of the twenty people wanting to work with you (because marketing is getting you a steady stream of applicants!); etc.? We recognize that in the beginning you have to say yes to everyone and everything. But you say yes only until you have the luxury to say no (read that sentence again). Those with a well-honed strategy know when to say yes and more importantly, when to say no.

Deep strategy work is time-consuming, as the marketplace constantly changes. To paraphrase the great Prussian General Carl von Clausewitz, strategy is only as good as your next encounter with the enemy (or decision of your competitor). Therefore, it's critical that the senior leadership team work on it each week, free from day-to-day firefighting. The tools and routines in the "Execution" section will set you free to do this.

Top strategists are often compared to grandmaster chess players. However, there is a misconception that these players are thinking more moves ahead of mere masters or novices. They are not. Their advantage is in having 10 times the NEXT moves in their repertoire, depending on the latest gambit of their opponent. Therefore, get help from mentors, advisors, and consultants who have developed strategies for hundreds of companies — they'll have more "next moves" in their bag of tricks.

## Keys to Dominating Your Market

Verne's mentor Hermann Simon wrote the definitive book on privately held growth firms called *Hidden Champions of the 21st Century*. For an excellent summary of the seven lessons he discerned from studying thousands of mid-market firms that dominate their niches globally, read Simon's article, "Hidden Champions (1): What German Companies Can Teach You About

Innovation." It details a key formula for crushing your competition and is worth the 7 minutes to review Simon's 7 lessons.

In addition, Salim Ismail's breakthrough book *Exponential Organizations: Why new organizations are ten times better, faster, and cheaper than yours (and what to do about it)* is a must read if you want to 10x your organization using the same strategies Silicon Valley's "unicorns" (startups that zoom to $1 billion in valuation) have used to scaleup. For a comprehensive online course by Ismail go to *www.ScaleUpU.com*.

# Section Overview

**The first chapter, The 7 Strata of Strategy,** guides you through a framework for constructing an industry-dominating plan. It integrates several of the best-known components of strategy — from Michael Porter, Jim Collins, Frances Frei, and Bob Bloom — into a single framework. The accompanying one-page 7 Strata of Strategy worksheet will help you do the strategic thinking for the One-Page Strategic Plan (OPSP) and determine your company's Brand Promises, Big Hairy Audacious Goal (BHAG®), and other components.

**The second chapter, The One-Page Strategic Plan,** introduces the new SWT (strengths, weaknesses, and trends) tool, which augments the standard SWOT (strengths, weaknesses, opportunities, and threats) analysis in preparing your strategic plan. We will guide you through the OPSP and a new one-page Vision Summary, which provides a more visually pleasing and simpler way to communicate your strategic plan.

**The third chapter, The Planning Process,** details a dozen key steps in preparing for a quarterly or annual planning session with suggested agendas and recommendations on follow-through after the offsite meetings. It also includes a sample completed One-Page Strategic Plan.

Four one-page Strategy tools will be covered in this section:

1. **7 Strata of Strategy:** a framework for integrating several important strategic components into one coherent plan

2. **Vision Summary:** a simplified OPSP, useful for sharing your vision with employees, customers, shareholders, etc.

3. **SWT:** a new strategic-planning preparation tool that augments the SWOT

4. **OPSP:** a one-page worksheet for capturing the company's vision, from the Core Values to the Quarterly Theme, and everything else in between

## Strategy: 7 Strata

Organization Name:

---

**Words You Own (Mindshare):**

---

**Sandbox and Brand Promises:**

| Who/Where (Core Customers) | What (Products and Services) | BRAND PROMISES | KPIs |
|---|---|---|---|
| | | | |

---

**Brand Promise Guarantee (Catalytic Mechanism):**

---

**One-PHRASE Strategy (Key to Making Money):**

---

**Differentiating Activities (3 – 5 Hows):**

---

**X-Factor (10x – 100x Underlying Advantage):**

---

| **Profit per X  (Economic Engine):** | **BHAG* (10 – 25 Year Goal):** |
|---|---|
| | |

*BHAG is a Registered Trademark of Jim Collins and Jerry Porras*

## **Strategy:** Vision Summary

SCALING UP
A GAZELLES COMPANY

| CORE VALUES | PURPOSE | BRAND PROMISES |
|---|---|---|
| | | |

**BHAG**

**STRATEGIC PRIORITIES**

| 3–5 yr | 1 yr | Qtr |
|---|---|---|
| | | |

Your Name: ______________________

| | Your KPIs | Goal |
|---|---|---|
| 1 | | |
| 2 | | |
| 3 | | |

**Critical #: People or B/S**

- ■
- ■
- ■ *Between green & red*
- ■

**Critical #: Process or P/L**

- ■
- ■
- ■ *Between green & red*
- ■

| | Your Quarterly Priorities | Due |
|---|---|---|
| 1 | | |
| 2 | | |
| 3 | | |
| 4 | | |
| 5 | | |

*BHAG is a Registered Trademark of Jim Collins and Jerry Porras.*

Download a full-sized copy of this tool at *scalingup.com*

# Trends

What are the significant changes in technology, distribution, product innovation, markets, consumer, and social trends around the world that might impact your industry and organization?

# Strengths/Core Competencies

What are the inherent strengths of the organization that have been the source of your success?

# Weaknesses

What are the inherent weaknesses of the organization that aren't likely to change?

# Strategy: One-Page Strategic Plan (OPSP)

Organization Name:

## People (Reputation Drivers)

### Employees

1. _____
2. _____
3. _____

### Customers

1. _____
2. _____
3. _____

### Shareholders

1. _____
2. _____
3. _____

| CORE VALUES/BELIEFS (Should/Shouldn't) | PURPOSE (Why) | TARGETS (3–5 YRS.) (Where) | GOALS (1 YR.) (What) |
|---|---|---|---|

| | | | |
|---|---|---|---|
| | | **Future Date** | **Yr Ending** |
| | | **Revenues** | **Revenues** |
| | | **Profit** | **Profit** |
| | | **Mkt. Cap/Cash** | **Mkt. Cap** |
| | | *Sandbox* | **Gross Margin** |
| | | | **Cash** |
| | | | **A/R Days** |
| | | | **Inv. Days** |
| | | | **Rev./Emp.** |

| | **Actions** *To Live Values, Purposes, BHAG* | **Key Thrusts/Capabilities** *3-5 Year Priorities* | **Key Initiatives** *1 Year Priorities* |
|---|---|---|---|
| | 1 | 1 | 1 |
| | 2 | 2 | 2 |
| | 3 | 3 | 3 |
| | 4 | 4 | 4 |
| | 5 | 5 | 5 |

| | **Profit per X** | **Brand Promise KPIs** | **Critical #: People or B/S** |
|---|---|---|---|
| | | | ■ |
| | | | ▨ |
| | | | ☐ *Between green & red* |
| | | | ▨ |

| | **BHAG®** | **Brand Promises** | **Critical #: Process or P/L** |
|---|---|---|---|
| | | | ■ |
| | | | ▨ |
| | | | ☐ *Between green & red* |
| | | | ▨ |

### Strengths/Core Competencies

1. _____
2. _____
3. _____

### Weaknesses:

1. _____
2. _____
3. _____

*BHAG is a Registered Trademark of Jim Collins and Jerry Porras.*

## Process (Productivity Drivers)

| *Make/Buy* | *Sell* | *Recordkeeping* |
|---|---|---|
| 1. _____ | 1. _____ | 1. _____ |
| 2. _____ | 2. _____ | 2. _____ |
| 3. _____ | 3. _____ | 3. _____ |

| ACTIONS (QTR)<br>(How) | THEME<br>(QTR/ANNUAL) | YOUR ACCOUNTABILITY<br>(Who/When) |
|---|---|---|

**ACTIONS (QTR)**

| Qtr # | |
|---|---|
| Revenues | |
| Profit | |
| Mkt. Cap | |
| Gross Margin | |
| Cash | |
| A/R Days | |
| Inv. Days | |
| Rev./Emp. | |

**THEME**

| Deadline: | |
|---|---|
| Measurable Target/Critical # | |

**Theme Name**

**YOUR ACCOUNTABILITY**

| | *Your KPIs* | *Goal* |
|---|---|---|
| 1 | | |
| 2 | | |
| 3 | | |

**Rocks**

*Quarterly Priorities* — Who

| 1 | | |
|---|---|---|
| 2 | | |
| 3 | | |
| 4 | | |
| 5 | | |

**Scoreboard Design**

*Describe and/or sketch your design in this space*

*Your Quarterly Priorities* — *Due*

| 1 | | |
|---|---|---|
| 2 | | |
| 3 | | |
| 4 | | |
| 5 | | |

**Critical #: People or B/S**
- ■
- ■
- ■ *Between green & red*
- ■

**Celebration**

**Critical #: People or B/S**
- ■
- ■
- ■ *Between green & red*
- ■

**Critical #: Process or P/L**
- ■
- ■
- ■ *Between green & red*
- ■

**Reward**

**Critical #: Process or P/L**
- ■
- ■
- ■ *Between green & red*
- ■

Trends

| 1. _____ | 4. _____ |
|---|---|
| 2. _____ | 5. _____ |
| 3. _____ | 6. _____ |

*BHAG is a Registered Trademark of Jim Collins and Jerry Porras.*

Download a full-sized copy of this tool at *scalingup.com*

# 6

# THE 7 STRATA OF STRATEGY
## The Framework for Dominating Your Industry

**EXECUTIVE SUMMARY:** *Without a powerful, industry-dominating strategy, you'll spend the next several years generating very little momentum in the marketplace. To address this challenge, we've integrated several of the best-known strategic concepts into one comprehensive framework titled the 7 Strata of Strategy. The 7 Strata defines the complete brand and provides an agenda for the strategic thinking team to create and maintain a competition-crushing, differentiated approach to a specific market. There are recommended resources to bolster your team's understanding of each stratum. It's hard work, which is why we suggest the CEO form a strategic thinking team Jim Collins labels a "council".*

The world leader in classic car and boat insurance, Traverse City, Michigan-based Hagerty continues to dominate its industry with a combined coverage larger than all of its specialty competitors combined. Growing to $674 million in 2021 and trending toward a billion by 2023, the company doesn't see growth slowing anytime soon. Why? Strategy!

When you nail your strategy, top-line revenue growth and fat margins come almost effortlessly. For those experiencing this kind of rapid and sustainable growth, skip this chapter. (We're serious!) Don't risk messing up your winning strategy. Your only challenge, like that of Hagerty, will be to heed the warning made famous by HP's Dave Packard, who was once advised that "more companies die from indigestion than starvation."

> *"More companies die from indigestion than starvation."*

For leaders of companies that are not buried by too much business, read on. Without an effective strategy, you're going to spend the next several years executing a plan that is less than optimal and leaving a pile of money on the table. Worse, you'll keep the doors open for savvier competitors to swoop in and take over your industry.

Using Hagerty as a case study (along with ample other examples), we'll walk you through the one-page 7 Strata of Strategy tool it used to dominate its industry. The 7 Strata is a comprehensive framework for creating a robust strategy that differentiates your company from the competition and helps you establish the kind of roadblocks that allow you to dominate your niche in the marketplace.

For those familiar with the One-Page Strategic Plan (OPSP), think about the 7 Strata framework as the "page behind the page" — a worksheet drilling down into the details of your Sandbox (WHAT you sell to WHOM and WHERE), Brand Promises, and the Profit per X and Big Hairy Audacious Goal (BHAG®), which are highlighted in columns 2 and 3 of the OPSP.

## Scaling Up

The idea is to use the 7 Strata worksheet to answer a series of strategic questions and plug some of the answers into the appropriate spaces on the OPSP. The questions will help you make key strategic decisions. Why aren't there spaces for all the 7 Strata answers on the OPSP? Because some should be kept confidential, and others cover details behind a few specific decisions summarized on the OPSP.

With each of the 7 Strata (levels) of decision-making, we'll share a KEY RESOURCE to help you dig deeper into that particular aspect of your strategy. In most cases, entire books have been written about the Strata, and where an appropriate one exists, we refer to it. We strongly suggest dividing up the workload and having each executive team member read one of the recommended books or articles and then brief the rest of the executives. Strategy is what a senior team should be spending the bulk of its time on, anyway — not fighting fires on a day-to-day basis, which is best left to the middle managers.

 **NOTE:** *If this work were easy, every company would have a killer strategy. The process can be very uncomfortable for CEOs, who might feel they should already have all the answers. After all, it's the CEO's primary job to set and drive the strategy of the business. At the same time, it's a very messy and creative process requiring lots of learning and talk time with a myriad number of customers, advisors, and team members. This can be particularly difficult for engineering types who want to follow a sequential process to finding the right answers. It just doesn't happen that way.*

Of all the methods we teach, this is the one where you must truly "trust the process." Persevere, keep searching (it took Wayne Huizenga, a very savvy serial entrepreneur, several years to find the key to making AutoNation's strategy work), and the magic will occur.

## Strategic Thinking Team — The Council

As mentioned in "The Overview," it's helpful to think about strategic planning in terms of two separate and distinct activities (and teams): strategic thinking and execution planning. The 7 Strata framework is one of the key tools guiding the strategic thinking agenda of the company. The 4Ps of marketing (Product, Place, Price, and Promotion) is the other guiding framework. From our perspective, marketing strategy = strategy. For an update to the 4Ps, search the Internet for ad agency Ogilvy & Mather's 4Es of marketing (Experience, Everyplace, Exchange, and Evangelism), and add these to your marketing meeting and strategic thinking agendas.

The first step in completing the 7 Strata and working through the 4Ps or 4Es of marketing is designating a strategic thinking team. Select no more than three to five people to meet for an hour or so each week to discuss each of the Strata and other issues of strategic importance. It's not sufficient to schedule strategic thinking time once every quarter or year. It's all about iterations: making a few decisions, testing them, and coming back to the table the following week for discussion. It's these ongoing weekly meetings that will keep your strategy relevant and fresh.

*"It's not sufficient to schedule thinking time just once every quarter or year."*

Jim Collins refers to this team as "the council." Grab a copy of Collins' *Good to Great: Why Some Companies Make the Leap... And Others Don't* and read the three most important pages ever written in business — Pages 114 to 116 — where he describes the 11 guidelines for structuring such a council. Included are recommendations on who should be on this council. Besides a few key members from the senior team, you might include someone with specific industry or domain knowledge underpinning your strategy.

The council doesn't accomplish its work in isolation. The council members are expected to spend time each week talking with customers and employees and checking out competitors, extracting insights and ideas to fuel their strategic thinking. People get the sense that geniuses like Steve Jobs sat around humming in a lotus position, hoping divine intervention would strike. To the contrary, Jobs spent most afternoons engaged directly with customer concerns, much to the chagrin of his team. And, underscoring the link between strategy and marketing, he chaired only one function — marketing — via a three-hour, Wednesday-afternoon meeting.

Jim Collins emphasizes that holding the council isn't a consensus-building exercise. The team members are there to give advice (council) to the CEO. And they are there to help the company illuminate the winding road ahead, which is why strategist Gary Hamel calls these groups "head-light teams." The key is to help the CEO see beyond the speed at which the company is growing so he or she can keep the company from careening off the side of the road.

In the end, strategic decisions need to be made, and it's the job of the CEO to make them. Yet it's advisable to recruit several pairs of eyes (and to have frequent contact with the market) to help the CEO navigate.

## Lords of Strategy

The creation of the 7 Strata of Strategy framework was inspired by a book written by Walter Kiechel III, a former *Fortune* editor and Harvard Business Publishing editorial director. Titled *Lords of Strategy: The Secret Intellectual History of the New Corporate World*, it chronicles the relatively short 50-year history of corporate strategy and the four men who were the pioneers in the field. For leaders interested in the topic of strategy, it's an invaluable resource documenting, in one easy-to-read package, the frameworks used by Boston Consulting Group, Bain & Co., McKinsey & Co., Porter Consulting, and many others.

What struck us, as we read the book, is how overly complex many of the models are. They were designed for large global conglomerates. At the same time, stating a simple definition of one's market (or Sandbox) and a few Brand Promises, as required on the OPSP, was too simplistic.

There needed to be something in the middle — for middle-market firms — that integrated several important aspects of strategy, and thus was born the 7 Strata of Strategy framework. We tested it with several firms for three years and found that it drove the exact kinds of strategies that helped companies like Hagerty dominate their industries. We knew then that we had something powerful, yet simple enough to help organizations scale.

Again, for those interested in the relationship between the 7 Strata and the OPSP, think of the 7 Strata as the pure "strategic thinking" piece of the strategic planning that the OPSP guides. As we take you through each of the 7 Strata, we suggest that you download the one-page worksheet at *scalingup.com* and follow along. Here are the 7 Strata:

## Scaling Up

1. Words You Own (Mindshare)

2. Sandbox and Brand Promises

3. Brand Promise Guarantee (Catalytic Mechanism)

4. One-PHRASE Strategy (Key to Making Money)

5. Differentiating Activities (3 to 5 How's)

6. X-Factor (10x – 100x Underlying Advantage)

7. Profit per X (Economic Engine) and BHAG® (10- to 25-year goal)

 **NOTE:** *Most strategy frameworks include some kind of competitive analysis. As you work through the 7 Strata, it's illuminating for the team to discuss how the competition might fill in each level — and to do the same for firms you highly respect outside your industry. This will give you additional insight into the market, the competition, and ways to differentiate your strategy.*

## S1 Words You Own (Mindshare)

 **KEY RESOURCE:** Search engine tools (Google, Bing)

No one can own the word "automobile" in the minds of the marketplace, but Volvo owns "safety." Meanwhile, BMW has molded every decision about the design and marketing of its cars around two words: "driving experience." Though BMW is also considered a luxury and performance vehicle, the company's obsession with the driving experience is what continues to differentiate the car from other mass luxury vehicles.

If you're lucky, the name of your company becomes the word you own, like Facebook. Or your company name can clearly describe what you do and represent the words you want to own in the minds of your market, like "trench safety." If you're entrepreneurial, you can name a new niche and then own it by default. J. Darius Bikoff did this in the bottled water industry in 1996. No one could own "bottled water," but he added some vitamins and minerals and created the first new beverage category in 25 years, called "enhanced waters." Though consumers were unaware of this term, Bikoff's Glacéau brands captured the attention of the big players in the industry. Coke snatched up the company for $4.1 billion just over a decade later.

The developers of Snapchat combined these ideas, creating a new category of chat and cleverly naming the venture after the two words the application now owns in the minds of the market. Launched in September 2011, the company now has a multibillion-dollar valuation.

It's a fun and useful exercise to think of well-known brands (and your competition) and discern the words they own. In the end, that's what branding is all about: owning a small piece of the mind-space within a company's targeted market, whether that's in a local neighborhood, an industry segment, or the world. If you want to hurt a competitor, steal its word, as Google did with Yahoo, becoming the "search" engine of choice.

**Brand Your Approach:** As we'll explore below in Strata five (S5), real differentiation occurs at the "activity" level of the business i.e. how you deliver your products and services in a way that's different to everyone else in the industry. One way to brand this differentiation is to name your unique approach.

Gauss & Neumann (G&N), a Barcelona-based search engine marketing (SEM) firm, employs the same kind of "quants" Wall Street uses to trade stocks — physicists and PhD mathematicians to optimize search engine results — which is a much different workforce than other SEM firms use. And this involves optimizing over a million keywords, different than the standard 5,000 to 100,000 keywords other SEM firms might utilize. The resulting revenues this differentiated approach generates is magnitudes greater than the traditional SEM methods which is why G&N is landing some of the most prestigious accounts around the globe.

G&N has taken it one step further and branded this approach MASK™ marketing. MASK is an acronym for Massive Array of Structured Keywords and represents a new category of SEM. Since G&N created the category it initially owns it — and it's become a term in the industry associated with G&N's brand. As with J. Darius Bikoff's "enhanced waters," clients can now say to others "we use the MASK™ marketing approach to SEM." By naming it you make it easier for happy customers to spread the word.

Private equity firm Riverside has done something similar. It has named/branded its approach to helping small to mid-size firms increase their market valuation. Riverside coined the acronym SPARCLE! (yes, it's a "C" instead of a "K"), to represent the eight attributes Riverside enhances to improve the valuation of the firms it acquires.

This branding helps potential customers find Riverside and G&N. They might not remember the names of the firms but they'll search for "the SEM firm utilizing MASK" or "the private equity firm with that SPARKLE methodology" (yes, clients will try the right spelling).

## Dominate Search Engines

Since 87% of ALL customers (business, consumer, and government) search the Internet to find options for purchasing products and services, you need to dominate these online search engines. The key is owning words that matter — the ones people think about and use to search for your products and services.

These search engines are useful tools for discerning your company's or competitors' success at owning a certain set of words. Take a moment to search the words or phrases you think you should own in the minds of your customers, and see how high your company ranks — or whether your lesser competitors are outranking you. Then go to the Google AdWords Keyword Planner to see how many times someone has searched for your target word

*"The key is owning words that matter."*

or phrase. More important, this tool will show you what related words are searched and with what frequency, both locally and globally. This will help you refine the words you choose to dominate.

The tool will tell you how many advertisers are bidding for a particular term in the Google AdWords program. It also gives you a sense of the difficulty you will face if you want to own that search term, letting you know if the competition is low, medium, or high.

Your first instinct may be to go after the most popular terms, whether you are planning to use paid advertising or "organic" search engine optimization techniques. However, you may be better off picking slightly less used but still popular terms to point potential customers to specific products or services you offer.

Then take a page from the best-selling book *The New Rules of Marketing & PR: How to Use Social Media, Online Video, Mobile Applications, Blogs, News Releases, and Viral Marketing to Reach Buyers Directly*. As author David Meerman Scott says, "You are what you publish." Hire writers and videographers to create case studies, white papers, and videos that naturally catch the attention of the search engines (and media) and educate the customers about the words you want to own. Videos and images have dominated over text ever since Google purchased YouTube.

G&N, for instance, has written a whitepaper comparing MASK marketing to MASS marketing which it distributes widely to those interested in better SEM results. Articles have been published by associates at Riverside on their SPARCLE process to attract acquisition candidates.

In Hagerty's case, its team publishes an informative and entertaining magazine titled "Hagerty" with a tagline "For People Who Love Cars." In addition, they've created the definitive pricing guide for classic cars called "Hagerty Price Guide." Both publications serve to brand Hagerty as the classic car experts in their field (and thus owning those words) and allows them to connect with classic car owners in general.

For more on how to use content to drive revenue, read Joe Pulizzi's highly insightful *Epic Content Marketing: How to Tell a Different Story, Break through the Clutter, and Win More Customers by Marketing Less.*

If you focus on only one of the 7 Strata, this first one is the most important in driving revenue. The rest help you defend your niche, simplify execution, and turn your revenue into huge profit.

 **NOTE:** *Owning a word or two also applies to your personal brand (e.g., Tim Ferriss owns the term "4-Hour.") If you're a LinkedIn member, read the piece Verne wrote as a LinkedIn Influencer titled "Your Career Success Hinges on One Word: Do You Know It?"*

Dominating the search engines isn't the only test. Your identity as the maker of the safest car or the "king of enhanced waters" might be well-entrenched in the minds of the right people, and therefore it might not be necessary to pop high in searches. The key is picking a niche and owning (or creating) the words in the minds of the people you want as your core customers.

## S2 Sandbox and Brand Promises

 **KEY RESOURCES:** Robert H. Bloom and Dave Conti's book *The Inside Advantage: The Strategy That Unlocks the Hidden Growth in Your Business*, and Rick Kash and David Calhoun's book *How Companies Win: Profiting From Demand-Driven Business Models No Matter What Business You're In*

There are four key decisions to make on stratum 2:

1. **Who/Where** are your (juicy red) core customers?

2. **What** are you really selling them?

3. What are your three **Brand Promises**?

4. What methods do you use to measure whether you're keeping those promises? (We call these the Kept Promise Indicators, a play on the standard definition of **KPIs**.)

**Who/Where:** Bloom and Conti, authors of *The Inside Advantage*, implore companies to get crystal clear about Who and Where their juicy red core customer is — the customer from whom the business can mine the most profit over time. Their warning is to define customers beyond a pure demographic. For Nestlé's Juicy Juice, pigeonholed early on as just another sugary drink for children, Bloom's team redefined the Who as "a mom who wants her young children to get more nutrition." For a particular nurse-staffing firm, the core customer is actually members of its team — the traveling nurses it places with hospitals — due to a global shortage of nurses. Bloom and Conti's book will help you discern a concrete definition of your core customer.

Kash and Calhoun, authors of *How Companies Win*, further suggest that there is a niche within any industry that represents no more than 10% of the total customers but holds a disproportionate percentage of the profit — what are termed profit pools. For instance, in the dog food industry, Kash's team segmented the market based on the relationship between an owner and her dog (vs. the size of the dog) and found a group of owners they labeled "performance fuelers." These are owners who are active — biking, hiking, jogging, and running — and want their dog with them. Though they represent only 7% of all dog owners, they account for more than 25% of the profitability in dog food purchases. The key is finding that same niche in your industry and owning it through a highly focused product or service offering.

Once you know more specifically Who they are, it's much easier to know Where to find them. The performance fuelers can be reached locally on a few key trails and via a couple of popular news sites and blogs.

For Hagerty, the core customer was anyone owning a classic car or boat and since the company also owns the most influential publication in the industry, it is already dominating one of the key distribution channels in the market. More recently, Hagerty has expanded its appetite for newer vehicles (from the eighties up to present day) driven by enthusiasts. A new Corvette, Porsche etc. may very well qualify for their special membership program now. This has expanded Hagerty's potential market extensively to where it estimates the market size to be approximately 29 million vehicles. Though Hagerty only owns 6% of this expanded market, it garners 20% of the profitability, much like the dog food example above.

**What:** Bloom and Conti suggest that the primary mistake companies make in describing What they sell is to focus on the benefits and features. All sales are emotional, initiated through the heart ("No one was ever fired for buying IBM") and then justified logically by the head. That's why established brands play on people's fear of purchasing from a new entry in the marketplace.

Summit Business Media (now Summit Professional Networks), an example that Bloom and Conti use in their book, offers "the indispensable source of authoritative information, data and analysis for the well-informed financial professional." The concepts that the company is (1) irreplaceable and

(2) helps its clients stay well-informed play to the financial professional's emotional needs as much as business needs.

Kash and Calhoun add that the What must encompass a 100% solution. Many business leaders are easily distracted by shiny objects; they move on too quickly to another product line, distribution channel, or niche before thoroughly locking down an existing one with an offering that completely does the job a customer needs to accomplish.

Winterhalter Gastronom GmbH, a German manufacturer of commercial dishwashing equipment, dominates the market in selling to large restaurant and hotel chains. These companies operate in a 24/7 environment and need dishes that not only are clean but look clean. Winterhalter engineered a complete solution for this niche, which included supplying water conditioners, specialty detergents, and a global quick-turnaround repair service to customers.

**Brand Promises:** Classic car owners need insurance and they have options, including many of the traditional auto insurance firms. So why should these owners buy from Hagerty vs. its competitors? There have to be some compelling reasons. We call these drivers the Brand Promises. Most companies have three main Brand Promises, with one promise that leads the list.

For Hagerty, the three Brand Promises are "We give a thumbs up to all car lovers" measured using the Net Promoter Score (NPS); "Helpful and delightful service each and every time" measured by new and retained members; and "Reasonable prices for a premium product and experience" measured by 100% satisfaction rating. The key is to define the company's Brand Promises quantitatively so they can be measured and monitored.

 **WARNING:** *Refrain from simply using the words "quality," "value," or "service" alone as Brand Promises. They are too vague. Their definitions may vary, depending on the group of customers you're facing. McDonald's delivers what many parents consider high value and service if it's noon on Saturday and they are looking for a place where they can grab a quick bite with their young children without standing in a long line, and get a few minutes of peace while the children play in the indoor playground. However, as a place to go on a date night, McDonald's has little value to them. McDonald's has defined its three measurable brand (value) promises as speed, consistency, and fun for kids. Getting clear about this and then delivering on these promises (including sending specific updates on these KPIs to its franchise owners daily) helped it pull off one of the most respected modern business turnarounds.*

The right Brand Promise isn't always obvious. Naomi Simson — founder of one of the fastest-growing companies in Australia, RedBalloon — was sure she knew what to promise customers who want to give experiences such as hot air balloon rides as gifts, rather than flowers and chocolates. Her promises included an easy-to-use website for choosing one of over 10,000 experiences; recognizable packaging and branding (think Tiffany blue, only in red); and onsite support.

It wasn't until a friend and client mentioned that she was using the website as a source of ideas — but buying the experiences directly from the vendors — that Simson had an "Aha!" moment. She realized that other customers might be doing the same thing, assuming that RedBalloon must be marking up the price of the experiences to cover the costs of the website, packaging, and onsite support. To grow the business, she promised customers they would pay no more for the experiences they bought through RedBalloon than for those purchased directly from the suppliers; otherwise, customers would get 100% of their fee refunded. The company calls this promise, which is technically a pricing guarantee, a "100% Pleasure Guarantee," to fit its brand.

**KPIs (Kept Promise Indicators):** A promise has no weight if you don't keep it, resulting in lost customers and negative word-of-mouth publicity. Thus, it's critical that you know how to measure daily whether you're keeping your promises. At RedBalloon, Simson created a team that monitors pricing of its roughly 10,000 experiences to make sure that her customers can't buy the experiences more cheaply from other vendors. This isn't easy. The prices that suppliers charge for experiences like jet boating are subject to constant change because of factors such as fuel price fluctuations and insurance costs.

Rackspace, offering cloud-based hosting, is another company that has mastered Brand Promise KPIs. The company, based in San Antonio, has built its brand around the promise of "fanatical support." This phrase appears smack in the middle of its website: "Fanatical Support: Over 1,400 trained cloud specialists, ready to help."

The company measures its success in meeting this Brand Promise in three ways. The #1 measurement is uptime of a client's site. Rackspace offers a money-back guarantee if there's any downtime. If there is a problem, and a customer has to call in, that call will be answered in three rings. Rackspace installs red lights in its call centers that start to spin if a call is getting ready to go to a fourth ring. So that a customer doesn't get transferred, that call will be answered by a level two tech who has the skill to handle escalated problems. That's what the customers want. Rackspace measures its performance on these three things, obsessively, every moment: uptime, calls answered in three rings or fewer, and lack of call transfers. The data is streaming all over its facilities. That's how Rackspace grew from nothing to a market cap of more than $6 billion in a dozen years.

The Hagerty team, similarly, has various Kept Promise Indicators it monitors to make sure everyone is keeping the company's Brand Promise. As mentioned above, Hagerty uses the Net Promoter Score to gauge overall delight (not just satisfaction). And its policies, on average, are 40% less than a standard market policy. Hagerty is often told that its insurance delivers "twice the value at half the price" given all of the product features.

## 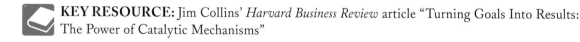 Brand Promise Guarantee (Catalytic Mechanism)

**KEY RESOURCE:** Jim Collins' *Harvard Business Review* article "Turning Goals Into Results: The Power of Catalytic Mechanisms"

It needs to hurt to break a promise; otherwise, it's too easy to let the moment pass. This is why Collins labeled what we call a Brand Promise Guarantee "a catalytic mechanism." By promising to refund 100% of a RedBalloon gift voucher's cost if the customer can find the experience for a cheaper price, the company's guarantee puts heat on Simson's team to keep its pricing promise.

The Brand Promise Guarantee also reduces customers' fear of buying from you. In its early days, Oracle promised that enterprise software would run twice as fast on its database software as on competitors' (in full-page ads on the back of *Fortune* magazine), or it would pay customers $1 million.

Today, it offers a similar guarantee on its Exadata servers, except the reward is $10 million.

Professional service firms might offer "short pay" guarantees, giving the client an option to pay whatever he thinks reasonable if there are issues. Though 99% of clients won't spend less, the existence of the guarantee gives them the confidence to do business with the service firm and encourages customers to share their concerns.

Jim Collins' article will give you many more examples, as will the marketplace, when you start paying attention to what other companies are doing to guarantee their promises.

For Hagerty, the challenge classic car owners have is making sure the real value of their auto is reflected in their insurance coverage. Since Hagerty has literally written the definitive pricing guide for classic cars, it has a "Guaranteed Value®" promise: We use our industry-leading tools to help you determine the true value of your classic, then create an agreed value policy that covers it."

##  One-PHRASE Strategy (Key to Making Money)

**KEY RESOURCE:** Frances Frei and Anne Morriss' book *Uncommon Service: How to Win by Putting Customers at the Core of Your Business*

Do you dare to be bad? Even risk alienating or upsetting a large segment of potential customers? This is precisely what highly profitable and successful companies do, according to Frances Frei, a leading strategy professor at Harvard Business School, and Anne Morriss, Executive Founder of The Leadership Consortium.

The first three Strata — owning mindshare, making and keeping promises, and backing them up with a guarantee — are expensive to accomplish. Making matters worse, in trying to address ever-increasing customer demands, the marketplace ends up "want, want, wanting" your margins away as the competition ramps up the "feature set and added services" war.

This is why it's critical to identify your One-PHRASE Strategy. This phrase represents the key lever in your business model that drives profitability and helps you choose which customer desires to meet and which ones to ignore.

Take IKEA's business model, based on "flat pack furniture." Since IKEA doesn't have to ship or warehouse air, its costs are considerably lower than competitors', giving it a huge price advantage (its #1 Brand Promise). Add to this a flair for design and the best Swedish meatballs on the planet, and you have three Brand Promises that outweigh all the things people hate about IKEA — and it's a long list!

Yet it's specific trade-offs that power IKEA's success and serve as a blocking strategy to competitors. Others simply don't have the stomach to make people drive out of their way to visit a warehouse designed like a labyrinth, committing customers to a lengthy shopping experience. Pile on the need for assembly after the purchase, and it's crazy to think anyone would shop at IKEA. And a lot of people don't. But with just 6.8% global market share, IKEA is the world's largest and most profitable furniture chain. NOTE: given the aging population which has all the money, IKEA purchased TaskRabbit in 2017 to make it easier for people to purchase and assemble their furniture.

Apple's One-PHRASE Strategy has been its "closed architecture," the source of its phenomenal profitability. It also serves as a powerful blocking strategy, since Google and Microsoft are beyond the point of no return and would never be able to close their open systems. Again, most of the consumers in the world don't find the trade-offs worth it, but that hasn't kept Apple from being the most valuable company in the world.

Frei and Morriss' overarching point is that great brands don't try to please everyone. They focus on being the absolute best at meeting the needs/wants of a small but fanatical group of customers, and then dare to be the absolute worst at everything else. In turn, competitors, in striving to be the best in everything for everyone, actually achieve greatness in nothing — and end up as just average players in the industry.

We would share Hagerty's One-PHRASE Strategy, but we strongly suggest that the company keep it a strategic secret. Again, you don't want to run around bragging about the key driver of your business's profitability, at least in the early years.

The book *Uncommon Service* will give you a myriad number of examples and walk you through how to both "be bad" the right and highly profitable way and "be great" via a few Brand Promises. It takes real guts to ignore or even alienate 93% of customers, focusing instead on the 7% of the market that is fanatical about you and willing to put up with the trade-offs.

##  Differentiating Activities (3 to 5 Hows)

**KEY RESOURCE:** Michael E. Porter's classic 1996 *Harvard Business Review* article titled "What Is Strategy?"

Underpinning the One-PHRASE Strategy is a set of specific actions that represent HOW you execute your business differently from the competition. According to well-known strategist Michael Porter at Harvard Business School, it's at the "activity" level of the business where true differentiation occurs and the business model is revealed.

 NOTE: *This is the first time the term "differentiation" has been used. Competitors can pursue owning the same words, make the same Brand Promises, and offer the same guarantees. However, it's HOW you deliver on your promises where differentiation occurs. Adds Kevin Daum, author of* ROAR! Get Heard in the Sales and Marketing Jungle: A Business Fable, *"a true differentiator can only be defined as*

*something your competitor won't do or can't do without great effort or expense. Often these can take years to de-velop since if it can be done cheaply, easily and quickly it provides little or no competitive advantage."*

Again, Porter's point is that this happens at the activity level of the business, as illustrated by the Southwest Airlines case he highlights in his *HBR* article referenced above. Southwest has a handful of hard-to-copy activities that differentiate it from competitors. In addition to not having advance-res-ervation seating, the airline flies just one type of aircraft (reducing the number of repair parts needed

and giving it more flexibility to swap pilots), utilizes second-tier airports to reduce landing fees, favors point-to-point flights vs. the more expen-sive hub-and-spoke system, and nurtures a quirky culture that helps customers put up with all the negatives.

Southwest Airlines even prices differently, being the first with no change, baggage, or hidden fees. And they have gone so far as to sub-brand this difference as "Transfarency."

These activities serve as blocking factors precisely because all the other airlines, except European copycat Ryan Air, are already invested in multiple aircraft, provide advance-reservation seating (it's hard to take away something you've already given the customer), are locked into

expensive hubs, and have built cultures of unhappy employees!

The key is to choose HOW you go about delivering your products and services in your industry in ways that are nearly impossible for your competition to copy. Notice that these activities derive from Southwest's One-PHRASE Strategy — "Wheels Up" (its expensive hunks of metal make money only when they are in the air) — helping the airline achieve this key result that drives profitability. Each layer of the 7 Strata of Strategy builds upon and reinforces the others.

In Hagerty's case, they are specialists and their products and services are uniquely designed ac-cordingly. Examples include guaranteed flatbed towing (vs. a tow hook) when roadside assistance is needed in order to minimize any potential damage to the collectible car during towing. Their claims handling is designed for the types of vehicles they insure. Imagine calling to say you cracked your windshield on a car built in the 1920's with a standard market insurer. These insurers wouldn't know what to do (how to source, pricing, etc.) yet Hagerty handles this kind of claim all the time. Last, it might seem minor but Hagerty refers to their customers as members and has created a club-like atmosphere for classic car owners through their publications and other activities.

Read Porter's article, along with *Uncommon Service*, and establish a set of activities — "how" you run the business — that is different from the norms of the industry, helps you drive profitability, and blocks the competition. This is a lot for a handful of activities to accomplish, but this is the source of your differentiation. Do the work!

As Porter summarizes, "A company can outperform rivals only if it can establish a difference that it can preserve."

#  S6 X-Factor (10x-100x Underlying Advantage)

**KEY RESOURCE:** Verne's *Fortune* article titled "The X-Factor"

Why would Hagerty allow us to share the details of its strategy? It's because of a hidden X-Factor — a 10x-100x underlying competitive advantage over its rivals. Normally invisible to customers, this edge underpins the strategic activities described above and blocks competitors from even trying to copy Hagerty. And it typically addresses a huge, established choke point in an industry.

Once you have such an advantage, it will allow you to sustain the kind of rapid growth that Hagerty has achieved for years.

As Verne details in his *Fortune* piece, Chris Sullivan made the Outback Steakhouse restaurant chain successful by focusing on an early X-Factor. After working extensively in the restaurant industry, he knew the primary challenge for large restaurant chains is maintaining consistency in food quality and service. But why? As he continued to peel back the layers, he concluded that it was due to the industry's average six-month turnover of general managers in stores, a statistic considered to be "just the way it is in the restaurant business." Good managers were typically moved around to take over for bad managers, and great managers would eventually leave and start their own restaurants.

Recognizing manager turnover as the choke point in the industry, Sullivan and his team asked themselves a key question: What if we could keep a restaurant manager in the same restaurant for five to 10 years? This would represent a 10x to 20x improvement over the existing situation in the industry.

The key for Sullivan turned out to be an unusual compensation plan (think "differentiated activity"). Young people interested in becoming managers were asked to "invest" $25,000 in an Outback restaurant. Imagine one of your children coming home and sharing that they found a job managing a restaurant. After expressing your initial skepticism ("What, managing a steakhouse after obtaining a four-year degree?"), you get around to the all-important question: "So what does it pay?" Whereupon she explains that she actually needs to pay the company to get the job!

Here was the deal Sullivan pioneered: New managers would invest $25,000 and commit to staying for five years. Outback would take the first three years to train them to run a restaurant, paying a competitive wage. During the last two years, the new managers would get to run a restaurant on their own. If they hit certain performance milestones by the fifth year, they would get a $100,000 bonus — a 4x return on their investment — which would vest over the next four years. If they signed on to stay at the same restaurant another five years, they would receive the $100,000 in one lump sum, plus $500,000 worth of stock that would vest over the next five years.

The company ended up turning a bunch of people in their 20s into millionaires; 90% of managers stayed in the same restaurant for five years; and 80% stayed for 10 years or more. Most important, Outback's theory was correct. The longevity of management led to consistency in products and service, helping Outback become the third-largest restaurant chain in the US, and the most profitable, before Sullivan stepped aside as CEO.

So how do you figure out an X-Factor? Start by asking: What is the one thing I hate most about my industry? What is driving me nuts? What is the choke point constraining the company? It could be a massive cost factor. It could be a massive time factor. The challenge is that you're often too close to the situation and as blind as everyone else to the real problems that have been accepted as industry norms.

One clue to the source of the X-Factor is going back to your last 10 trade association meetings and gathering the titles of the various breakout sessions. Put them in an Excel spreadsheet, and see if there are any patterns of challenges facing your industry over the past decade. By focusing on these roadblocks, and figuring out a 10x to 100x advantage, you'll have a huge leg up on the competition.

And you don't have to run a business the size of Outback to put this principle into practice. Barrett Ersek, founder of lawn care company Happy Lawn, reduced the typical sales process from three weeks to three minutes. Using the latest digital technology and tax map data to estimate lawn measurements and offer instant quotes while customers were on the phone, he eliminated the need to have salespeople visit prospects' homes and take manual measurements, write up quotes, and then schedule appointments. It's not surprising that industry giant ServiceMaster bought Ersek's $10 million company. At Holganix, Ersek's new company — which manufactures and distributes organic fertilizer — he's identified another X-Factor. But, like his One-PHRASE Strategy, he's keeping it a secret.

Hagerty's X-Factor remains a secret, as it should. But you can go to Verne's *Fortune* article for additional examples. Then start brainstorming with your strategic thinking team about some possible 10x advantages.

##  S7 Profit per X (Economic Engine) and BHAG® (10- to 25-Year Goal)

**KEY RESOURCE:** Jim Collins' Hedgehog Concept in *Good to Great: Why Some Companies Make the Leap... And Others Don't*

The final two decisions cap the strategy with a single overarching KPI that Jim Collins labels "Profit per X" and a measurable 10- to 25-year goal referred to as a BHAG®, a term that Collins and Jerry I. Porras introduced in their book *Built to Last: Successful Habits of Visionary Companies*. Both decisions round out Collins' strategic framework that he calls the Hedgehog Concept in *Good to Great*.

The Profit per X metric represents the underlying economic engine of the business and provides the leaders with a single KPI they can track maniacally to monitor the progress of the business (a great luxury to have). Though the numerator can be any metric you like — profit, revenue, gross margin, pilots, routes, etc. — the denominator is fixed and represents your company's unique approach to scaling the business. And it generally ties back to the One-PHRASE Strategy (all of this stuff links together). While most airlines focus on profit per mile or profit per seat, Southwest focuses on maximizing profit per plane, which aligns with its One-PHRASE Strategy of "Wheels Up."

As we saw in Alan Rudy's story in Chapter 2, he took a similar approach in the business of answering phones. While everyone else focused on revenue per minute and profit per minute, he looked at the industry through a different lens and drove the business to maximize profit per booked appointment. The result: revenue reached an industry high of $5 per minute, vs. an average of $1.25 per minute. At Scaling Up, we used to obsess over profit per event; now it's profit per city with our new 20,000 Scaleups initiative aimed at serving 150 scaleups in each of 150 cities around the globe.

## Big Hairy Audacious Goal (BHAG®)

As leaders set the ultimate long-term, 10- to 25-year goal for their companies, we see a lot of sloppy work — a random number or statement of aspiration with no real connection to a company's underlying strategy.

### Microsoft's BHAG®

*"When Paul Allen and I started Microsoft over 30 years ago, we had big dreams about software. We had dreams about the impact it could have. We talked about a computer on every desk and in every home. It's been amazing to see so much of that dream become a reality and touch so many lives. I never imagined what an incredible and important company would spring from those original ideas."*

— Bill Gates at a news conference announcing plans for full-time philanthropy work and part-time Microsoft work, June 15, 2006, Redmond, Washington

Collins placed the BHAG® in the center of his Hedgehog Concept, noting that it must fully align with all the components of your strategy. It's why we've made it the seventh and final stratum. And we've discovered that the best unit of measure for the BHAG® is the X from the Profit per X.

 **NOTE:** *Your BHAG® should be measured in the same units as the X. This is a key point. Since Southwest Airlines is focused on profit per plane, it made sense that the company set a long-term goal to have X number of planes in the air. The Profit per X and the BHAG® need to align very tightly.*

The BHAG® must also align with the Purpose of the company, as we explain in the chapter on the One-Page Strategic Plan. RedBalloon set an aggressive BHAG® to sell 2 million experiences in 10 years, a goal established in 2005, when it sold only 7,500. Simson, founder and CEO, reasoned that to truly change gifting in Australia forever (tapping people's desire for experiences vs. stuff), RedBalloon needed to touch the lives of 10% of Australians. At the time, there were 20 million Australians, so reaching 2 million experiences sold was the goal. It then made sense for RedBalloon's primary KPI to be profit per experience. RedBalloon ended up reaching the 2 million goal two years early (2013) and as detailed in the opening Introduction is aiming to deliver an experience every second by 2030.

Hagerty's BHAG is to scale from 1.7 million members in 2017 to 6 million by 2025 with a corresponding profit/member as their overarching KPI. Perfect alignment between these two final strategic decisions.

# 7 Strata Summary

Hagerty's strategy can be stated simply, yet there is nothing simple about it in terms of execution. If you're a classic car owner (and/or high-end luxury car owner with their new expanded reach) and need car insurance you'll find the company easily via the search engines. This owner will likely find the 40% savings an appealing value proposition, along with the delightful customer service and less than 24-hour response time to any questions and inquiries. Classic car owners know their questions are often more difficult to answer than owners of newer vehicles i.e. what is the cost to replace a windshield on a vintage automobile.

And the owner has no fear that Hagerty's insurance coverage will fall short. Hagerty's "Guaranteed Value®" promise assures the owner that through its industry-leading tools, it can "help you determine the true value of your classic, then create an agreed value policy that covers it."

Hagerty doesn't mind that we share its strategy because its top-secret X-Factor, which took years to perfect, provides a 10x advantage over any competitor that might try to copy the rest of its strategy. That's why the leadership team at Hagerty sees a clear growth path from 1.7 million members to 6 million within the next few years while dominating one of the most profitable sectors in the auto insurance industry. This focused strategy allowed Hagerty to go public via a SPAC in 2021 with an initial market cap of $3 billion and the family maintaining control.

The payoff is huge if you figure out all of the attributes of the 7 Strata. As with all of our tools, nail down what you can and keep moving. Set up your strategic thinking team, have each member read (and master) one of the referenced books or articles, and start testing your theories and honing your strategy to perfection. You'll know you're on the right track when sustained revenue growth and great margins start coming more easily.

It's very difficult work, and your strategic thinking team may feel both lost and outright dumbfounded in the beginning, but trust the process. Keep meeting each week and talking through the ideas, and answers will come to you. If you need help, Scaling Up has some top-notch strategy consultants, with experience helping many companies work through these Strata, who can help you do some of the heavy lifting.

In the next chapter of the "Strategy" section, we'll take several decisions from the 7 Strata and integrate them into the OPSP: the one-page vision around which to align the entire company.

# 7

# THE ONE-PAGE STRATEGIC PLAN
## The Tool for Strategic Planning

---

**EXECUTIVE SUMMARY:** *The bigger your company, and the faster it's growing, the harder it is to keep everyone on the same page. The problem, of course, is that there isn't a single page around which to align. Instead, there are likely more than a dozen actual and imaginary ones, along with memos and emails, each purporting to describe your company's vision, values, strategies, goals, and priorities. Many of these messages may be riddled with unclear and even contradictory statements about your company's identity, what it does, and how it accomplishes this. This chapter will introduce you to the One-Page Strategic Plan (OPSP), updated since it was first introduced more than a decade ago and used by more than 80,000 companies worldwide. It's a simple yet powerful tool that helps you edit down your vision to a single, action-oriented page. We'll also introduce the SWT, a tool to augment the traditional SWOT analysis as you prepare your OPSP, along with a Vision Summary which provides a succinct way to communicate your vision.*

---

The One-Page Strategic Plan (OPSP) has been critical to the growth of JSJ Corporation, the Michigan-based parent company of six durable-goods firms. With 2,700 employees spread out around the world, the family-owned firm, which celebrated its 100th anniversary in 2019, began using the OPSP in 2006.

After hearing about the OPSP, Nelson Jacobson, the CEO of JSJ, sent the company's head of organizational development to a two-day "Mastering the Rockefeller Habits" workshop. Executives also spoke with leaders of a local company who were using it, to learn how the tool had helped them scale up and manage business performance.

"I had been the chief operating officer of JSJ since about 2000," recalls Jacobson, a member of the third generation of one of the founding families. "We went through the post-9/11 recession. At that point, it became a very different company. When I became the CEO in 2005, I was searching for a tool that would make us a more cohesive operating entity. The OPSP gave us a way of tracking and driving business performance."

## Everyone on the Same Page

Confident that the OPSP could help JSJ grow cohesively, Jacobson introduced it to his seven-member leadership team. "I was looking for something to bring the company together," he recalls.

Each of JSJ's six companies has a different focus, so each creates and updates its own OPSP. These, in turn, influence JSJ's plan for the entire company. There is a rhythm to this: Each business typically develops its own plan in time for the company's Annual Operating Planning session in October.

Over the next several months, the six companies' plans get finalized, so JSJ can utilize them to further shape its own plan. JSJ's plan, in turn, becomes final at a February board meeting.

Jacobson says the OPSP helped the leadership team make one of its toughest decisions: to sell one of its companies, a lithographic printing firm in California. "It helped us to evaluate which were the right businesses to hold," he recalls. "That one didn't fit." Fortunately, the parent sold it at a good time. "We used those funds to invest in and grow the remaining businesses," Jacobson says.

JSJ's efforts have taken commitment, but there's been a big, measurable payoff. The company has developed new technologies, launched additional product lines, and expanded geographically as a direct result of decisions it made while using the OPSP. "We've had continuously improving profit and growth since we started," says Jacobson. "The OPSP has brought better alignment, accountability, and execution."

In this chapter, we'll examine in detail the components of an effective OPSP, and how JSJ and tens of thousands of other firms have used it to drive engagement, alignment, and focus throughout their organizations. But first, we want to introduce a simplified version of the OPSP: the Vision Summary. Many companies can start with this and then progress to the more comprehensive OPSP as their sophistication in strategic planning increases.

# Vision Summary

The Vision Summary provides a simplified OPSP framework for companies just getting started with implementing the Rockefeller Habits and for firms with 50 employees or fewer. For larger firms that are taking advantage of the more detailed aspects of the OPSP, the Vision Summary provides a one-page format to communicate key aspects of the company's vision to employees, customers, investors, and the broader community.

At *scalingup.com*, you can download a copy of the Vision Summary without the Scaling Up or Gazelles logo in the upper right. Then list the following for your company:

- Core Values
- Purpose
- Brand Promises
- Big Hairy Audacious Goal (BHAG®)

We detailed these strategic components of the Vision Summary in the two previous chapters in the "People" and "Strategy" sections. They represent the key components of the company's vision that every employee should know and understand thoroughly, making this summary useful as a key onboarding tool for new employees.

Under these components is a place to list the strategic priorities. In the first column, list the three-to five-year Key Thrusts/Capabilities from the OPSP. These are the handful of major medium-term priorities, which we will describe in more detail later.

In the middle column, list the year's #1 Priority and the Key Initiatives necessary to achieve it. And in the last column, list the quarter's #1 Priority and the "Rocks" required to reach this goal. We will provide more detail on how to set these priorities in "The Priority" chapter.

These strategic components and priorities provide a quick snapshot of the company's vision. Underneath them is a place for every employee or team to personalize the plan. There, they can list a handful of key performance indicators (KPIs), priorities, and a Critical Number for the quarter, which should support and align with the company's vision. These come from decisions made when completing the last column of the OPSP, and we detail them later in this chapter, as well.

We encourage team members to post this Vision Summary in their cubicles, their offices, or the cabs of their sanitation trucks as visual reminders of the organization's strategic plan and their part in making it a reality.

## One-Page Strategic Plan (OPSP)

Many people have dreams. However, a vision is a dream with a plan: a One-Page Strategic Plan.

To flesh out the vision, you need to answer seven basic questions: *who, what, when, where, how, why*, and the often challenging question, "But *should* we or *shouldn't* we?" These questions anchor the seven columns of the OPSP. If you ever feel confused by the terminology that comes with strategic planning, always come back to these seven simple questions.

*"A vision is a dream with a plan."*

The terminology can be hard to follow. We are working to get our industry to align around a common language, agreeing on standard definitions of vision, purpose, values, priorities, etc. We are also using the OPSP to integrate the various visioning frameworks of thought leaders like Jim Collins, Gary Hamel, Jack Stack, and Stephen Covey, to name a few.

The tool is designed to align both horizontally and vertically, providing a logical framework to organize your strategic vision and guarantee that you have all the pieces to make it whole. The physical structure of the OPSP forces prioritization and simplicity. There's not a lot of space to write, so you must be concise.

As you fill in the document, think of it as a giant crossword or Sudoku puzzle. Figure out what you can, and let that help you determine the rest (e.g., Purpose and Brand Promise will triangulate back to the BHAG®). "Get it down; then get it right" is our mantra. A good plan now is better than a great plan too late.

*"Get it down; then get it right."*

There is one other important design element to the OPSP. Jim Collins discovered that enduring companies operate with a dual dynamic that he labeled "preserve the core/stimulate progress." This duality is built into the OPSP. The first three columns describe the core, which holds steady over time. The balance of the plan, as you move right, becomes more dynamic, stimulating progress to meet the trends, opportunities, and challenges of the marketplace.

To summarize, the OPSP process provides the organization with:

1. A **framework** that details your corporate vision.

2. A common **language** with which to express that vision.

3. A well-developed **routine** for keeping the vision current.

To get started with the OPSP, download the document, available in various languages from *scalingup. com*. If you print it out, place the first page to the left of the second page. This will give you a continuous single-page document on an 11-by-17-inch (A3) piece of paper. It will be helpful to have a physical copy as you read this chapter (a three-quarter-size copy appears at the front of the "Strategy" section). A sample completed plan can also be found at the end of the next chapter "The Planning Process.".

 **NOTE:** *The OPSP is for internal consumption. It's designed to help a team get the technical aspects of the strategic plan correct vs. craft marketing messages (e.g., taglines). However, once you construct the plan, it will be faster and less costly, if you are using an outside marketing or ad agency, to create the external messaging to communicate your vision to employees, customers, and the broader community.*

## OPSP Experiences: Holganix, Markitforce, and Towne Park

Barrett Ersek, co-founder of natural-lawn-care firm Holganix in Pennsylvania, has created five companies over 20 years, his first when he was 17 years old. He describes the OPSP and other strategic habits of this methodology as a blueprint for what he needs to do to grow his business. "When I was in my 20s, I was running a business with a checkbook in my back pocket, and then for the first time in my life, someone gave me an instruction booklet," he says.

For Alan Higgins of Australia-based Markitforce, a point-of-sale and warehouse fulfillment firm, the OPSP is an "automatic decision-making machine." The founder and chief engagement officer notes: "If there's ever a fork in the road or a decision to be made, we refer back to the tool to see if we're on strategy. If we're not, we chat about whether we should walk away from the opportunity."

The OPSP is one of the most valuable tools at 15,000-employee Towne Park, a hospitality services firm based in Maryland, according to founder Jerry South. "It allows me to think strategically about the business and compartmentalizes some of the big decisions we are wrestling with and breaks them down to bite-sized pieces," South says. "Plus, it creates the clarity needed around what's important in the business."

Let's walk through the seven columns of the OPSP:

**Column 1 (Should/Shouldn't):** Lists a handful of rules defining the boundaries for decision-making — the *Shoulds* or *Shouldn'ts* represented by the Core Values.

**Column 2 (Why):** Expresses the impact the company wants to make in the world (or neighborhood), providing the meaning — the *Why* — behind everyone's efforts. It requires two main decisions:

- **Purpose** (often referred to as "mission"): the aspirational North Star or Southern Cross providing direction to the business
- **BHAG®** (**Big Hairy Audacious Goal**): the measurable piece of the Purpose that the business can achieve in the next 10 to 25 years

**Column 3 (Where):** Defines *Where* the company is headed in the next three to five years. Includes a description of the Sandbox in which the company wants to play (e.g., in terms of customers, geography, and product/service mix) and its measurable Brand Promises to those customers. It also summarizes a handful of major Capabilities and Key Thrusts the company must pursue.

**Column 4 (What):** Describes *What* results need to be achieved in the next 12 months. These are driven by a measurable #1 Priority (Critical Number) and a handful of "Rocks" (see Pages 133-134).

**Column 5 (How):** Details *How* the company plans to achieve its vision, focused on a measurable "next step" 90-day #1 Priority (Critical Number) and a handful of "Rocks."

**Column 6 (Finish Lines and Fun):** Describes the theme, celebration, and rewards associated with the #1 Priority for the quarter or year. The theme celebrations give everyone a definitive finish line and a chance to have some fun.

**Column 7 (Who):** Delineates *Who* is accountable for various aspects of the OPSP, detailing the KPIs, Rocks, and Critical Numbers for each employee or team. Last, the *When* question is represented by each column's time frame.

## Filling In the OPSP

Alignment and clarity start at the very top of the OPSP with the Organization Name. Organizations must align around a name that customers and employees (including the receptionist answering the phones) can remember and say. Finding that everyone called the company FedEx, Federal Express changed its name. Minnesota Mining and Manufacturing worked for a while, but the corporation is 3M today. HVLS Fan Company, whose large industrial fans were designed to be high-volume and low-speed, adopted the name Big Ass Fans after years of having customers use that moniker instead. Today, the business — recently renamed Big Ass Solutions — is one of the most widely recognized, fastest-growing companies in its niche. Other companies have exceedingly long and complex names that include generic terms like "Group" or "Inc." which no one ever uses. Consider dropping those extra words.

The "Organization Name" line can be used to signify whether the strategic vision applies only to a division or department within a firm. At JSJ, each of the six companies will list its respective name (e.g., "Sparks, a JSJ Business").

Finish the title area by adding your own name and the date. A few key points:

1. Some of you have names that are difficult to pronounce and spell. It might be best to simplify them, like many of our clients in Malaysia who go by their initials (hi, H.K. and C.K.!) or like my friend Nick Alexos, whose original name was Nicholas Alexopoulos. Or mimic performers and consider adopting a more memorable and business-friendly nickname (Gordon Sumner is known the world over as Sting).

2. To eliminate confusion over whether the month or day is listed first in the date, we suggest trying the global standard used by Cisco: the two-digit designation of the day, followed by the three-letter designation of the month, and then the four-digit designation of the year (e.g., 02 Feb 2022.)

We hate to be so picky, but alignment starts with getting agreement on the organization's name, your name, and the format of the date.

## Strengths, Weaknesses, and Trends

Along the bottom of the OPSP is a place to summarize the company's top three inherent Strengths/ Core Competencies and Weaknesses. There is also room to highlight the top six trends that will likely hit the company and its industry like meteors. These serve as the foundation upon which the Vision is built. Later in this chapter, we'll introduce a new one-page SWT tool to help you fill this in. It supplements the age-old SWOT that companies have used for decades.

## OPSP Column 1: Core Values/Beliefs

Moving up to the body of the form, list the firm's Core Values in the first column. These three to eight phrases broadly define the *shoulds* and *shouldn'ts* that govern your company's underlying decisions and describe the personality of the organization. "The Core" chapter discusses in more detail Core Values and how to use them to drive the people (HR) systems inside your company.

**NOTE:** *Do not feel compelled to call these concepts Core Values. Label them however you like: beliefs, rules, the HP Way. The key is to figure out what they are so your team can utilize them to keep the culture strong and drive decisions as the company scales.*

## OPSP Column 2: Purpose, Profit per X, and BHAG®

If the first column represents the soul of the organization (or organism), then column 2 presents its heart. Column 2 answers some very basic *Why* questions: Why is this company doing what it's doing? What's its higher purpose? Why should I have passion for what we're doing?

It also provides a clue as to why certain seemingly small incidents send the founder into a tirade, while other situations, which may be bigger and more costly, slide by almost without comment. For example, Scaling Up's Purpose revolves around the word "contribution." We're excited to support the contribution scaleups make to their local and global economies and the contribution they make to all the families supported by the organization.

Find what rankles the CEO in your firm, and you'll have a leg up on figuring out your company's purpose. An example is Wal-Mart's purpose: "To give ordinary folks the chance to buy the same things as rich people." Sam Walton, founder of Wal-Mart, was bothered by the inequality between the rich and poor and had a passion for giving people in rural areas access to reasonably priced retail goods.

Again, "The Core" chapter provides more detail on how to determine the company's Purpose and how to use it to create a stump speech the leadership team can use to ignite employees' hearts.

Under the Purpose on the OPSP, you'll see an "Actions" section. It's easy for companies to create a list of Core Values, Purpose, and BHAG®, and then forget them. This "Actions" box is meant to drive a quarterly conversation about what's necessary, in the short run, to keep these long-term Vision items alive in the company and generate a handful of actions to bolster these core elements.

We had a client with a Core Value that emphasized the importance of having some "serious fun" as part of its culture. Having just gone public (which is no fun), the executive team decided at the next quarterly planning session to present the employees with a foosball table as a symbol that they didn't want to lose this fun aspect of the culture just because they were now part of a public company.

This is the kind of specific action item you would list under "Actions" in the Purpose column — specific ways to reinforce the Core Values, Purpose, and BHAG® in the next 90 days.

The Profit per X and BHAG® (Big Hairy Audacious Goal) were discussed in detail in "The 7 Strata of Strategy" chapter. To review, the Profit per X is a single KPI that represents the company's primary economic engine (e.g., the driving element of the business model). Southwest Airlines, for example, has a relentless focus on profit per airplane vs. other airlines' focus of profit per seat or profit per mile. The BHAG® represents the quantifiable 10- to 25-year target that aligns with the Purpose and Profit per X.

The key is for everything to align in column 2 and tell a compelling story that excites and engages the people to scale up the business. For a moving example, watch the five-minute, 25th-anniversary video tribute to Southwest Airlines' employees featuring then-President, CEO, and Chairman Herb Kelleher.

## OPSP Column 3: Targets, Sandbox, and Brand Promises

As we move to column 3, the plan becomes more detailed, listing specific financial targets and priorities over the next three to five years. These define the "camps" on the way to Everest (BHAG®), recalling the analogy shared in "The Overview."

The first decision is choosing whether to look ahead three, four, or five years. The key question to ask is, "In what time frame do we plan to double the revenue/size of the company?" If the plan is to grow at 15% per year, then you'll double in five years. If it's 25% per year, then choose a three-year time frame. If you're growing 100% per year, then your company is living in "dog years," when one year is like three to five for everyone else. In this case, choose a one-year time frame for column 3, a quarterly time frame for column 4, and a one-month time frame for column 5 (your month is like everyone else's quarter).

Since everything between the BHAG® and the next 90 days is a WAG (wild-ankle guess), the three- to five-year financial targets might as well be aspirational and aggressive. Specifically, looking at the top of column 3:

1. **Future Date:** Set the ending date for this medium-term planning period (e.g., 31 Dec 2023).

2. **Revenues:** Consider hitting a target revenue that's twice what it is today. Again, this is the definition of a camp on the way to your Everest: the point at which you're going to double the size of the business next.

3. **Profit:** Consider targeting three times industry average profitability. This is the definition of a great vs. good company, so go for it!

4. **Mkt. Cap/Cash:** If you lead a public company, set a goal for what the company will be worth (market cap). If you're at a private company, set a target for how much cash you would like to have in the bank or the market share you'd like to own within your industry.

Next, summarize the **Sandbox** in which the company plans to play over the next three to five years. This is a summary of Stratum 2 off the 7 Strata worksheet: a short description of the core customers *(Who and Where)* and *What* it is you plan to sell them.

Then jump to the bottom of the column and clearly articulate the key needs you're going to satisfy for this Sandbox: the measurable **Brand Promises**. Note these specific metrics in the **Brand Promise KPIs** (Kept Promise Indicators) box. Recall from the last chapter how Rackspace measured Fanatical

Support in terms of answering customer calls within three rings. FedEx's promise of 10 a.m. delivery and Oracle's Exadata 5x promise are additional examples of Brand Promise KPIs.

Once you've decided on the financial targets, Sandbox, and Brand Promises, choose the three to five Key Thrusts/Capabilities the company must pursue over the next three to five years. These might include a number of important acquisitions or the launch of a new product or service line. They might also represent a dramatic refocus of the core business, like Steve Jobs' decision, when he became Apple's CEO in 1997, to pull it out of all of its current business lines and focus on producing just two desktops and two laptops.

For Scaling Up, some earlier Key Thrusts/Capabilities included international expansion outside of the US and Canada; the launch of a software-as-a-service offering to support our methodologies; the creation of a high-end membership organization; a significant global expansion of our coaching organization; and the creation of an online learning platform.

These examples represent the kinds of significant medium-term priorities that a company should list in column 3 and are meant to provide a clear strategic direction for the next several years. To support the company's efforts, assemble a board of advisors. Recruit the smartest people you can find to advise you on each Key Thrust/Capability. It's always helpful to learn from those who have already been *Where* you're about to go.

## OPSP Column 4: Goals

Moving to column 4, if you're going to get to your next camp, *What* are the #1 Priority and Key Initiatives for the company year — sometimes referred to as OKRs (Objectives and Key Results)? Addressing this starts with setting some very specific and expanded financial outcomes at the top of the column. Feel free to edit or add to the categories listed (e.g., some of you might not have significant inventory; tracking staff utilization instead might be more appropriate).

Next, jump to the bottom of the column and determine THE **Critical Number** for the year: "the main thing that will be the main thing." Yes, we recognize that your metrics are all critical, but this Critical Number designation is specific to one metric each year. "The Priority" chapter will walk you through this Critical Number decision for the year and for the next 90 days (columns 4 and 5) and explain how to set Critical Number targets: Super Green, Green, and Red. Think of them as giving your team the chance to earn a gold, silver, or bronze medal this coming year.

In general, you'll pick a Critical Number that will address either an opportunity or a challenge on the **People/Balance Sheet** side of the business (e.g., reduce employee turnover, improve customer service scores, or dramatically reduce a credit line with the bank) or the **Process/Profit & Loss** side (e.g., improve gross margins, reduce production cycle time, or increase sales close ratios). And depending on which side you choose, you will want to pick a counterbalancing number from the other side to monitor (e.g., you want to improve relationships but don't want to give away the store, or you want to improve processes but not damage relationships along the way).

Last, move to the middle of the column and ask, "What are a handful of Key Initiatives we must complete this year to achieve our financial outcomes and hit our Critical Number?" Think of these initiatives as your corporate New Year's resolutions (Less is more) and plan to revise them each time you close the books on your fiscal year — or as the marketplace demands — while keeping an eye on the longer-term goals.

These are NOT a random set of priorities. Choose them to achieve the Critical Number. Again, jump to "The Priority" chapter for more details.

*"Less is more."*

## OPSP Column 5: Actions

Column 5 mirrors column 4, only it details *How* you're going to contribute this quarter to accomplishing the one-year goals, driven by the Critical Number and Rocks for the next 90 days. Given this short time frame, management should have sufficient clarity and foresight to set financial outcomes precisely (at the top of the column) and a Critical Number (at the bottom of the column) that the company can achieve.

 **KEY:** *The quarterly Critical Number represents a key step in achieving the annual Critical Number. For instance, Verne's brother-in-law worked for a company that set a specific cash target for the year. He then chose a Critical Number in process improvement for the quarter. The goal was to reduce the dollars spent on parts to repair machines, therefore saving significant money for his division and contributing to the cash goal.*

Last, choose a handful of Rocks* — priorities that must be accomplished to achieve the quarterly financial outcomes and Critical Number. Again, less is more. Finally, place the initials of the person accountable for each Rock in the small corresponding "Who" box.

Think of these Rocks as a series of three to five simultaneous 13-week sprints that provide focus and direction to the rest of the organization.

***Rocks:** This term honors the late Stephen R. Covey, author of *The 7 Habits of Highly Effective People: Powerful Lessons in Personal Change*. He would demonstrate how, if you have a limited amount of time (a bucket) and put in a bunch of pebbles first (email, distractions, etc.), there's not much room for the big important stuff (Rocks). But if you reverse the process — take care of the big things first — then there's room for all of it. To see an excellent demonstration of Covey's rock analogy, go to YouTube and search "Big Rocks in First" and watch the six-minute video with your team.

## OPSP Column 6: Theme, Scoreboard Design, and Celebration/Reward

We will cover details for the Theme column, including some theme examples, in "The Priority" chapter. To give you a quick overview, the idea is to build a fun and memorable theme around the Critical Number from the Quarterly column. Specifically, starting at the top of the Theme column 6:

1. **Deadline:** Normally the end of the current quarter.

2. **Measurable Target:** The quarterly Critical Number from the bottom of column 5.

3. **Theme Name:** Brainstorm a fun and relevant title for the Quarterly Theme. Current movie or song titles work well (*Fast & Furious* is always popular). Or try a play on a common phrase, like The City Bin Co.'s "Life Begins at 40" (the goal: generate 40,000 euros more in monthly earnings).

4. **Scoreboard Design:** It can be a hand-drawn chart on the wall or a whiteboard, or a more elaborately printed or electronic version. You ultimately want something visible so everyone can see the score, which is updated daily or weekly.

5. **Celebration:** The Quarterly Theme gives you a reason to host an event to either celebrate the accomplishment of a big goal or commiserate. It can be as simple as a barbecue in the parking lot, or it can be a significant trip. It is even more fun if you pick a celebration destination that aligns with the theme (e.g., a "Fast & Furious" theme culminates in a go-carting experience).

6. **Reward:** This might be prizes that align with the theme, or it can include a monetary incentive.

The key is giving your team finish lines and an opportunity to have some fun together.

## OPSP Column 7: Your Accountability

Once the vision has been set, sit down with each individual or team in the company to establish what they can do over the next quarter to help the organization succeed. This creates "line of sight," through which everyone is able to see how his or her daily actions link to the company's goals. In some cases, doing a great job so that others are free to focus on a special initiative might be sufficient. Specifically, look at:

1. **Your KPIs:** Every employee or team should have an ongoing KPI or two that enables them to quantifiably answer the question, "Did we have a productive day or week?"

2. **Your Quarterly Priorities:** In addition to an individual's ongoing work, what are a few priorities for the quarter that will raise his/her performance or drive a special project that aligns with the employee's Critical Number and the #1 Priority of the company?

3. **Critical Number:** What is the single most important quantifiable quarterly achievement for that person or team that will help the company achieve its vision?

## Scaling Up

One of the keys to keeping people engaged is making a connection between their day-to-day efforts and the goals and vision of the company. If everyone can accomplish one thing in addition to his or her daily job, that's a dozen improvements every quarter, or hundreds, depending on the number of employees.

## People and Process (Reputation and Productivity)

To realize a vision, you need people doing stuff! Otherwise, the vision is just words on a piece of paper. These two main components — People and Process — are listed just above the main body of the OPSP.

On the left side, we have listed the three main groups of People involved in any business: employees, customers, and shareholders. The goal is to continually improve the company's Reputation with all three as you balance the potentially competing demands between each group.

On the right side, we have listed the three main Processes that drive any business: Make/Buy, Sell, and Recordkeeping. The goal is to continually improve the company's Productivity in all three as you balance the potentially opposing demands between each process.

The big challenge is balancing the competing demands among all six, like juggling spinning plates. You want to keep all the people happy (Reputation), but you can't give away the store (Productivity). You want to continually improve your Processes to drive better results, but you don't want to greatly upset any of the groups of People as you do so. Maintaining this balance between the demands of the People and Process sides of the business, as you scale up your Reputation and Productivity, requires frequent feedback and metrics to keep you from dropping any plates.

To complete the top portion of the OPSP, choose one or two KPIs you can track weekly to monitor the company's Reputation with all the stakeholders and the Productivity of the three main processes.

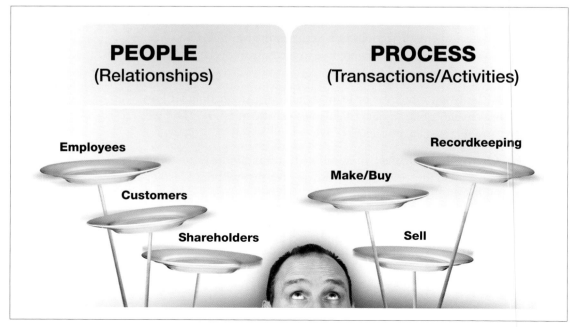

Here are some suggestions:

**Employees:** Happiness and engagement scores (TINYpulse and 15Five have simple systems for tracking these)

**Customers:** Kept Promise Indicators and Net Promoter System scores

**Shareholders:** Cash and company valuation

**Make/Buy:** Speed of processes (Lean), costs, and quality measurements

**Sell:** Close ratios, sales cycle, and revenue metrics

**Recordkeeping:** Relevance, speed, and accuracy of data

## A Better Balance

The Balanced Scorecard™, popularized by Robert S. Kaplan and David P. Norton in their book by the same name, has been an industry-standard performance management tool for more than two decades. We align with Kaplan and Norton on the People side of the equation, emphasizing the need to balance the demands of employees, customers, and shareholders equally. Where we diverge is on the Process side. Kaplan and Norton lump all the processes into a single fourth category, whereas we break it into its three components: make/buy, sell, and recordkeeping. We believe this adds balance to the People side of the business. In the end, they balance four components, while we balance six.

Many nonaccountants struggle with understanding the basic functions and structures of a balance sheet and an income (profit & loss) statement. Considering the People and Process sides of the business from an accounting perspective often gives them a better grasp.

Let's look at the People side of the business. Track how the cash flows through the business with this equation:

**Customers:**          Cash from anyone who pays you

minus (-)

**Employees:**          Cash to anyone you pay ("employ"),
such as traditional employees, contractors, suppliers, partners, etc.

equals (=)

**Shareholders:**       What is left to pay back investors, banks, sweat equity, etc.

The balance sheet simply documents who owes you, whom you owe, and what is left over. It also notes how much cash you have. The goal is to generate sufficient cash to fuel growth as the company faces the First Law of Business Dynamics: Growth sucks cash!

*"The First Law of Business Dynamics: Growth sucks cash!"*

Now let's look at the Process side of the business. Track how the business generates profit through these factors:

**Make/Buy:** The processes that generate expenses

**Sell:** The processes that generate revenue

**Recordkeeping:** The processes for tracking all of these transactions

The profit & loss (P&L) statement simply documents the revenue and expenses and determines if there is a profit. The goal is to abide by the Second Law of Business Dynamics: Buy low, sell high!

*"The Second Law of Business Dynamics: Buy low, sell high!"*

What's sad is that companies unknowingly violate this fundamental every day. In "The Cash" chapter, we'll discuss why the #2 weakness of growing companies is the lack of sufficient financial data. You need data detailing the profitability of every customer, product, service, salesperson, location, etc., so you can see where the business is making a profit and where it is not.

In the end, the financial goals of the company are to collect cash from customers fast enough to pay everyone it needs to employ and to reward the shareholders — and to sell things for more than they cost in order to generate a sufficient profit. Leaders must manage this balance between generating Cash and Profit, which mirrors the equilibrium between keeping the People happy and the Processes productive.

## Preparing for a Strategic Planning Session

To complete the OPSP, JSJ Corporation finds that surveys are valuable tools. When it comes time to do a SWOT analysis, JSJ goes straight to its customers for feedback that influences its planning decisions. And to make the right calls about talent development, the company surveys its employees for insight.

CEO Jacobson believes that giving his team a chance to step back from the business and get reinspired has been vital to its planning process. JSJ typically sends its leadership team and members of its business team to our spring and fall ScaleUp Summits. JSJ's senior team arrives a day and a half early to do a deep dive into the OPSP and make updates. "It forces a discipline of getting away and taking the time to think deeply," says Jacobson.

To mirror JSJ's routine, there are four main activities in preparing for a strategic planning session (quarterly or annual):

1. Leaders at all levels gather feedback from employees and customers.
2. Team leaders complete a SWOT analysis and submit a Top 3 Priority list.
3. Senior leadership completes a SWT analysis and submits a Top 3 Priority list.
4. Everyone aims to keep learning and growing as a team.

Nothing can emerge from the collective brain of the team that doesn't enter it first. JSJ sparks its team's thinking through the reading and executive education delivered in Scaling Up's book club and participation in our Scaling Up Summits. It also taps into the many decades of experience that company employees have accumulated.

## Employee and Customer Feedback

The first preparatory activity is to send out a short Start/Stop/Keep survey to all the employees:

1. What do you think [company name] should **start** doing?
2. What do you think [company name] should **stop** doing?
3. What do you think [company name] should **keep** doing?

These are broad enough to solicit responses ranging from "We need a new microwave in the break room" to "We need to start looking at robotics technology."

Ask the same three questions of your customers. It could be a random sample if you have thousands of retail customers; or it might be more appropriate to have account managers query business-to-business customers face-to-face or over the phone. Use your best judgment, but be sure to incorporate customer feedback into the process.

The weekly routine of collecting and reviewing ongoing feedback from customers and employees will also feed into the decisions made during the planning process. We will outline more details of these ongoing routines in "The Data" chapter.

## SWT and SWOT

We've observed for decades how market-leading firms eventually fall behind start-ups because they are blinded by their current reality. This is what Harvard Business School professor Clayton M. Christensen labeled the "innovator's dilemma" (detailed in his book by the same name).

So why do leaders miss seeing sweeping global trends that are about to broadside them? We put a big part of the blame on the standard SWOT analysis. It's time to update this methodology.

## Inside/Industry Myopia

Almost by definition, the SWOT process drives leaders to look inward at both their company and industry challenges, creating what we term "inside/industry myopia." The traditional SWOT analysis, while helping executives see the forest and the trees, tends to lead them to forget that there's a world outside the forest. The SWOT, with this introspective focus, isn't the right tool to spot the trends in other industries and distant markets that CEOs must factor into their plans.

## Scaling Up

We don't want to throw away the SWOT. It still has its place in the strategic planning process. It's an excellent tool for gathering ideas and input from middle managers, who are more internally focused and closer to the day-to-day operations of an organization.

## SWT Instead

For senior leaders, we propose replacing the SWOT with the SWT: an updated approach that identifies inherent *Strengths* and *Weaknesses* within their firms while exploring broader external *Trends* beyond their own industry or geography.

As we've mentioned several times, the *strategic planning* process comprises two distinct activities: *strategic* thinking and execution *planning*. Strategic thinking is coming up with a few big-picture ideas. Execution planning is figuring out how to make them happen.

The traditional SWOT is a great tool for execution planning — the focus of middle management — resulting in a laundry list of accolades and fixes. However, for the senior team, the SWOT can be a trap. It tends to pull executives down into operational issues, distracting them from the much bigger forces around the globe that can take the company by surprise if it is not prepared.

### It's Time to Build

Marc Andreessen, co-founder and general partner of Silicon Valley's premier venture capital firm Andreessen Horowitz (known as "a16z"), penned a blog at the beginning of the pandemic titled "It's Time to Build." The piece was so well received and timely (we promoted it!) that a16z changed its tagline from "Software is eating the world" to this phrase. And we grabbed ahold of this idea of building to serve as an analogy for the pivots many companies need to continue to make with their business models and markets — build, rebuild, build, rebuild — as they move from plan A to Z.

Taking the building model literally, there are two components critical to success: laying down a rock- solid foundation and getting the roof on as quickly as possible. Then you can take your time completing the rest, knowing it's built to last.

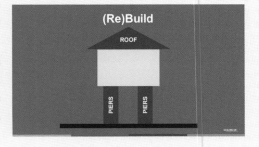

This is the role of the SWT. It starts with a deep understanding of your organization's core **S**trengths (core competencies) and core **W**eaknesses — the foundational piers, anchored in bedrock, upon which the rest of the plan is built.

Next the roof. Actually, you want to get on the roof! You want to see over the forest and the trees of your industry and look to the horizon for tidal waves coming your way. It's important you recognize and get ahead of these market forces or **T**rends, so your firm is prepared to ride them successfully vs. get washed over by them.

Therefore, to anchor strategic thinking, senior leaders need to complete the SWT. It will help them face the brutal facts about the company's inherent strengths and weaknesses, and the global trends threatening to wash over their industry.

Let's look at the components of the SWT.

## Trends

In addition to sizing up the immediate opportunities and threats that the SWOT tends to surface, the senior team needs to rise above all of this. Leaders should look at major trends, such as significant changes in technology, distribution, product innovation, markets, and consumer and social developments around the world that might shake up not only the business but the entire industry.

Forget about the competitor down the street. Is there a company on the other side of the globe that might put you out of business? Is there a new technology coming onto the start-up scene that could lead to an overnight change in the way all companies must do business? How is robotics changing the very nature of work? These are the kinds of questions the strategic thinking team must explore.

Choose four to six trends most likely to shake up your industry and business, and list them on the bottom of the OPSP. Recalling Jim Collins' dual dynamic, mentioned earlier, these trends are meant to anchor the "stimulate progress" right side of the OPSP.

To up your game in seeing trends, we encourage that each senior leader on your team attend one tradeshow a year in an industry that couldn't be more different from your own. If you're in a heavily industrial business, choose a consumer industry show (someone on your team, no matter the industry, should attend the Consumer Electronics Show!). If you're in manufacturing, attend a professional services show. Mix it up and see what ideas you can shamelessly steal from another industry and install in yours.

To further stimulate your thinking, we recommend reading Peter Diamandis's book *Abundance: The Future is Better Than You Think* and attend his annual A360 conferences. In addition, Frost & Sullivan's team of futurists publish annual "Mega Trends" insights for various industries. Acquire the one for your industry and a few others.

## Core Strengths and Weaknesses

Like you, an organization has innate strengths and weaknesses. Coping with them is less about changing who you are and more about leveraging the hand you've been dealt (evolution!). Play to your strengths and avoid your weaknesses.

Core Strengths, often called Core Competencies, are a handful of resources and capabilities that anchor a firm's strategic advantage in the marketplace and emerge over time. In "The Core" chapter we shared BIC corporation's core competencies, which have allowed it to pivot beyond pens into lighters, razors, and other consumer products. We encourage you to read the famous *HBR* article titled "The Core Competence of the Corporation" by Gary Hamel and C.K. Prahalad. You can also Google for a myriad of examples from various firms.

Core Weaknesses, on the other hand, are attributes of an organization that are inherently weak and not easily fixable (and you shouldn't try to fix!). Many are cultural and foundational in nature. 3M, for instance, has a core weakness around selling directly precisely because it's such a "science" culture (its tagline is "Science. Period." — with science being one of its two core strengths). Scientists like to innovate more than "sell," especially to the public.

To offset this lack of a direct sales culture, 3M developed a Core Strength around partnering, measured by the number of annual partner and "supplier of the year" awards the company receives. 3M serves as the science partner to thousands of companies, helping them innovate solutions to tough industry challenges — with over 60,000 solutions to date. These companies, in turn, help distribute these solutions.

Verne helped his children's international school, Ben Franklin International School (BFIS), discern their core strengths and weaknesses as part of a five-year strategic plan he was asked to facilitate. After months of "council" meetings held each week over lunch in the Head of School's office, the group concluded that the school's location in Barcelona was a key strength.

Being one of the most attractive cities in the world to live, especially for expats from Silicon Valley (Barcelona is the San Francisco of Spain, with 300 days of sunshine), BFIS was able to focus its recruiting efforts in the Bay area of the US. This was helpful because it offset a weakness of being in Barcelona. Most international schools pull students from the families of expats working in the overseas offices of Fortune 500 firms or government agencies/embassies. Those are all in Madrid.

In turn, BFIS's physical location was a weakness because there was no adjacent land near the school for expansion. Though the school had contemplated moving many times, during this planning cycle it chose to accept its location as a structural reality and to limit the number of students it could accept. BFIS also partnered with competitive schools nearby to use their sports facilities.

Like trends, the core strengths (core competencies) and weaknesses need to be identified as part of building a successful long-term plan and anchoring the base (along the bottom) of the OPSP. Given the relative long-term permanence of core strengths, they anchor the "preserve the core" side of the OPSP, on the left.

## Mining All Levels

In summary, to feed the strategic planning process properly, the key is using different techniques to mine ideas from all levels of the organization. With frontline employees and customers, ask the Start/Stop/Keep questions. With middle management, require a standard SWOT and inquire about their top three priorities for the quarter or year.

And demand that the senior team go deeper and broader using the SWT. Knowing what trends are going to shake up your industry — and having a plan for dealing with them — will help you stay ahead of the competition, and sniff out new rivals who want to take over your turf while you can still do something about it. At Amazon, one of the questions founder Jeff Bezos asks his team each week is what competitors have entered their market in the last seven days!

The next chapter will provide more detail in how to prepare and lead a strategic planning session.

# 8

# THE PLANNING PROCESS
## Preparing and Leading

---

**EXECUTIVE SUMMARY:** *The key to success in most endeavors requires the right preparation, execution, and follow-through. In this chapter, we share a dozen key steps to prepare the team for a quarterly or annual planning session; suggested agendas; and recommended follow-through after the offsite meetings. And at the back of this chapter is a sample completed One-Page Strategic Plan.*

---

## Preparation:

1. **Set Dates:** It's advisable to set the dates for the quarterly and annual planning retreats (some people call them "advances") well in advance. And it's best if a specific rhythm is established (i.e., the second Friday and Saturday before the end of the quarter). The annual planning session is normally two to three days and the quarterly sessions one to two days. Specific agendas are detailed below.

2. **Scan *Scaling Up*:** Have the executive team scan *Scaling Up (Rockefeller Habits 2.0)*, especially the first two chapters in the Strategy section and The Priority chapter in the Execution section. The book is available on Amazon.com or you can save some money and order in bulk (box of 20 copies) at *www.scalingup.com*.

3. **Complete Scaling Up Assessment (optional):** Have the executive team take 15 minutes to complete the complimentary Scaling Up Assessment to see which of the Four Decisions — People, Strategy, Execution, or Cash — needs the most attention in the upcoming planning session. Visit *www.scalingup.com*.

4. **Read Collins' Articles:** Read (and re-read) Jim Collins' *Harvard Business Review* article titled "Building Your Company's Vision" (download for a fee at *www.hbr.com*). Do this in the first few annual planning sessions until you're comfortable with your Core Values, Purpose, Profit/X, and BHAG — key elements of the first two columns of the One-Page Strategic Plan (OPSP). Also go to *www.jimcollins.com* where Collins has several free interactive tutorials to help discover Core Values, discern a Purpose, choose a BHAG, etc.

5. **Strategic Thinking "Council":** Form the council as discussed in *Scaling Up* and start meeting weekly to get some critical talk time around the strategic decisions driven by the Strengths, Weaknesses, Trends (SWT) and 7 Strata worksheets. Also discuss the 4Ps of marketing: Product, Price, Place, and Promotion. In most firms, marketing strategy = strategy. Search the internet for Ogilvy's 4Es of marketing and add those to the ongoing discussions/debates. Even if it's just for a few weeks prior to the planning session, these weekly discussions will get the strategy juices flowing.

6. **Employee Survey:** A few weeks prior to the planning offsite, conduct an employee survey. Employees' insights are helpful in determining quarterly or annual priorities since they are closer to the customers and are immersed in the daily processes of the business. Many firms use an online survey tool such as SurveyMonkey to make it easier to administer. We suggest three simple questions:

    a. What should (enter company name) **start** doing?

    b. What should (enter company name) **stop** doing?

    c. What should (enter company name) **keep** doing?

7. **Customer Input:** Along with employee feedback, formally gather customer input. At a minimum, ask them the same three "start, stop, and keep" questions. As discussed in The Data chapter, it's easier to pick up patterns and trends if there is a weekly rhythm of gathering input from customers and employees, but this simple three-question survey will get you started if you are new to the process.

8. **Top Three Constraints:** Send out an email to those attending the planning session to ask them to send back the top three constraints they feel MUST be addressed/explored/answered at the upcoming planning session for them to feel it was a success." Compile these for review at the beginning of the planning session or just prior.

9. **(Optional) Strengths, Weaknesses, Opportunities, and Threats (SWOT):** If you want to dig deeper than what the "top three constraints" question uncovers, lead a separate SWOT exercise with the broader leadership team prior to the planning session. Or simply send out an email to your team seeking their input on the SWOT and compile the results for the planning session.

10. **(Advanced) SWT**: As part of the activities leading up to the planning session, have the senior team complete the SWT worksheet as outlined in earlier. Helpful resources in identifying important trends are *Frost & Sullivan's annual trends report* and Peter Diamandis's Abundance 360 annual event and quarterly updates.

11. **(Optional) One-Page Personal Plan (OPPP):** Encourage all team members to update their OPPPs. It's best if one's personal and professional goals are aligned.

12. **Get Someone to Facilitate:** Find someone outside the company to facilitate your planning sessions. Ask a colleague from another firm or bring in a professional facilitator like those we have at Scaling Up. This allows everyone on the team, including the CEO, to actively participate rather than worry about facilitation. And trained facilitators will know how to discern Core Values, define a powerful Purpose, discover a key strategy, and help the team uncover the underlying constraints in establishing priorities and setting key performance indicators (KPIs).

## OPSP Form Preparation:

1. **Replace Logo:** Feel free to take all references to Scaling Up off the OPSP document, except the copyright, and replace them with your own logo and company information. There are versions of all the Growth Tools, in 25 languages, you can download at *www.scalingup.com*.

2. **Replace Headings:** Call them Core Values, Core Purpose, Brand Promise, Rocks, etc. —OR NOT!!! Feel free to come up with your own unique language within the firm. HP calls its Core Values The HP Way. Some firms prefer the term principles or guidelines instead of Core Values. Similarly, some firms find the term Rocks as a label for quarterly priorities to be awkward. Again, it's up to you. The document is meant to serve as a guideline.

3. **Use Blank Documents:** There's a tendency to provide team members with completed or semi-completed one-page plans during planning sessions (i.e., with Core Values, Purpose, etc. already filled in). We highly suggest you pass out blank OPSPs at the beginning of the session and have everyone fill them in by hand. There's something about re-writing the Core Values, Purpose, BHAG, etc. each quarter that helps hardwire them into the brain and better connects each person to what is said and decided. Besides, there's not that much to write!

4. **Project up on a Screen:** To facilitate the process, project the OPSP on a large screen. Designate someone to fill it in electronically so it can be immediately emailed to all of the participants after the planning session. Doing this also helps people stay focused and makes it easier for everyone who is filling in documents by hand simultaneously.

5. **Software Offering (optional):** Manage your Scaling Up implementation in our official software, Scaling Up Scoreboard. Get flexibility, visibility, and accountability not just during your planning session, but also throughout the year. The software allows you to track progress on company and individual priorities to ensure that you are on track to hit your targets. At the end of each period, update your strategic tools to match your growth trajectory and use historical data to guide you in setting goals in your next planning session. In preparation for your planning session, set up your account — go to *scalingup.com/software* and request a demo to get started. Once you have your account set up, use the One Page Strategic Plan WIZARD to load your plan contents as the team makes decisions. This will give you the ability to display the OPSP on the screen during planning and make real-time adjustments as you go, with everything safely stored and accessible to the whole team. We suggest you start with your leadership team to create and track KPIs and Priorities. Then cascade priorities down through the organization as you expand the implementation of the Scaling Up. (Scaling Up Scoreboard can manage the entire process for you.) Need help? Your dedicated account manager will assist you in getting started. Email *scoreboard@scalingup.com.*

## AGENDA (OVERVIEW):

Quarterly vs. Annual (timing and agendas): The annual planning session is typically two to three days; the quarterly (or trimester) planning sessions are one to two days. Executive Team Dinner: We recommend the senior team have dinner together and then meet afterwards for a couple hours the night before the start of the planning session. Dinner allows time for catching up, and the two-hour session following dinner gives the team a chance to focus on reviewing the SWT and share stories from the last quarter where the company "lived" its Core Values and Purpose. It's also a good time to do some blue sky thinking about the company with questions like "If our team were to launch a new business, what would we do instead of this business?" and "How would we put our own company out of business?" It also gives the team an extra night to sleep on the conversations generated that evening.

# Scaling Up

The first third of each planning session (day one of the annual planning session; three hours of a quarterly session) is spent reviewing the SWOT (optional), and the first three columns of the OPSP. Also update the Functional Accountability Chart (FACe) tool and focus on the one functional position that needs support.

The next third (day two of the annual planning session; afternoon of the quarterly session) is spent on the 1 year column of the OPSP, including a review of the company's financials and using the CASh and Power of One worksheets to focus on ways to improve cash flow.

> *"How would we put our own company out of business?"*

The final third (day three of the annual session; day two of the quarterly) is focused on completing the entire right hand page of the OPSP. Review the Process Accountability Chart (PACe) tool and choose one process to design or redesign that supports achieving the Critical Number (#1 Priority). Last, review the Rockefeller Habits Checklist and choose one or two of the 10 habits to execute (or execute better) the next quarter.

 **WARNING:** *"When I go slow, I go fast" notes the Chinese proverb. There is a tendency in planning sessions to rush through or ignore the Strengths, Weaknesses, and Trends along the bottom of the OPSP and the first two or three columns of the OPSP (Core Values, Purpose, BHAG, Sandbox, and Brand Promises), especially after team members feel like they've nailed down the decisions in previous sessions. However, spending sufficient time reviewing and updating the SWT and first three columns almost always makes the decisions in the Annual and Quarterly columns come more quickly and effortlessly. Trust us on this!*

> *"When I go slow, I go fast"*

## Sample Quarterly Agenda:

### Day 1:

*17:30 - 18:00* — Reception/arrival

*18:00 - 20:00* — Dinner (Snacks in Europe)

*20:00 - 22:00* — Opening Session — Review core values and purpose stories, SWT, and host open discussion about the future (continue into the night!).

*22:00 - ?* — Dinner in Europe

### Day 2:

*8:30 - 10:00* — Opening Remarks by CEO, Good News Stories/OPPPs, and Top 3 Issues (what will make this a successful meeting for everyone)

*10:30 - 12:00* — SWOT, FACe, and review first three columns of OPSP

*13:30 - 15:00* — Review Annual column of OPSP

*15:30 - 17:00* — CASh and Power of One

*18:00 - ?* — Dinner, finish up what didn't get completed earlier (further work on 7 Strata)

**Day 3:** (invite team leaders)

> *8:30 - 10:00* — Review previous day, and complete Quarterly column OPSP
>
> *10:30 - Noon* — PACe (review key process supporting Quarterly Critical Number),
>
> *13:30 - 15:00* — Establish column 6 Quarterly Theme (leave for middle management to design/drive) and review Rockefeller Habits Checklist. Choose one or two areas for improvement.
>
> *15:30 - 17:00* — Everyone updates their own column 7 — individual KPIs, Critical Number, and Priorities. Then go around the room and have everyone share their Critical Number (top 1 priority for the quarter).

## AGENDA (DETAILS):

**Opening Remarks by CEO:** Reflect on the past quarter/year and then set the stage for the major conflict that will be resolved this planning session.

**Details:** Great meetings are structured like great movies according to Pat Lencioni in his book *Death by Meeting*. At the heart of all movies is a "conflict, then resolution" structure. Rather than open with something like "I'm glad all of you can be here to participate in this planning session (yawn)," instead set the stage with an opening line like "We face stiff competition from XYZ, the marketplace for our services is heating back-up, and we're being hindered by our … so this next two days are critical in figuring how we address these challenges and maximize our opportunities…" Or opt for something like "we've been offered the greatest opportunity to gain market share in five years. It is for us to figure out how to make it happen…" or "This is the year we must make the kinds of profits we expect from a great company." Pick up your hints from the preparation work you've done — the employee survey, the customer feedback, top three issues lists, and the SWT/SWOT analysis.

**Good News Stories and OPPP:** Share a round of good news stories. Sometimes this precedes the opening remarks by the CEO or occurs the night before if you host the optional evening session. It is your decision. (Optional) Go around a second time and share a couple highlights from each executive's OPPP — a key relationship, achievement, and ritual for the coming quarter or year.

> **Details:** Following the opening remarks, you want to set a positive tone, loosen everyone up, and help the team connect as people by taking 10 to 20 minutes to have everyone share good news personally and professionally from the previous week and a reflection on the previous quarter or year. Keeping it current helps make it relevant and fresh. The professional good news allows the team to count its blessings and the personal good news always brings a laugh or two — a powerful way to de-stress, slow the brain down to the alpha state (7 to 14 brainwave cycles per second), and help keep even the most dreaded issues in perspective. Also use it as an early gauge if someone is particularly stressed or disturbed coming into the meeting.
>
> **(Optional)** Go around a second time — and make it a separate round, not one combined with the good news round. Share a few key decisions from each executive's OPPP for the coming quarter or year. This awareness will prove helpful in setting the company goals and strengthen bonds

between the team members. Maintaining a healthy team dynamic (and handling conflict) starts with being vulnerable with each other according to Pat Lencioni's book *Five Dysfunctions of a Team*.

**New Team Members:** Pat Lencioni suggests all teams complete a personality test (Myers Briggs or equivalent) and review the results. This helps them understand and appreciate each other's differences (and generates a laugh of two). He also suggests reviewing each other's lifeline: the five high points and five low points in their life that have shaped who they are. This is something members of Young Presidents' Organization and Entrepreneurs' Organization do to form a healthy forum. *Here's a link to learn more* about drawing lifelines, a powerful exercise for bonding teams when you share your lifeline with each other.

 **NOTE:** *When a new executive is added to the team, the lifeline exercise should be repeated. Adding someone to a team makes it a new team. It's not the old team plus one.*

**Start Filling in One-Page Tools:** The rest of the planning session is using the Growth Tools to drive the right questions and discussions. Go back to *Scaling Up (Rockefeller Habits 2.0)* Strategy section for specific instructions in completing the OPSP. Be sure to also review the other onepage tools according to the suggested agenda overview above.

 **WARNING:** *It's your call, but we would resist jumping in and reviewing the past quarter or year (columns 4 and 5 of the OPSP) in detail at the beginning of the meeting (beyond the brief opening remarks of the CEO as outlined above). Once you open that Pandora's Box, it's hard to get it shut. Teams tend to get sucked right into the minutia, getting caught up in the details and making it difficult to step back from the trees and talk more strategic about the direction of the firm (could we have incorporated more clichés in one sentence!!). We suggest you start more broadly reviewing the SWT and the first three columns of the OPSP — after all, it's a strategic planning session, not a weekly executive team meeting or monthly review session. And if those weekly and monthly meetings have been effective, the quarter has been covered and everyone should be well briefed on the current state of the company.*

## Quarterly/Annual Employee (Town Hall) Meeting

Gather all the employees (or travel around to various offices) and share the results from the last quarter and the theme/priority for the next quarter. This meeting is usually 30–45 minutes long.

The first half of the meeting is a review/celebration of the previous quarter. The key is to get the employees talking and sharing victory stories from the previous quarter. The CEO starts this dialogue by saying something like "Welcome to the quarterly meeting. We said we were going to do X, and we achieved Y — congratulations." Now, rather than drone on about how everyone pulled together and worked hard (as if the CEO has a clue), the CEO should ask the most powerful question you can ask anyone (team or child) after they've accomplished something — "how did you do it?"

The leader can seed the conversation by saying something like "Lisa, you were telling me how your team pulled an all-nighter to win that Acme deal. Please share that with everyone." Obviously, choose someone who you know likes to talk/share. This will then get the conversation started. Lisa will likely say, "yes, we pulled the all-nighter, but we couldn't have done it without Sam's team…" and now Sam is invited to share. The key is for people to relive what it took to accomplish the goals.

In turn, if you failed to reach the goal (discussed in *Scaling Up*) and the team's trust levels are good, it's worthwhile discussing as well.

After this past quarter review, it's time to introduce the theme for the next quarter. Turn down the lights, fire up the music, and make a grand transition. Doug Greenlaw at VTC came running in wearing a red jumpsuit to the music from the movie "6 Million Dollar Man" (add $6 million to the sales pipeline in the next quarter). Appletree Answers typically opened with a video — this one introducing their *Idea Flash initiative* mentioned in *Scaling Up*.Let each executive explain how their function will support the Theme/Critical Number and the "rocks" which will need to be moved to achieve the goal and quarterly outcomes (Revenues, GM, Profit, etc.). Also discuss the one process that will be designed or redesigned to support achieving the Critical Number (Appletree built an app inside Salesforce.com to support Idea Flash). Then handout a copy of the Vision Summary to all employees and give everyone a few minutes, in the meeting, to begin filling in their individual goals at the bottom of the Vision Summary. Everyone's immediate supervisor can follow-up after the meeting with their teams to coach them if they need help determining appropriate KPIs and priorities that align with the company's vision.

## Daily/Weekly Updates:

After the quarterly meeting, put your plan in action. Use the Rockefeller Habits to create relentless repeatability and track the daily/weekly progress on Company Priorities and Critical Numbers. Many CEOs, like Larry Page did of Google's parent company Alphabet, keeps employees updated weekly on progress either through email or an all-employee meeting. Page called them TGIF meetings (used to be on Fridays, now on Thursdays). Our Scaling Up Scoreboard software takes that one step further. Using the software makes it easy for everyone to track progress on all devices, desktop, mobile, or large flat screens scattered throughout the office. No need to email; instead, everyone spends a couple of minutes a day updating progress and their huddles, and you stay on track all year. Here's a critical number and a priority tracking screenshot from Scaling Up Scoreboard:

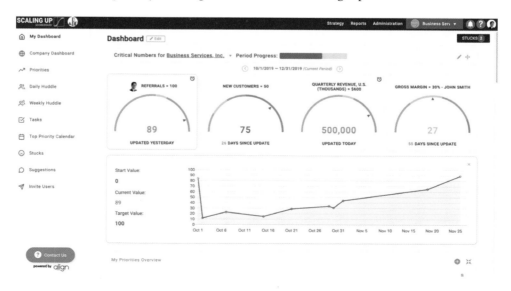

## Scaling Up

We hope you find this helpful. If we can be of assistance or you would like someone to facilitate these meetings, email *verne@scalingup.com* and put "Scaling Up Coach Facilitation" in the subject line.

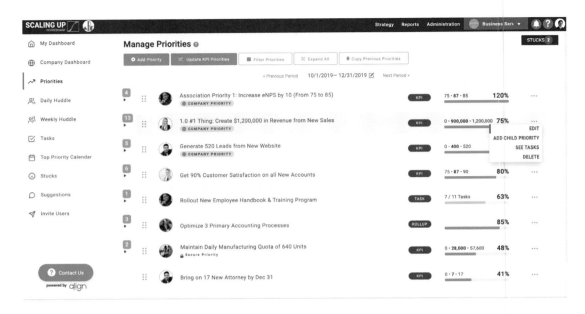

## Sample One-Page Strategic Plan

On the next two pages is a sample One-Page Strategic Plan for a fictitious company called TestCo (we know you're not exactly like them!). BEST OF LUCK with your strategic planning process.

# Strategy: One-Page Strategic Plan (OPSP)

**Organization Name:** Testco

## People (Reputation Drivers)

### Employees
1. Appreciation every 7 days KPI = 100% a
2. Employee Net Promoter Score KPI = 60+
3. Voluntary A-Player Retention - KPI = 95%

### Customers
1. Delivery - KPI = Daily report 10 minutes
2. Client 'contact'- KPI = 3 Contacts per Client
3. NPS - KPI = Net Promoter Score at 8.5

### Shareholders
1. Cash increase daily - KPI = % of increase
2. Revenue Increase - KPI = 20%
3. Gross Margin - KPI = 55%

| COREVALUES/BELIEFS (Should/Shouldn't) | PURPOSE (Why) | TARGETS (3–5 YRS.) (Where) | GOALS (1 YR.) (What) |
|---|---|---|---|
| We live to hear the word "speed" We never say no! We always give options We cultivate trust with clients | EASY! - We make using data easy so that it helps rather than hurts people! | **Future Date** 31 Dec 2023 / **Revenues** $14,250,000 / **Profit** $2,850,000 / **Mkt Cap/Cash** $1,425,000 <br><br> **Sandbox** $500M+ Corporations - US, Canada, Europe | **YR Ending** 31 Dec 2020 / **Revenues** $6,875,000 / **Profit** $1,375,000 / **MKT Cap** / **Gross Margin** $3,781,250 / **Cash** $687,500 / **A/R Days** 32 / **Inv. Days** 15 / **Rev./Emp.** $225,000 |

| Actions *To Live Values, Purposes, BHAG* | Key Thrusts/Capabilities | Key Initiatives |
|---|---|---|
| 1. Post Core Values and Purpose visually in the office | 1. UK - Germany - France launch and profitable | 1. Automate proposal process |
| 2. Post in ALL marketing materials and online | 2. Database developed for automated marketing | 2. Dashboard/KPI metrics updated and reviewed weekly |
| 3. Host one on one - quarterly - CV, CP, BHAG Reviews | 3. Zero human touch in request fullfillment | 3. Hiring/onboarding plan and process in place- filled openings |
| 4. | 4. Named the Best Place to Work Award | 4. Ensure every TestCo team member 'understands' and 'lives' our CP/CV/BHAG |
| 5. | 5. | 5. |

| Profit per X | Brand Promise KPI's | Critical #: People or B/S |
|---|---|---|
| Profit Per Installation 2014- $125,000 2015- $155,000 2016 - $200,000 | 10 days or less - installation NPS scoring 60+ 7 business days to measurable results | ◼ 6 PhD Hires ☐ 5 PhD Hires *Between green & red* ◼ 3 PhD Hires |

| BHAG® | Brand Promises | Critical #: Process or P/L |
|---|---|---|
| 'GLOBAL #1' ~ The #1 Global Data Analytics Solution. 1,000 installations within the Fortune 2,500 - globally! | Speed of installation Easy to do business with Results in a week | ◼ 60% Gross Margin ☐ 55% Gross Margin *Between green & red* ◼ 50% Gross Margin |

### Strengths/Core Competencies
1. Deep analytic capabilities
2. Culture inducive to PhDs
3. Live for Speed

### Weaknesses:
1. Arrogance -- we're good and we know it
2. Sales Capabilities -- lacking, so better be the best
3.

*BHAG is a Registered Trademark of Jim Collins and Jerry Porras.*

# Process (Productivity Drivers)

## Make/Buy
1. Pipeline Full - KPI = 60 qualified leads
2. Active Proposals - KPI = 14 active
3. Close Ratio - KPI = 75%+

## Sell
1. Time on Project - KPI = 90% of Budget m
2. Help Tickets - KPI = 95% SLA's met
3. Utilization Rate - KPI = 85%

## Recordkeeping
1. Invoice within 24 hours
2. Cash Conversion Cycle minus 18 days
3. Timely reports -- daily, weekly

| ACTIONS (QTR) (How) | | THEME (QTR/ANNUAL) | YOUR ACCOUNTABILITY (Who/When) | |
|---|---|---|---|---|

### ACTIONS (QTR) (How)

| Qtr # 1 | ending 31 March 2020 |
|---|---|
| Revenues | $2,185,000 |
| Profit | $37,000 |
| Mkt Cap | |
| Gross Margin | $1,201,750 |
| Cash | $145,000 |
| A/R Days | 35 |
| Inv. Days | 18 |
| Rev./Emp | $225,000 |

### THEME (QTR/ANNUAL)

| Deadline: | 3/31/2020 |
|---|---|
| Measurable Target/Critical # | |

1,200 face to face meetings with decision makers, clients and partners

#### Theme Name
Race to 1,200

#### Scoreboard Design
*Describe and/or sketch your design in this space*

### YOUR ACCOUNTABILITY (Who/When)

| Your KPIs | | Goal |
|---|---|---|
| 1 | Proposals Closed | 50 |
| 2 | Prospects Contacted | 250 |
| 3 | Face to Face Meetings | 125 |

#### Rocks

| | | Who |
|---|---|---|
| 1 | Training Program - created - implemented - every team member | Lisa |
| 2 | Complete Business Plan | John |
| 3 | Increase Google Presence | Jane |
| 4 | Reduce A/R Time - to 60 days less than 10% | Tom |
| 5 | 1,200 client meetings with whole team | Angel |

#### Your Quarterly Priorities

| | | Due |
|---|---|---|
| 1 | Hire 3 Sales Associates | 3/31/2020 |
| 2 | Increase Google Presence | 3/31/2020 |
| 3 | 1200 Client Meetings with Whole Team | 3/31/2020 |
| 4 | Get 10 Stories from Clients on Core Values | 3/31/2020 |
| 5 | | |

### Critical #: People or B/S
- ■ 22 Service Contracts
- ☐ 20 Service Contracts
- *Between green & red*
- ■ 18 Service Contracts

### Celebration
A BIG dinner where we will bring our families - loved ones - together to celebrate the accomplishment

### Critical #: People or B/S
- ■ 1500 Client Meetings
- ☐ 1200 Client Meetings
- *Between green & red*
- ■ 900 Client Meetings

### Critical #: Process or P/L
- ■ 89% Utilization Rate
- ☐ 85% Utilization Rate
- *Between green & red*
- ■ 75% Utilization Rate

### Reward
$12,000 donated to the groups top 12 favorite charities - $1,000 per charity! $10 for every contact made!

### Critical #: Process or P/L
- ■ 150 Referrals
- ☐ 100 Referrals
- *Between green & red*
- ■ 75 Referrals

### Trends
1. Artificial intelligence and how it will evolve
2. The speed at which technology is evolving
3. Generational views on the use of our solutions
4. Communication mediums shifting -- social
5. Information flows (speed and type) changes
6. The value being placed of data as a tool

*BHAG is a Registered Trademark of Jim Collins and Jerry Porras.*

# SCALING UP
# EXECUTION

# THE EXECUTION INTRODUCTION

**KEY QUESTION:** *Are all processes running without drama and driving industry-leading profitability?*

In the largest investment in an e-commerce company in Canadian history, Coastal.com, a Vancouver-based eyewear company, was purchased by Essilor International, one of the world's largest lens manufacturers, for CAD$430 million. Roger Hardy, Coastal.com's founder and CEO, credits the disciplined execution of the Rockefeller Habits with these stellar results.

Case in point: Some German industrialists sat in on Coastal.com's daily executive team huddle while the company's leaders stood up and reported on their Critical Numbers. The executives discussed quickly their key opportunities, issues, highlights, problems, and threats. "They were blown away with our operational efficiencies and knowledge of the business," Hardy noted.

Hardy's team also introduced the Net Promoter System (NPS) to measure how likely customers were to recommend the business to others and to single out a few (from over 2 million) who indicated they were not raving fans, so the senior team could call them. These weekly conversations with customers, debriefed at the weekly huddle, gave Hardy and his leadership team the kind of gut feel for the market that drives ongoing improvements. One change, which we'll share in "The Data" chapter, caused revenue to jump 60% in one market. Coastal.com also tapped into the innovative ideas of its employees in its own *Shark Tank* type of competition. Implementing those ideas generated another 15% lift for Coastal.com's revenue.

Coastal.com excelled at execution precisely because it listened to customers and employees; had a meeting rhythm to discuss and implement quickly what's being learned; and relied on a process for setting priorities based on all this input. This excellence in execution wowed customers, engaged employees, and delivered stunning financial results for the shareholders. It also resulted in an outstanding exit for Hardy himself.

At the end of this Introduction is the Rockefeller Habits Checklist™. Take a few minutes to go through it. Don't worry if you don't have many items checked. Neither did Hardy's executives when they attended their first Rockefeller Habits workshop. "It gave me a blueprint on how to run a team in a successful way and is a key part of why we have achieved $200 million in sales while keeping everyone aligned and heading in the same direction," says Hardy.

Hardy advises CEOs to review the Checklist every three months. "You're not going to get it perfect every quarter," he says. "It's a work in progress. It forces you, though, to be objective and to realize there are blind spots. Like a pilot taking off, you don't want to forget to lift the landing gear. It may be the things you take for granted that can hurt you the most. A Checklist is a good way of reminding you what's missing."

Jim Collins and Morten T. Hansen, in their book *Great by Choice: Uncertainty, Chaos, and Luck — Why Some Thrive Despite Them All,* note: "Greatness is not a function of circumstance. Greatness, it turns out, is largely a matter of conscious choice, and discipline." We couldn't agree more, and hope you'll consciously choose to implement the 10 Rockefeller Habits detailed in this section.

# Section Overview

This section is structured around the 10 Rockefeller Habits, divided into three disciplines (routines) fundamental to execution:

1. **Priorities:** Less is more in driving focus and alignment.

2. **Data:** Qualitative and quantitative feedback provides clarity and foresight.

3. **Meeting Rhythm:** Give yourself the time to make better/faster decisions.

**The first chapter, The Priority,** highlights Rockefeller Habits #1 and #2, emphasizing the importance of having a "healthy team" that is able to face the brutal facts and support the kind of constructive debate necessary to set a main priority that everyone can support. This chapter also reviews important routines centered around Rockefeller Habits #4, #7, and #8 that were covered in earlier chapters.

**The second chapter, The Data,** highlights Rockefeller Habits #5, #6, #9, and #10, and the importance of gathering both quantitative and qualitative data to properly fuel decision-making. It's particularly critical for the senior leadership team and team leads to engage in weekly conversations with customers and employees (and to shop competitors).

**The third chapter, The Meeting Rhythm,** highlights Rockefeller Habit #3 — the importance of setting a routine of daily, weekly, monthly, quarterly, and annual meetings to address the communication challenges that exist whenever you get a group of people together. These structured meetings also create the space and time for teams to debate and make the important decisions needed to scale the organization.

Two one-page Execution tools will be covered in this section:

1. **Rockefeller Habits Checklist™:** 10 routines for driving relentless repeatability in your execution

2. **Who, What, When (WWW):** Quick summary of actions and accountabilities — the only "notes" you need to keep from a meeting of an hour or longer

*A special thank-you to Kevin Lawrence for contributing to this "Execution" section and serving as an early collaborator on the book.*

**1. The executive team is healthy and aligned.**
- [ ] Team members understand each other's differences, priorities, and styles.
- [ ] The team meets frequently (weekly is best) for strategic thinking.
- [ ] The team participates in ongoing executive education (monthly recommended).
- [ ] The team is able to engage in constructive debates and all members feel comfortable participating.

**2. Everyone is aligned with the #1 thing that needs to be accomplished this quarter to move the company forward.**
- [ ] The Critical Number is identified to move the company ahead this quarter.
- [ ] 3-5 Priorities (Rocks) that support the Critical Number are identified and ranked for the quarter.
- [ ] A Quarterly Theme and Celebration/Reward are announced to all employees that bring the Critical Number to life.
- [ ] Quarterly Theme/Critical Number posted throughout the company and employees are aware of the progress each week.

**3. Communication rhythm is established and information moves through organization accurately and quickly.**
- [ ] All employees are in a daily huddle that lasts less than 15 minutes.
- [ ] All teams have a weekly meeting.
- [ ] The executive and middle managers meet for a day of learning, resolving big issues, and DNA transfer each month.
- [ ] Quarterly and annually, the executive and middle managers meet offsite to work on the 4 Decisions.

**4. Every facet of the organization has a person assigned with accountability for ensuring goals are met.**
- [ ] The Function Accountability Chart (FACe) is completed (right people, doing the right things, right).
- [ ] Financial statements have a person assigned to each line item.
- [ ] Each of the 4-9 processes on the Process Accountability Chart (PACe) has someone that is accountable for them.
- [ ] Each 3-5 year Key Thrust/Capability has a corresponding expert on the Advisory Board if internal expertise doesn't exist.

**5. Ongoing employee input is collected to identify obstacles and opportunities.**
- [ ] All executives (and middle managers) have a Start/Stop/Keep conversation with at least one employee weekly.
- [ ] The insights from employee conversations are shared at the weekly executive team meeting.
- [ ] Employee input about obstacles and opportunities is being collected weekly.
- [ ] A mid-management team is responsible for the process of closing the loop on all obstacles and opportunities.

**6. Reporting and analysis of customer feedback data is as frequent and accurate as financial data.**
- [ ] All executives (and middle managers) have a 4Q conversation with at least one end user weekly.
- [ ] The insights from customer conversations are shared at the weekly executive team meeting.
- [ ] All employees are involved in collecting customer data.
- [ ] A mid-management team is responsible for the process of closing the loop on all customer feedback.

**7. Core Values and Purpose are "alive" in the organization.**
- [ ] Core Values are discovered, Purpose is articulated, and both are known by all employees.
- [ ] All executives and middle managers refer back to the Core Values and Purpose when giving praise or reprimands.
- [ ] HR processes and activities align with the Core Values and Purpose (hiring, orientation, appraisal, recognition, etc.).
- [ ] Actions are identified and implemented each quarter to strengthen the Core Values and Purpose in the organization.

**8. Employees can articulate the following key components of the company's strategy accurately.**
- [ ] Big Hairy Audacious Goal (BHAG) – Progress is tracked and visible.
- [ ] Core Customer(s) – Their profile in 25 words or less.
- [ ] 3 Brand Promises – And the corresponding Brand Promise KPIs reported on weekly.
- [ ] Elevator Pitch – A compelling response to the question "What does your company do?"

**9. All employees can answer quantitatively whether they had a good day or week (Column 7 of the One-Page Strategic Plan).**
- [ ] 1 or 2 Key Performance Indicators (KPIs) are reported on weekly for each role/person.
- [ ] Each employee has 1 Critical Number that aligns with the company's Critical Number for the quarter (clear line of sight).
- [ ] Each individual/team has 3-5 Quarterly Priorities/Rocks that align with those of the company.
- [ ] All executives and middle managers have a coach (or peer coach) holding them accountable to behavior changes.

**10. The company's plans and performance are visible to everyone.**
- [ ] A "situation room" is established for weekly meetings (physical or virtual).
- [ ] Core Values, Purpose and Priorities are posted throughout the company.
- [ ] Scoreboards are up everywhere displaying current progress on KPIs and Critical Numbers.
- [ ] There is a system in place for tracking and managing the cascading Priorities and KPIs.

Download a full-sized copy of this tool at *scalingup.com*

| Who | What | When |
| --- | --- | --- |
|  |  |  |
|  |  |  |
|  |  |  |
|  |  |  |
|  |  |  |
|  |  |  |
|  |  |  |
|  |  |  |
|  |  |  |
|  |  |  |
|  |  |  |
|  |  |  |
|  |  |  |

# 9

# THE PRIORITY
## Focus, Finish Lines, and Fun

**EXECUTIVE SUMMARY:** *"The main thing is to keep the main thing the main thing,"* noted the late *Stephen R. Covey, author of* The 7 Habits of Highly Effective People: Powerful Lessons in Personal Change. *Individuals or organizations with too many priorities have no priorities and risk spinning their wheels and accomplishing nothing of significance. In turn, laser-focusing everyone on a single priority — today, this week, this quarter, this year, and the next decade — creates clarity and power throughout the organization. In this chapter, we'll press hard for you and your company to stay focused. We'll show you how to wrap a memorable theme around your priority; achieve it — or at least make substantial progress toward it — by a specific due date; and host a celebration with rewards to provide the requisite finish lines and fun, pumping up the energy and engagement of the team members as they achieve something significant together.*

Gene Browne didn't know how to drive a garbage truck when he started a waste collection company, The City Bin Co., in Galway, Ireland, in 1997—and he still doesn't. In fact, he thinks this is one of the keys to success in his business.

By staying out of his trucks and focusing on steering the company instead, he has scaled the business to $37 million in annual revenue, 160 employees, and 3x the profitability in 2019, up from 80 in 2013 — while leading and managing a successful turnaround for a 1,000-person company across four countries in the Middle East, which he exited in 2019. The City Bin Co. is now working toward a Big Hairy Audacious Goal™ of "20 Cities, $500 million" by 2030. This is its long-term "main thing."

In 2011, it became clear to CEO Mark Zuckerberg that "Facebook's first priority needed to be figuring out a wireless strategy," noted a 2013 article in *Fortune* magazine. Jessi Hempel, senior writer, explained: "He was maniacal about it. In December 2011 he reorganized the company to embed mobile engineers in all product teams. In June 2012 he began Facebook's annual all-hands meeting by explaining that the company's most pressing priority was to become a mobile company." Every acquisition, hiring decision, and software development project was focused on one thing for the next 18 months: to go mobile. And in April of 2013, Facebook did. It achieved mobile ad revenue that exceeded all expectations in the next six months, reaching 50% of total revenue in the fourth quarter of 2013. It was an amazing pivot that saved the company. This was Facebook's medium-term "main thing."

Ignite Social Media President Jim Tobin had a "rock in his shoe." His 28-member team wasn't using its newly installed project-management system. With a month left in the year, he wrote on a whiteboard in the break room, "Late: 241; Unassigned: 728" and dated each metric "12/1." After sending out a short email to his team focusing everyone on getting both metrics to zero by 12/31, he was blown away to find that within 24 hours, late tasks had dropped by 25%, to 193, and unassigned tasks by

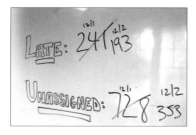

over half, to 353. By the end of the month, both were at zero. The team was now ready for the coming year. This was the short-term "main thing" at Ignite.

Decades ago, Charles Schwab, CEO of Bethlehem Steel, asked management consultant Ivy Lee to show him how to get more done. As the famous story goes, Lee asked Schwab to write down and prioritize his six most important tasks to complete the next business day. Then he instructed Schwab to start on item #1 the next day and not move on to item #2 until item #1 was completed. "Don't be concerned if you've only finished two or three, or even one, by quitting time. You'll be working on the most important ones, and the others can wait." Lee encouraged Schwab to share this approach with his executives, judge the value, and "send me a check for whatever you think it's worth." Two weeks later, Lee received a check for $25,000 — a king's ransom in those days — and an accompanying note in which Schwab said it was the most profitable lesson he'd ever learned. This priority list was Schwab's daily "main thing."

As the above examples demonstrate, priority-setting is as applicable today as it was 100 years ago, and as critical in the short run as in the long term. As Confucius said, "He who chases two rabbits catches neither." The key is sequencing a series of #1 priorities that keep everyone focused and heading in the same general direction together.

Throughout the book, we have emphasized setting priorities (that includes deciding which of the 4 Decisions to focus on first and which box on the FACe chart needs to be updated next). On the One-Page Strategic Plan (OPSP), there is a progression of #1 priorities:

1. Core Purpose: the **one** word/idea/speech driving the business
2. BHAG®: the **one** 10- to 25-year goal for the company
3. Profit per X: the **one** overarching KPI representing the core economic engine of the enterprise
4. Brand Promise: the **one** most important measurable promise (of three) representing the brand
5. The Critical Number: the **one** key driver for the year and the quarter

And in the chapter on "The Meeting Rhythm," we'll continue this focus on priorities, imploring the team to pick one key topic to discuss/solve at the weekly meeting and one big issue/opportunity to address at the monthly leadership meeting. Again, it's just a matter of sequencing these initiatives so they align and build upon each other. This way, you can tackle the hundreds of decisions and activities that need to be addressed without overwhelming and defocusing the team. As the well-known analogy suggests, you can only eat an elephant one bite at a time. The same is true with scaling up a business.

# Rockefeller Habits Checklist™

Throughout this "Execution" section, we'll cover the 10 routines listed on the Rockefeller Habits Checklist™. Flip back to "The Execution: Introduction" and take a few minutes to review the list, placing a checkmark next to each routine you feel is present (even if not perfect) in your organization. Or download a copy of the Rockefeller Habits Checklist™ at *scalingup.com* and mark it up, if you prefer.

Leaders who've completed the checklist often ask us two questions:

1. How did we survive/thrive for all these years and yet have nothing checked off on the list?

2. Are the habits in any kind of order?

Responding to the first question, we remind executive teams that this is an execution checklist. It's not necessary to implement any of these habits to build a long-lasting organization. It just means you've been leaving massive amounts of money and time on the table. And if you have a killer strategy and/or heroic people willing to work 18-hour days, eight days a week, these will make up for the messes created by sloppy execution and lack of discipline.

To answer the second question, you can't implement any of what we've taught in this book unless Rockefeller Habit #1 — "The executive team is healthy and aligned" — exists. The order in which you implement the other habits doesn't matter. Choose just one or two each quarter, based on what will give you the most immediate benefit, as you would with the rest of our crossword puzzle-like tools. Over 24 to 36 months, you'll have moved through all 10 habits.

## Why Checklists — Safest Place to Be!

Where is, physically, the safest place to be? Not your home, nor walking down the street or eating lunch, but in a US or European commercial airliner. In the US, if you exclude the 265 passengers who died aboard the four 9/11 planes that crashed, there were 11 fatal crashes and 247 deaths between the years 2000 and 2009 — roughly one crash and 25 deaths per year. To put this in perspective, there are almost twice as many deaths from lightening per year in the US.

As impressive as this is, between 2010 and 2020 there were only two fatal crashes and two deaths the entire decade — over a hundred-fold improvement in the commercial airline safety record in the US (thankfully for all who fly). In contrast, the third leading cause of death in the US is medical error — almost 249,000 deaths per year! The difference? One, the pilot and crew are going down with the passengers — not so with doctors and their teams! And second, we can credit checklists.

So disturbing are these medical statistics that Dr. Atul Gawande, a medical doctor, wrote a book titled *The Checklist Manifesto: How to Get Things Right*. In this book he details how the commercial aviation industry was the first to adopt checklists. And when there is an incident, the black/orange box is retrieved, and the data is studied until a root cause is found and checklists are updated. Not so in the medical world. The biggest barrier? Three letters — E.G.O.

*"A professional does all parts of a job; an amateur only the fun parts."*

As Gawande highlights, it's professionals that need checklists as much or more than others, as in, "A professional does all parts of a job; an amateur only the fun parts." I'm so thankful, again, that the mechanics and pilots don't skip over a single item on their checklists.

## Piloting Your Organization

As the pilot and crew of your organization, it's just as critical that you do all the parts of the checklist and not just the fun parts. It's no time for amateur hour or people are going to get hurt (figuratively or literally). And as noted above, you don't have to do any of the items on the Rockefeller Habits Checklist. It just means you're likely wasting time and money and creating unnecessary drama for you, your team, and your clients. The goal is to create a drama-free organization, driving relentless repeatability throughout the organization.

The commercial airline industry also learned, after the fatal crash of United flight 178 in 1978, the importance of having a "healthy team" aboard each airliner. The result of that investigation led to significant changes in the way teams interact and communicate, giving every team member permission to be more forceful in speaking up and for the captain to be more open to input.

This mirrors what Google found is key to team effectiveness — psychological safety and the importance of equal talk time — more on this later — and why Rockefeller Habits #1 is number one.

### Crew Resource Management (CRM)

Crew Resource Management (CRM) is the effective use of all available resources for flight crew personnel to assure a safe and efficient operation, reducing error, avoiding stress and increasing efficiency.

CRM was developed as a response to new insights into the causes of aircraft accidents, which followed from the introduction of flight data recorders (FDRs) and cockpit voice recorders (CVRs) into modern jet aircraft. Information gathered from these devices has suggested that many accidents do not result from a technical malfunction of the aircraft or its systems, nor from a failure of aircraft handling skills or a lack of technical knowledge on the part of the crew; it appears instead that they are caused by the inability of crews to respond appropriately to the situation in which they find themselves.

For example, inadequate communications between crew members and other parties could lead to a loss of situational awareness, a breakdown in teamwork in the aircraft, and, ultimately, to a wrong decision or series of decisions that result in a serious incident or a fatal accident.

CRM is concerned not so much with the technical knowledge and skills required to fly and operate an aircraft but rather with the cognitive and interpersonal skills needed to manage the flight within an organized aviation system. In this context, cognitive skills are defined as the mental processes used for gaining and maintaining situational awareness, for solving problems and for making decisions.

Interpersonal skills are regarded as communication and a range of behavioral activities associated with teamwork. In aviation, as in other fields, these skill areas often overlap with each other, and they also overlap with the required technical skills. Furthermore, they are not confined to multi-crew aircraft, but also relate to single-pilot operations, which invariably need to interface with other aircraft and with various ground support agencies in order to complete their missions successfully.

(The above paragraphs were taken from a paper by the CRM Standing Group of the Royal Aeronautical Society (RAeS) — Source: SkyBrary

# Rockefeller Habit #1 — Healthy Team

**1. The executive team is healthy and aligned.**
- ☐ Team members understand each other's differences, priorities, and styles.
- ☐ The team meets frequently (weekly is best) for strategic thinking.
- ☐ The team participates in ongoing executive education (monthly recommended).
- ☐ The team is able to engage in constructive debates and all members feel comfortable participating.

Patrick M. Lencioni's best-selling book *The Five Dysfunctions of a Team: A Leadership Fable* defines the unhealthy situations that can derail your leadership team: an absence of trust, fear of conflict, lack of commitment, avoidance of accountability, and inattention to results. If one or more of these afflictions exist, address it before you tackle any other aspect of execution. We strongly suggest purchasing Lencioni's affordable "Team Kit." Take your leadership team through his assessment and training process to strengthen the levels of trust, healthy debate, commitment, accountability, and results. It's a great tune-up for even healthy teams. At a minimum, require all leaders and managers to read his book once a year. It's a quick read, and doing a refresher can prevent new problems from arising within the team as you scale up.

*"The #1 habit is the most important and first."*

Many of the Rockefeller Habits reinforce routines that keep the team healthy, like taking a few minutes to share personal and professional good news at the start of a weekly or monthly meeting (discussed in "The Meeting Rhythm" chapter). Other ways to help the team build trust:

- Personality and leadership style assessments, which help team members appreciate each other's differences
- Meal and social time during offsite planning sessions and monthly management meetings
- Shared learning experiences
- Take your team through a lifeline exercise — see grey box

Once the team is healthy, then it is ready to tackle the tough work of setting priorities successfully.

### Lifeline Exercise

The lifeline exercise is a critical tool that YPO and EO forums use to quickly deepen their relationships among forum members. Pat Lencioni's team uses it, as well, with leadership teams. In essence, each member of the team takes an 8.5" x 11" (A4 in metric) sheet of paper and turns it horizontally. Drawing a horizontal line through the middle, label the line from zero to your current age.

Then note, at the age it occurred, your top five "highlights" and the lowest moments in your life. Don't include marriage or children. Connect the dots and you'll see the roller coaster ride you've been on (or river flow, going back to that analogy in the opening of the book). Next, take 10 – 15 minutes each, to share your stories with your teammates.

Kevin Rhodes, owner of FMI, a leading contractor cosmetic manufacturing firm, learned about the lifeline exercise at our CEO Boot Camp. A year later, when he came back, he noted that his wife shared something on her lifeline with the team of which he was not even aware — deepening their relationship. It's a powerfully simple tool. Take the time to do it with your team.

 **NOTE:** *When you add someone new to a team, it's not the old team plus one. It's an entirely new team. Take the time to go through the lifeline exercise, again, to introduce them to the team and vice versa.*

# Rockefeller Habit #2 — The #1 Priority

**2. Everyone is aligned with the #1 thing that needs to be accomplished this quarter to move the company forward.**
- ☐ The Critical Number is identified to move the company ahead this quarter.
- ☐ 3-5 Priorities (Rocks) that support the Critical Number are identified and ranked for the quarter.
- ☐ A Quarterly Theme and Celebration/Reward are announced to all employees that bring the Critical Number to life.
- ☐ Quarterly Theme/Critical Number posted throughout the company and employees are aware of the progress each week.

To simplify our methodology, there are two main vision decisions: the BHAG® and the measurable next step (one with a 90-day to one-year focus). Everything else in between is just a WAG — a wild-ankle guess. The BHAG®, derived from your strategy, is the main long-term priority anchoring the *strategic thinking* in the vision. The quarterly or annual Critical Number is the main short-term priority anchoring the *execution planning* side.

Rockefeller Habit #2 starts with identifying this Critical Number, introduced and popularized through Jack Stack's classic book *The Great Game of Business: The Only Sensible Way to Run a Company*. Though all your metrics are critical, reserve the term "Critical Number" for your measurable #1 priority, even when other metrics are nearly as important.

To derive the one Critical Number, imagine the hundreds of important things you need to accomplish lined up like dominoes. Find the lead domino: the one initiative that, when pursued, makes it easier to accomplish everything else. Or identify the constraint — the choke point or bottleneck — and address it first. For more on how to choose this "critical" constraint, read my favorite biz book of all time titled *The Goal* by the late Eli Goldratt. Scaling up is all about eliminating constraints — in the business and for customers.

At ProService Hawaii, a human resources firm based in Honolulu, President Ben Godsey determined that one fiscal year, his Critical Number was getting 600 referrals. This was a major stretch goal. The company, which has $385 million in annual sales (2021), had previously averaged fewer than 200 referrals a year, despite its focus on developing a great service culture and innovative products — indicated by a Net Promoter Score (NPS) consistently above 70% (on par with Apple).

After Godsey's team talked about how great it would be to get more referrals from satisfied clients, the company created an annual theme around the plan. It set that stretch goal: getting 600 leads from clients in 12 months, three times more than it had ever achieved. And sure enough, the company accomplished this with a couple of weeks to spare— and the entire team celebrated with a trip to Waikoloa Beach.

In addition to tripling leads, this single focused and measurable priority helped to knock over a bunch of other dominoes. "We've now made referrals, by far, the biggest driver of our growth — which shows quality and value to clients — through achieving a goal we thought was pretty far-fetched," says Godsey. "More important, the focus on referrals has become embedded in our culture, reinforcing our service ethic." Clients and staff understand that as the company grows, getting more referrals helps the firm invest in improving its services and products, and brings new projects that are good for staff development. "We call that the virtuous cycle of growth," Godsey says.

So, what is the most important and measurable choke point you need to fix/control in your business this coming year? Figure it out. Then give your team a chance to win gold, silver, or bronze rewards (Super Green, Green, or Red at the bottom of column 4 of the OPSP). ProService Hawaii normally has a three-tiered set of goals in its themes. However, in upping its game in lead generation, "we did not have Red and Green goals this time," notes Godsey. "We set one high bar [Super Green]; the Critical Number of hitting 600 referrals. It was like going to the moon and back: Either we were going to do it, by all working together toward this singular goal [like Apollo 13], or die trying."

Godsey's team is experienced in using themes and therefore was ready for this all-or-nothing challenge. For those new to this routine, give your team some wiggle room in the beginning by setting a three-tiered target. Using the ProService example, we might recommend setting 200 leads as the minimum target (Red), with the reward being a party in the company's parking lot; 400 leads as the goal (Green), with the reward a local beach party; and 600 leads as the stretch goal (Super Green), with a company trip to Waikoloa Beach.

## Quarterly Themes

The Quarterly Theme is a fun motif you can use in your internal marketing to rally everyone around achieving your Critical Number.

 **NOTE:** *Especially for those new to the process, we encourage teams to start with a few initial themes that last no longer than a quarter. It takes several quarters to master choosing and setting Critical Numbers.*

Gene Browne thought he had tapped into the ideas covered in *Mastering the Rockefeller Habits* as he grew The City Bin Co., but with Ireland's economy hit hard by the global economic crisis, he decided he needed to dig deeper into the habits in 2009. "Ireland was in a deep recession," he recalls. "I thought we needed to do something new. We needed to get out of the quagmire."

That year, he flew his leadership team to Orlando, Florida, for a two-day "Mastering the Rockefeller Habits" workshop. There, he realized that he hadn't been focusing enough on using Quarterly Themes to align his company's employees as their numbers grew. "It was stuff we thought we were doing, but weren't, really," Browne says.

When Browne and his team returned to Ireland, they decided to put the Quarterly Themes front and center. Every quarter, they ask themselves: What is the single most important thing going on in the business in the next 90 days that we want everyone to be aligned on? Then they assign a "Champion" to prepare a presentation, using guidelines from a sheet of best practices for Quarterly Themes that the company outlined. A designer in the software division creates a humorous visual theme to align everyone in the company around it. The Champion who selects the theme can be any employee, but Browne and his managing director have final approval.

The presentation is shared in an hourly meeting with all of The City Bin Co.'s employees each quarter. Within each theme, the company lists smaller "Rocks" (column 5 of the OPSP) that need to be addressed in order to achieve the company's big goal for the next 13 weeks, helping to focus everyone on execution. Though employees do not discuss the themes during daily huddles, which are focused on daily operations, they devote 30 minutes at weekly meetings to addressing progress toward the Quarterly Theme. Particular employees are asked to take ownership of the Rocks in their areas of responsibility, and the company's managing director and finance manager track progress toward meeting the goals, using key metrics. "It transformed the company," Browne says.

Here are several examples of The City Bin Co.'s Quarterly Themes:

## Saving Mrs. Ryan

With price pressure in his industry especially high, one of the quarterly themes that Browne introduced was "Saving Mrs. Ryan." Borrowing from the military theme of the movie *Saving Private Ryan,* the 90-day campaign focused on attracting 10,000 individual new customers, homemakers now identified as "Mrs. Ryan" (the company's core "Who"). The cover of the presentation was illustrated with the silhouette of a soldier, flanked by the company's trash cans. "Competitors' contracts were coming up for renewal, and we wanted to bring onboard 10,000 new Mrs. Ryans," says Browne. "We wanted to save these Mrs. Ryans from the 'Soviet era' service of a rival firm, so we sent a door-to-door 'assault' team to rescue them."

Giant posters in the company's main office and depot reminded employees of each quarter's theme. In this case, above office workers' cubicles were "Saving Mrs. Ryan" posters, designed to look like the movie poster from the Tom Hanks film. A board in the company's main office tracked the number of contracts being signed, providing daily progress reports to the entire company. At weekly meetings, there were more detailed updates, in which the managing director presented a slide — in military green, with a stencil font similar to the one used by the US Army — showing progress in meeting the subsidiary goals, or rocks. The City Bin Co. provided bonuses to particular employees who moved the needle toward the goal each month, to keep the momentum going. "Instead of waiting until the end, this is better," says Browne.

To motivate its team to exceed its goals, The City Bin Co. sometimes picks a Super Green benchmark that is above and beyond its target for a given theme. For the "Saving Mrs. Ryan" theme, the company selected a Super Green target of saving 12,000 Mrs. Ryans.

### Life Begins at 40

The City Bin Co.'s themes have varied along with the constraints confronting the company each quarter. To raise profitability while recovering from the recession, the company ran the "Life Begins at 40" quarterly campaign, with an image of a Las Vegas slot machine hitting the jackpot gracing the guidebook's cover. The idea was to increase the company's monthly earnings by 40,000 euros a month, either through annual savings or recurring revenue. Employees were invited to submit ideas to raise cash or slash the budget.

The theme was lighthearted, but Browne knew it was necessary for the long-term survival of the company. "The economy had contracted so much that a lot of companies in Ireland were closing down," says Browne. "'Life Begins at 40' was saying that if we can get to this magic figure, it'll ensure that we can ride through this economic storm." The company managed to achieve its goal to fuel growth.

### 180 to One

Another lighthearted, betting-oriented quarterly theme, "180 to One," focused on having each of Browne's 60 employees spend one day a month job-sharing (60 employees x 3 job-sharing days = 180), to improve customer service throughout The City Bin Co. "We wanted to get people thinking outside of their own department and get an appreciation of what the other departments do," says Browne. That meant having the accounts people work in the call centers, asking the customer center workers to ride around in the company's garbage trucks, and enlisting the truck drivers to answer the phones at the customer center.

Customer service and staff cohesiveness improved tangibly. A truck driver now knew what types of complaints would come into the call center if a bin was not picked up. "We've seen a big change in relation to the culture," says Browne. "If you ask people what the one thing The City Bin Co. is about, they will say, 'Customer service.'" At the end of the quarter, the company celebrated beating the odds and accomplishing its goal by inviting its team to the dog races.

### Bin it

Some quarterly themes have focused on improving efficiency. One was called "Bin it." It asked employees to submit index cards listing wasteful practices and unnecessary tasks they wanted to stop doing — anything that was depleting time, money, energy, or space without a valuable result. "People like me, in senior management, ask people to do things and load them on," says Browne. "We never take away stuff." Often, employees may hesitate to speak up or to question a leader about why they're doing something, even if it's obvious to them that it isn't necessary.

Browne had one reminder of how much time could be wasted this way after he asked a team member to keep track of customer sign-ups on a spreadsheet that he intended to monitor for three months during a marketing campaign. Nearly three years later, in a casual conversation, the employee mentioned that she was still keeping the spreadsheet.

"You're still doing that?" Browne asked. "I haven't looked at it in two and a half years."

To inspire employees to clear the decks of projects like this and focus on what really matters, the "Bin it" campaign awarded prizes — ranging from tickets to the cinema to a weekend break — to those who submitted items that were approved to be "binned." As with its other Quarterly Themes, The City Bin Co. introduced this one with a launch party; it celebrated with a barbecue upon meeting its goals. And lest employees forget about the theme, floor-to-ceiling red posters at the company's offices reminded them to "Bin it."

"We binned more than 150 activities over that quarter, many of which affected several individuals, so the total impact was huge," says Browne. "It also brought a new phrase and philosophy to the company culture."

### The Price is Right

Taking a clue from our Power of One cash tool (see chapter 13), Gene's team took a quarter to focus on "right pricing" all 10,000 of their customers, something that is especially critical in inflationary times.

He recognized that pricing is often left to salespeople and isn't thought about strategically. And the lesson from the "unicorns" is that pricing is based on demand, not pure costs. Whereas taxis charge the same per 1/8th of a km or mile; Uber and Lyft charge based on demand. By making similar changes to its pricing, City Bin was able to increase revenue 7% that quarter, most of which went straight to the bottom line.

### Bin's Health

After the company invested heavily in a marketing campaign, it introduced the "Bin's Health" quarterly theme. The presentation of the theme was a play on the magazine *Men's Health* — complete with David Beckham on the cover, with an image of The City Bin Co.'s logo superimposed on his chest. The company had been splurging on marketing spending as it made a major move into a new market that helped grow its customer base 250%. "However, at a certain point, there's no more bang to your buck" says Browne — and it was time to get lean again. The presentation outlined the company's goals for cutting spending by set percentages in salaries, transportation, advertising and design, legal and professional services, vehicle hires, and landfill costs.

In this case, The City Bin Co. didn't meet its goals, but it made progress toward them. "It was very clear some time into it that we were probably a bit too aggressive on our goal," Browne says. While the company held its customary parties to kick off the theme and to celebrate the end of the 13 weeks, it did not offer any awards, as it did when the team met goals in other quarters.

 **NOTE:** *The City Bin Co. alternates between a Critical Number and Quarterly Theme that are focused on improving the People side of the business ("180 to One," "Saving Mrs. Ryan") and the Process side of the business ("Life Begins at 40," "Bin it," "Bin's Health"). It's important to find the same kind of balance as you sequence your #1 priorities.*

## SMART and FAST Goals

The acronym SMART — Specific, Measurable, Achievable, Relevant, and Time-bound — has been associated with proper goal setting for decades. More recently, we've adopted the acronym FAST. Proposed by Donald Sull and Charles Sull, FAST speaks more broadly to both setting and acting on those goals — and springs to mind the popular one to two week "sprints" powering most tech firms. Specifically, the acronym stands for:

**F**requently discussed — key to maintaining focus through daily/weekly review

**A**mbitious — more energizing than attainable/achievable (or outrageous) goals

**S**pecific — implies measurable as well

**T**ransparent — powerful in driving accountability through peer pressure

Recognizing the overwhelming popularity of SMART goals, if you want to keep using that acronym, we strongly suggest an alternative set of definitions for each letter. This brings SMART goals much more in line with the broader spirit of FAST goals:

**S**pecific — implying it's measurable as well

**M**eaningful — assuring it aligns with the broader goals and BHAG of the organization

**A**mbitious — stretching people but not demoralizing them

**R**eview Routinely — keeping the goal front and center in everyone's minds

**T**ransparent — posting and sharing to drive accountability and peer pressure

Whether you choose SMART or FAST to define your goals, the three disciplines of Priorities, Data, and Meeting Rhythms accomplishes, automatically, the spirit of both acronyms.

## To Reward or Not To Reward

What if in the middle of a Quarterly Theme or an annual one, you feel the team is going to miss the Critical Number, maybe substantially? Do you adjust midstream? Do you lower the target?

If the organization misses the mark, you have three options:

1. Repeat the Critical Number in the next quarter if it's still crucial that the organization achieve the target. We've seen this when a quality or a customer service score needs to be reached.

2. Move on to another Critical Number if you sense that enough momentum was created with the previous target to keep the organization trending in the right direction.

3. Do a root-cause analysis to uncover the reasons your organization didn't achieve your Critical Number. Choose one of those reasons to fix in the next quarter. For instance, The City Bin Co.'s "180 to One" theme addressed an organizational health issue. Browne felt team members needed to step back and gain more empathy for each other's situations so they would be ready to work as one to achieve the next target.

Like the river making its way from Everest to the ocean, your organization will have to constantly navigate obstacles and take a step back (or pause) every once in a while. One reason we encourage organizations new to this process to start out with Quarterly Themes, rather than annual ones, is that it isn't uncommon for teams to fall short of their goals in the beginning. Don't change the goals. It can be inspiring to stick with a target to see if the team can pull out a victory in the last few days.

At the same time, no one's paycheck should suffer because the senior team chose an overly aggressive goal or one that the team was not prepared to achieve. Pick celebrations and rewards that are mostly for fun.

And having three potential targets — Super Green, Green, and Red — ups the odds that the team will earn a medal. Even if you don't hit the minimum goal, convene the team for an event to announce the results. One company promised a barbecue at which management would cook if the team achieved certain employee-retention goals. The higher the target, the better the menu. If the team hit 75% retention (Red), employees would dine on hot dogs and hamburgers. If they reached 80% (Green), management would serve chicken and ribs. The company promised steak if the business held on to 85% of employees (Super Green). When the team missed even the minimum, management instead hosted a soup kitchen.

Last, as the company matures in the use of quarterly and annual themes, you can dial up the rewards. At Jack Stack's SRC Holdings Corporation, a group of companies with revenue totaling over half a billion dollars, roughly 15% of employees' compensation is tied to the achievement of the Critical Number. Again, we strongly encourage you to read Stack's book *The Great Game of Business,* and have a team travel to Springfield, Missouri, to attend his two-day "Get in the Game" workshop. It's particularly useful for CFOs and COOs.

## Customer and Employee Feedback

Jack Harrington, CEO of Virtual Technology Corporation (VTC), was hosting the company's first quarterly offsite to determine the Critical Number and theme. Coming off a previous quarter of phenomenal growth, the senior team focused on continuing to drive revenue, aiming to add $6 million in revenue to the pipeline in the coming quarter.

While there, in preparation for an upcoming strategic-planning offsite, the company conducted an analysis of strengths, weaknesses, opportunities, and threats and a survey of management to learn their top three priorities. It also surveyed employees. It found that the frontline team was deeply concerned that VTC was in danger of failing to deliver on projects already in progress, risking the firm's stellar reputation.

Fortunately, the senior team was "healthy" enough that an executive spoke up during the offsite and advocated for the employees' viewpoint. In the end, Harrington and the team pivoted their focus to recruiting, hiring, and onboarding 16 hard-to-find distributed-simulation experts in the next quarter, to both relieve pressure on the existing team and prepare VTC for the additional business it planned to acquire. This removed the constraints on the company.

Going with a "Sweet Sixteen" theme (who would have imagined that a bunch of techies would enjoy such a thing!), VTC engaged all 120 employees in the process, structuring internal bonuses for anyone in the firm who could recruit one of these specialists. Mara Harrington, Jack's wife and the head of human resources, was relieved to get the help, and in the end, the company brought on board 20 of these critical team members, exceeding its goal. The following quarter, it followed up with a "Six Million Dollar Man" theme based on the classic '70s hit television series (people still talk about VP of Sales Doug Greenlaw running into the Quarterly Theme launch event dressed in a Lee Majors-like red jumpsuit!), where employees continued to pour on the gas and ramp up the sales pipeline.

Later that year, the company was purchased by Raytheon for a hefty multiple of EBITDA precisely because VTC had almost all the quality distributed-simulation experts on its team. It controlled a critical constraint/choke point in the industry! In the "Strategy" section, Verne shared Harrington's post-VTC story at Raytheon as he went on to head billion-dollar divisions for this global conglomerate.

 **WARNING:** *The Critical Number, like the rest of the organization's strategy, cannot be set in isolation from the realities of the company and the marketplace. Employees and customers will think the senior team was smoking something if they come down from the mountaintop with "the tablets" pronouncing the latest strategic plan without having completed the necessary preparation. And as Jack Stack strongly suggests, it's best if the Critical Number is benchmarked against an external standard (e.g., "If that company can achieve 12 inventory turns, why can't we?"), so employees don't think the senior team was just making stuff up!*

## Theme Creation and Celebration

At ProService, a group of employees who are not part of the executive team developed every aspect of the 600-referral theme. Their efforts included producing a "Happy" video to celebrate the achievement of their goal (search "Happy ProService" on YouTube).

"Basically, the team said, 'Let's put together a fun video to celebrate achieving our goal,'" says Godsey, the president. "They started to riff and innovate, and then invited people to participate in the celebration, saying, 'Show us your happy dance.' Different teams made up different fun little dances. And then bam! The end result of the video was even better."

As at ProService, you should delegate the actual creation of the theme to a nonexecutive team. Almost every company has a team member who is skilled in using a computer to create videos, posters, and other themed collateral. The senior team doesn't need another job, and it's best if an employee-run team drives the theme activities.

### Powerful Celebration Question

At the celebration, skip the usual speeches by the senior team about "How we couldn't have done this, that, or the other thing without so-and-so's help, etc." Instead, ask the most powerful question a leader can pose when a team has successfully completed anything: "How did you do it?" Stand up and say "Congratulations. We said we would do X, and we did it!! How did you do it?" Then pick someone who you know contributed to reaching the Critical Number, and have that person share his or her story. This hint is courtesy of Aubrey C. Daniels, author of *Bringing Out the Best in People: How to Apply the Astonishing Power of Positive Reinforcement* (a foundational business book that all leaders should read).

By the way, if you're a parent, this is a great question to ask your children when they come home with a success story. Rather than shower them with praise, simply say: "Congrats. So how did you do it?" and let them share their story.

Nothing builds momentum and energy like hitting specific targets. If your company has been through some rough times lately and the culture has taken a couple of body blows, pick some really short-term goals, focus everyone on the same thing, "play to win," and get back your mojo!!

# Rockefeller Habits #3, #4, #7, and #8

**Rockefeller Habit #3,** Meeting Rhythm, will be covered in its own chapter at the end of this section.

Rockefeller Habits #4, #7, and #8 have already been covered extensively. But here are quick recaps:

**Rockefeller Habit #4** — *Every facet of the organization has a person assigned with accountability for ensuring goals are met* — was covered in "The Leaders" chapter. We include a mention in the chapter on "The Priority" because the related worksheets focus on determining the **one** person accountable for the functions, outcomes, and processes of the organization.

4. Every facet of the organization has a person assigned with accountability for ensuring goals are met.
- ☐ The Function Accountability Chart (FACe) is completed (right people, doing the right things, right).
- ☐ Financial statements have a person assigned to each line item.
- ☐ Each of the 4-9 processes on the Process Accountability Chart (PACe) has someone that is accountable for them.
- ☐ Each 3-5 year Key Thrust/Capability has a corresponding expert on the Advisory Board if internal expertise doesn't exist.

**Rockefeller Habit #7** — *Core Values and Purpose are "alive" in the organization* — was covered in "The Core" chapter. It's important that the Core Values and the Purpose are given priority when making hiring (and firing) decisions — and when sharing praise and constructive criticism. It's also crucial that the leadership team formulate its **one** passionate stump speech that can be repeated to reinforce the bigger Purpose of the organization.

**7. Core Values and Purpose are "alive" in the organization.**
- ☐ Core Values are discovered, Purpose is articulated, and both are known by all employees.
- ☐ All executives and middle managers refer back to the Core Values and Purpose when giving praise or reprimands.
- ☐ HR processes and activities align with the Core Values and Purpose (hiring, orientation, appraisal, recognition, etc.).
- ☐ Actions are identified and implemented each quarter to strengthen the Core Values and Purpose in the organization.

**Rockefeller Habit #8** — *Employees can articulate the key components of the company's strategy accurately* — was covered in "The One-Page Strategic Plan" chapter. In essence, it speaks to the need for all employees to understand key aspects of the Vision and Strategy of the business, as reflected on the Vision Summary worksheet. And it helps drive alignment if all the employees have the same "elevator pitch" they share when asked the question, "What does your company do?"

**8. Employees can articulate the following key components of the company's strategy accurately.**
- ☐ Big Hairy Audacious Goal (BHAG) – Progress is tracked and visible.
- ☐ Core Customer(s) – Their profile in 25 words or less.
- ☐ 3 Brand Promises – And the corresponding Brand Promise KPIs reported on weekly.
- ☐ Elevator Pitch – A compelling response to the question "What does your company do?"

The balance of the Rockefeller Habits (#5, #6, #9, and #10) will be covered in the next chapter, "The Data."

# 10

# THE DATA
## Powering Prediction

---

**EXECUTIVE SUMMARY:** *The fundamental job of a leader is prediction, according to the late business consultant W. Edwards Deming. At the heart of a leader's ability to predict is data — and lots of it. Big data analysis has become mainstream and within reach of companies of all sizes. Yet leaders also need plain old human-gathered intelligence to get a gut feel for the market and what is happening in the company, so that they can make the right decisions. Talking weekly with customers and employees and then discussing what's been learned at the executive huddle is critical. And engaging all of your employees in data collection, with a middle-leadership team leading them, spreads out the work so the senior team doesn't get buried.*

---

When COE Distributing in Smock, Pa. was looking for the most efficient location for its new office furniture distribution center, it turned to data. CEO and President James D. Ewing — whose innovative employee recognition program you read about in the "People" section — tapped a team of data analytics students from the Graduate School of Business at the University of Pittsburgh, who worked on the site selection for three months.

"They took into account multiple bits of information available: distribution space, cost of distribution space, customer concentration, cost of logistics and so on," explains Ewing. After a three-month review, they chose a location in Houston, down to the block. With the location identified, the company leased a building that spans a quarter of a million square feet.

COE Distributing next turned to a group of students to use artificial intelligence (AI) to determine what products will be successful. They are using predictive analytics. "The more that model is used, the better and more accurate it is becoming," says Ewing.

Their latest initiative is "Olivia," a web widget created by Forethought.

### "Olivia" Check's Stock

Notes Jennifer Jubin, VP of Customer Experience (love the title), for COE:

> *You can interact with her (Olivia) directly at www.coedistributing.com (lower right corner). We made the focus of what she can and should accomplish to be repetitive tasks that our CS Team gets bombarded with. So far she can advise when an order will ship, check stock, advise on stock replenishment dates, provide product assembly instructions and directly contact our CS Team (via email). This is still pretty new for us, but it has been met with a wonderful reception. Checking stock is definitely the most popular feature in this climate of supply chain challenges. You can even add the item right to your shopping cart once you've looked up an item.*

## Scaling Up

Olivia is helping to improve both the customer experience (CX) and employee experience (EX) — this is a win-win-win for all stakeholders. Where can you apply data and AI to your business?

## Intelligence-Gathering

All wars, and markets, are won by intelligence — whoever has the best intel, the fastest, wins. That's why data analysis must be augmented with plain old human intelligence-gathering.

For all the big data computing power that Wal-Mart Stores Inc. possesses, it sends teams from the Bentonville, Arkansas, headquarters out to stores to gather insight Monday through Thursday, bringing them back Thursday night. On Friday morning, its executives pore over all the quantitative data from its computer systems, along with the qualitative intelligence picked up from talking with customers, meeting with employees, and shopping at competitors' stores during the week.

The late David Glass, former CEO of Wal-Mart and owner/CEO of the Kansas City Royals baseball team, recalled this routine well. "We would decide what corrective action we wanted to take [Friday morning]," he said. "And by noon on Saturday, we had all our corrections in place. Our competitors, for the most part, got their sales results on Monday for the prior week. Now they're 10 days behind, and we've already made corrections."

It's this "learn fast; act fast" cycle that put Wal-Mart ahead of the co petition. And as this example demonstrates, you don't have to be months or even weeks ahead, just 10 days ahead for more than 50 years.

*"Learn fast; act fast."*

Wal-Mart's routine is not just for large companies. Its habit of gathering data on employees, customers, and the competition started in 1962 with a 6 a.m. meeting every Saturday at Sam Walton's first store.

Two lessons:

1. Senior leaders need to be in the market 80% of the week, either figuratively or literally.
2. This routine must start on day one and continue through half a trillion in revenue!

Speed is the key. It was military strategist and United States Air Force Colonel John Boyd who articulated the OODA loop, which determined which fighter pilots prevailed in a dogfight. In essence, whoever could Observe, Orient, Decide, and Act faster than the competition, won! We call it the Learn – Decide – Act cycle — and whoever does this most quickly has a huge advantage in the market — like the 10-day advantage Wal-Mart created with its intelligence gathering, decision, and action approach on a weekly basis.

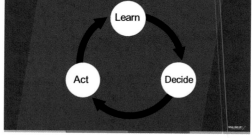

The OODA loop is why QuickBooks is still the preferred accounting software for more than 80% of small business owners after years of competitive threats from Microsoft and other major players who have tried to take this market from Intuit. The key? Five hundred times per year the company sends someone to a user's home or office, especially after a new release, and watches them interact with the software. Every pause and raised eyebrow by a client is a clue that QuickBooks needs a user interface fix.

Decades ago, I knew Ken DeLaski's firm Deltek would become the dominant player in the government contracting software space. With the company at 70 employees, Ken invited me in to work with his team. What I saw blew me away. In the technical support area were four people fielding customers' questions about the company's software. In the same area was a cubicle where each of the programmers was expected to work for a half-day a week.

They weren't answering calls, but they were overhearing all the questions and concerns. And if one of the technical support people couldn't answer a question, they could exclaim, "I have someone sitting right here who wrote the software." It was the perfect and rapid OODA or Learn-Decide-Act loop where customer concerns were being identified daily and making their way into the code.

In addition, Ken, himself worked one day a week in the same area, where he could pick up the same intel as the programmers. I knew then that his company would go big, which it did.

## Metrics Everywhere

Scaling Up's Growth Tools are replete with boxes asking you to pick Key Performance Indicators (KPIs) and Outcomes. We start with the functions and processes driving the business, then push for the company to set goals, delineate measurable Brand Promises, and pick Critical Numbers on the One-Page Strategic Plan, including KPIs for both the People and Process sides of the business so the leadership team has a balanced view of performance.

The challenge is choosing metrics that matter, meaning those that measure what's important to customers, and provide sufficient insight to help both the leadership team and all employees see problems and opportunities in time to react. We refer to these meaningful KPIs as "Moneyball" stats. What are the one or two KPIs that truly drive the outcomes you're seeking.

### What is Your "Moneyball" KPI?

Are you tracking too many things? Are you measuring what matters? The call center industry, where John Ratliff works, measures everything! John even helped his industry trade association create a "gold" awards program where member firms would be mystery-shopped and measured on dozens of call-center-specific attributes.

John employed this same mystery shopping program, at great expense, at all 24 locations and 500+ call center employees. He used this data to evaluate the quality of each location and performance of the local leader.

Then he read *Moneyball*! For those unfamiliar with the book or movie, it details how the Oakland A's, using data analytics, discovered that most of what baseball measures and uses to recruit and compensate players has no correlation to winning games and championships!

Like the team's GM Billy Beane (played by Brad Pitt in the movie), John wondered if any of what he was measuring correlated to outcomes that mattered. Choosing client retention, his COO then compared each location's retention numbers with its "gold" quality score. Because the universe likes to have the last laugh, the location with the highest quality score had the lowest client retention and the location with the lowest quality score had the highest! The rest of the diagram was scattered.

Searching for that one Moneyball stat, like on-base percentage in baseball, John's team discovered it was the employee Net Promoter Score (eNPS). It may seem strange, but having happy employees leads to happy clients! This became the Moneyball KPI that drove everything else — and ultimately led to employee turnover that was 1/10th the industry average, and profitability that was 5x what peers were averaging.

What is your Moneyball stat? In completing the FACe tool, it's better to start with the end in mind — filling in the last column (outcomes/results) and working backwards. Verify, using regression analysis, that the KPIs you're measuring correlate to the results for each function and the overall firm; then recruit leaders who can deliver on these KPIs.

However, quantitative metrics alone provide an incomplete view. Qualitative insights from conversations with the market and observations of customers and competitors fill out the data set needed to guide decisions. Input from advisors, experts, and "the crowd" also contribute. Piling all of this data into computers and our brains and engaging in healthy, frequent debate helps leaders make decisions — regarding hiring, product, marketing, etc. — with a high degree of confidence.

By following processes and routines like these, Roger Hardy and his team at Coastal.com, highlighted in the introduction to this section, have scaled up a company that's now worth almost half a billion dollars. Following are detailed recommendations and examples of growth firms that are putting these weekly habits in place to gather the kinds of data — quantitative and qualitative — that are critical to supporting the important leadership capabilities of prediction, delegation, and repetition.

 **WARNING:** *If talking with customers and employees routinely is so powerful, why do leaders stop doing it? It's because they continue to hear the same recurring issues or praise over and over — and have to take time from their busy schedules to listen to stories that seem to have zero relevance to their businesses. However, it takes only one or two key ideas to fuel a business model. So hang in there, embrace the human aspects of these conversations, and relish the moment the light bulb goes on — it will!!*

Let's now look at the details of collecting input from employees first: Rockefeller Habit #5.

# Rockefeller Habit #5: Gather Employee Input

**5. Ongoing employee input is collected to identify obstacles and opportunities.**
- [ ] All executives (and middle managers) have a Start/Stop/Keep conversation with at least one employee weekly.
- [ ] The insights from employee conversations are shared at the weekly executive team meeting.
- [ ] Employee input about obstacles and opportunities is being collected weekly.
- [ ] A mid-management team is responsible for the process of closing the loop on all obstacles and opportunities.

Have you noticed the humongous Big Ass Fans in airports and warehouses around the world? Manufacturer Big Ass Solutions, a rapidly growing Kentucky firm, rocketed from $34 million in revenue in 2009 to $240 million in 2016 before exiting for $500 million to a PE firm. More important, its employee retention ran 93% vs. a US average of 63%. Founder and Chief Big Ass Carey Smith (now that's a title!) accomplished all this through a series of initiatives. Besides offering top-tier perks — including an on-site health clinic, subsidized catered lunches, and a game room (hey, this isn't Silicon Valley) — Smith and his top leaders took half a dozen workers to dinner at one of the area's best restaurants each week. What better way to tap into the rumor mill, pick up ideas, and share a little bit of the company's DNA with the team?

## Bring Every Brain Into the Game

Walton, back in 1962, saw the value of meeting with employees weekly to seek their ideas for making the business better, which was quite progressive at the time. Without a formal routine to prompt members of your team to share their perspectives, you risk having those ideas walk out the door at the end of every day. Worse yet, your workers miss an opportunity to contribute and feel good about it.

At a minimum, we recommend that *all executives (and middle team leaders) have a Start/Stop/Keep conversation with at least one employee weekly.* Even though you might see a lot of your employees each week, stopping by for a casual chat or two, that is not the same as having a 15- to 45-minute focused conversation with an individual or a group of employees to gather feedback and ideas. Choose employees who work directly with customers and those newest to the company. Recent hires will have fresh eyes that lead them to notice things longer-term employees have come to accept.

Here are three simple questions that we recommend you use when holding these conversations:

- *What should we **start** doing?*
- *What should we **stop** doing?*
- *What should we **keep** doing?*

We encourage leaders to pay particular attention to the "stop doing" responses. They are likely destroying the motivation of the employees, as we discussed in "The Team" chapter.

 **NOTE:** *Some might equate these questions to the creation-preservation-destruction cycle from Hindu mythology.*

 **HINT:** *In some company cultures, this type of conversation may feel strange at first. Don't be surprised if there's awkward chitchat at the beginning of the conversations. What's important is that by the end, you've reminded your employees that it might be months before they have this opportunity for a one-on-one again. Ask them one more time if there is anything else they think should be started, stopped, or kept, and they will normally open up.*

### Markitforce's Employee Lunches

Founder and Chief Engagement Officer Alan Higgins spends a lot of time focusing on the culture at Markitforce, a Sydney-based firm that creates fulfillment campaigns and offers warehousing, distribution, and account management services in the warehousing industry. He takes one employee out for lunch each week to learn more about him. Before the meal, he asks the employee to answer a few questions that are discussed during lunch: What should Markitforce start doing, stop doing, and keep doing? What does the staffer love and loathe about his job? What are his 101 goals in life — both professional and personal? "I tell them to write this stuff down, because if they write it down, it will happen. Things just start to fall into place," says Higgins. "It's pretty powerful. And, as a leader, it's my objective to help them check things off their list."

## Discuss at the Weekly Management Meeting

Rather than create detailed reports that no one has the time to read, Higgins shares insights from his conversations with employees at the weekly executive team meeting. He includes 10 minutes on the agenda for sharing employee feedback (detailed in "The Meeting Rhythm" chapter). Hearing his stories gives the leaders a better feel for the pulse of the business.

If you plan to act on any concrete "start" or "stop" ideas, feed them into a more formal employee-suggestion process. Also include information from the "stucks" mentioned in the daily huddles, which we will also describe in the upcoming chapter.

## Ongoing Feedback

Collect weekly input from employees about obstacles and opportunities. To keep this from turning into a collection of gripes, provide some prompts. Ask employees to submit suggestions that will:

1. Increase revenue.
2. Reduce costs.
3. Make something easier/better for the customers or employees.

Ways to tap into employee ideas include 3M's "15 percent rule," launched in 1948, which allows employees to spend a proportion of paid time on projects of their own choosing. Google, Apple, and other companies now have similar policies. At Sydney-based software firm Atlassian, employees get 24 hours to produce innovations on "ShipIt" days. And Jimmy Calano, who built CareerTrack Inc. into the largest one-day-seminar company in the world, and sold it to cable conglomerate TCI, implemented what he called a 3I program.

Each month, every manager (Calano had 40 at the time) had to submit three ideas for increasing revenue, reducing costs, or making something easier at the Colorado-based company. Calano would spend the Sunday morning before the Monday monthly management meeting going over the 120 ideas and writing detailed responses, especially for concepts that needed more work to implement. He would then choose the top 20 ideas for the month and announce them at the management meeting, handing each winner a crisp $20 bill for fun.

The 3I program gave Calano real insight into the gaps in knowledge among his frontline and team leaders, affording him many "teachable moments" when responding to their submissions. And Calano could document millions of dollars' worth of improvements from these ideas. Equally important, having to submit three ideas every month forced all of his leaders to seek input from frontline employees and customers.

## Close the Loop

Gathering employees' feedback and ideas will backfire on the company if management doesn't close the loop and act on their suggestions. At a minimum, let an employee know why an idea can't be implemented.

The biggest obstacle is finding the time. The senior team doesn't need any more to-do's. Therefore, we strongly recommend *holding a middle-leadership team responsible for responding to employees' feedback on all obstacles and opportunities.* This is an excellent executive-development opportunity for a group of up-and-coming leaders as they gather and react to the suggestions and work cross-functionally to implement them.

And just as you probably track the number of days you take to pay your vendors (accounts payable days) or to get paid (accounts receivable days), we suggest that you track the number of days it takes to implement the ideas gathered from your employees. Have the middle-management team that is driving this process create a "Suggestion Aging Report" tracking how many ideas are 30, 60, and 90 days past due.

Last, be transparent with employees. Set up an internal Web portal where all suggestions are listed (unedited) with updates on progress, or simply write them on a huge whiteboard in the break room and erase them only when they've been addressed. In addition, publish updates in internal newsletters.

 **WARNING:** *Any submissions that single out individuals in a negative way should, of course, be handled privately and never be posted.*

# Rockefeller Habit #6: Gather Customer Input

6. **Reporting and analysis of customer feedback data is as frequent and accurate as financial data.**
   - ☐ All executives (and middle managers) have a 4Q conversation with at least one end user weekly.
   - ☐ The insights from customer conversations are shared at the weekly executive team meeting.
   - ☐ All employees are involved in collecting customer data.
   - ☐ A mid-management team is responsible for the process of closing the loop on all customer feedback.

Sanjeev Mohanty was CEO of India's #1 international fashion brand as of 2014, when Benetton India Private Ltd. surpassed Levi's to take over the top spot. He attributes the company's rapid growth and success to its intense daily interaction with its more than 5 million customers. Through a process launched after its first Rockefeller Habits workshop, he placed signs in the stores requesting that customers send feedback via email. In addition, as required by law, Benetton printed an email address on every clothing tag.

Most retailers merely pay lip service to the notion of listening to customers' complaints and suggestions. Mohanty automatically received a copy of every submission and replied directly to several every day (while his team followed up on all of the rest). If the customer gave a phone number, he would call the patron. This generated wildly positive word-of-mouth enthusiasm for Benetton India. And Mohanty and his team picked up clues from these conversations that drove many of the innovative clothing lines outside the company's main offering, which helped him rapidly scale up revenue and the brand.

 (**NOTE**: *Levi Strauss recruited Mohanty and in 2017 he become Managing Director & SVP — South Asia, Middle East & North Africa for the company! Mohanty went on to win the "Retail Icon" award in India in 2019)).*

Down the road in Bangalore, 4,200-employee QuEST Global Engineering Pvt. Ltd. landed a five-year, $50 million contract, thanks to its efforts to get feedback from customers. Competing with 2,000 vendors, QuEST made it into the final two. Ajay Prabhu, COO, made a winning move — right into the Marriott hotel across the street from the prospect's offices. Every day, Prabhu and a senior vice president met there with people at all levels of the potential customer's company, so they could improve QuEST's proposal in real time.

"We really gathered all the 'what ifs' and learned what issues might work against us," says Prabhu. "When we finally submitted the proposal, all the customer contact had been a game changer for us. The customer could see we were paying attention to them and to the details. And we were able to make decisions quickly while our competition, being a much larger company, had to go through several different layers of management back at HQ to get an answer. In our case, the decision-makers were right next to the customer. It was like we were camping out together."

QuEST also surveys customers immediately after completing projects. If the results are not satisfactory, it completes a detailed analysis of what went wrong. However, Prabhu notes, "While customer satisfaction is important, there has to be a balance." QuEST uses a triple scorecard approach to satisfaction — measuring satisfaction among customers, employees, and the company itself. The first two, customer (c-stat) and employee (e-stat) satisfaction, are benchmarked against industry standards. The third one, QuEST Satisfaction (q-stat), is used to evaluate whether or not to accept projects. "We don't take projects until they meet QuEST Satisfaction. It has to be a client that we can make more efficient and profitable, and it has to fit with our strategy," says Prabhu.

## Conversations With Customers

*We implore all executives and team leaders to have a 4 Questions (4Q) conversation with at least one end user weekly.* Particularly in business-to-business situations, you may have to bypass your distribution channels and purchasing agents (with permission) and talk directly with those benefiting from your products and services.

The 4Q refers to the four questions that we suggest leaders ask customers in person (not on a survey):

1. How are you doing?
2. What's going on in your industry/neighborhood?
3. What do you hear about our competitors?
4. How are we doing?

The key is to get them to talk about their favorite subject: themselves!! The first question will give you an understanding of their current situation: What are their pain points? What are their priorities for the coming year?

And for salespeople in a B-to-B situation, find out what the person's bonus is tied to. You don't need to know the amount, but your goal is to show how your products and services can help them achieve their targets.

The second question offers insight into industry trends in general. What are the newest changes or technologies? Who is buying whom in the industry? And if you are talking with consumers, what are they and their neighbors thinking/feeling/talking about?

The third query is probably most important, because it can help you cut through your own biases. It was this question that helped Coastal.com realize that it shouldn't lower its prices to ward off ankle-biting, low-price competitors. When Hardy's leadership team asked customers point-blank what they thought of its competitors, they raved instead about Coastal.com and its rapid response to phone calls and customer service.

Only after you've asked your customers these three questions should you ask about their reactions to your offerings, if they have not shared these already. Remember, this call is about them, not you!

In a business-to-business environment, have all senior leaders connect with their counterparts at customers' companies (e.g., your CFO should talk with the client's CFO). Communicating with other specialists in their area will allow them to pick up insights others will miss.

Look at these efforts as an investment in customer retention. At rapidly growing companies, the team is often so busy chasing new opportunities that the existing clients feel ignored. If companies were able to hold on to the customers they now lose from neglect, it would fuel at least half of their growth.

## Using Social Media

Coastal.com came out of a two-day planning session struggling with ideas on how to grow. So Hardy and his management team decided to call 30 to 40 customers every Friday for feedback. To Hardy's surprise, the same theme surfaced: Patrons wanted their contact lenses the next day. "Speed is very much a part of the business, and we heard that message from customers," says Hardy. When customers order contacts, they are often on their last pair. "We started overnighting everything, and sales grew 60% in one of our markets," Hardy says.

Today, Hardy reports that as consumers spend more time on social media, it can be challenging to get feedback through phone calls. "We were at a point where we were leaving 40 messages and not getting as much feedback. It was unproductive," he says. Now Coastal.com uses SurveyMonkey to get feedback immediately after a purchase, using the NPS. The company also relies on comments through Facebook, which can be left easily and quickly. "We try to figure out hot spots from the comments we get through social media," says Hardy.

## Discuss at the Weekly Meeting

*Share insights from conversations with customers at the executive team's weekly huddle.* Don't bog down the process with a bunch of written reports.

At global consulting firm Bain & Co., loyalty practice founder Fred Reichheld and his team found a company in almost every sector that was growing top-line revenue 2.5 times faster than its competitors. So they set out to identify what these companies did differently. At the "good" companies, the executive team spent zero time discussing what it was hearing from customers at its weekly meeting. The only time a customer's name came up was if there was a crisis. (Think about your own weekly meeting!) In contrast, the "great" companies — which, like Enterprise Rent-A-Car, were growing considerably faster — spent roughly 20% of their leadership team's meeting discussing feedback from customers.

## Involve All Employees (Especially Salespeople)

Whichever competitor has the most market intelligence, and uses it, wins. The fastest-growing companies of this century — Facebook, Google, Amazon, Booking.com, and Netflix — have built business models predicated on being able to tap into more input from customers than anyone else. Using powerful algorithms to discern correlations from users' actions gives them a great deal of their insight. Much of their data also emerges from enticing customers to make comments and leave ratings for innumerable products and services online. We're in an era in which people don't trust large institutions. Instead, they turn to "the crowd" to help them figure out which doctor or vacation spot to visit.

Appletree Answers, highlighted in the "People" section, built an application on top of its CRM system, called Idea Flash, to collect suggestions from its frontline call-center people by the minute. With this program, the agents log ideas and issues from customers during live conversations and add their own suggestions and observations into a central database so these valuable insights do not get lost. In the first 90 days (when Idea Flash was Appletree's Quarterly Theme), employees generated more than 8,800 ideas, and they have continued to supply the company with 3,000 to 5,000 every quarter since. Just one of the thousands of ideas submitted resulted in a $17,000-per-month profit for a client. Now that's turning customer feedback into customer service.

It's particularly important to encourage all your salespeople, distributors, and independent reps (in all of your sales channels) to gather and report market intelligence. Require all of them to call in daily to a voice mailbox and leave a three-minute update on any positive sales results. (Salespeople like to share good news.) Ask them to provide feedback from customers and about competitors and report on barriers they are facing in making sales. Do not ask them to put this information in writing, or it won't happen. (The only written report is the one you threaten to make them write if they don't call in daily!) Most Internet-based phone systems have the capability of converting voice messages into text messages, so you will have your salespeople's thoughts in writing without having to listen to a bunch of voice mails.

## Again, Close the Loop

As with employee feedback, *hold a middle-leadership team responsible for the process of closing the loop on all customer feedback.* This team normally reports to the senior leader accountable for the customer advocacy function listed on the FACe chart, which can be found in the "People" section.

### Getting the Most Out of Net Promoter Scores

We have mentioned the NPS several times throughout the book as our preferred way to measure customer satisfaction (advocacy) and engagement. Fred Reichheld popularized it in his book, *The Ultimate Question: Driving Good Profits and True Growth*, and today's revised and expanded version, *The Ultimate Question 2.0: How Net Promoter Companies Thrive in a Customer-Driven World*. In short, the idea is that satisfied customers can be passive, transacting with you but not necessarily engaged. For growing companies, engaged customers —those that are thrilled enough to tell others about you —are critical for profitable growth. The NPS measures the net percentage of your customers who are actively spreading the good word about your company. It is a system that Apple, Enterprise Rent-A-Car, and hundreds of our clients use to manage this aspect of their business.

Beijing-based Gung Ho! Pizza uses the NPS to measure customer satisfaction, linking the results each month directly to employee bonuses — along with the four Brand Promises and a sales

target. Each day, every store sends out two questionnaires with delivery people to randomly selected existing customers, for a total of 60 surveys per month. To keep it simple, the survey asks four questions, including the NPS question, "Would you recommend us to a friend?" It also includes a spot for the customer to add a phone number. Then the Gung Ho! Team calls these customers to learn how the company might do better.

## Rockefeller Habit #9: KPIs for Everyone

**9. All employees can answer quantitatively whether they had a good day or week (Column 7 of the One-Page Strategic Plan).**

- ☐ 1 or 2 Key Performance Indicators (KPIs) are reported on weekly for each role/person.
- ☐ Each employee has 1 Critical Number that aligns with the company's Critical Number for the quarter (clear line of sight).
- ☐ Each individual/team has 3-5 Quarterly Priorities/Rocks that align with those of the company.
- ☐ All executives and middle managers have a coach (or peer coach) holding them accountable to behavior changes.

This habit is linked directly to column 7 of the One-Page Strategic Plan, discussed in the "Strategy" section. It is important to have a clear plan for the company for the next quarter. In turn, each team and person needs individual quarterly goals that align with the plan. This creates "line of sight," as discussed in the "People" section, so every employee feels connected to the vision and direction of the company.

## Did I Have a Great Day or Week?

Every member of the team, from the senior leadership to staffers, needs to be able to answer objectively the question, "Did I have a great day or week?" The key: Each person must report on *one or two KPIs weekly.*

Australia-based Shine Lawyers has five measurable goals. All employees in the business have the same goals, with their corresponding KPIs changing depending on their role. "We get alignment this way," shares Managing Director Simon Morrison. "And when you go into anyone's office, you'll see their five goals." Shine creates a strategy card for each of the five goals and their corresponding KPIs. "Previously we counted 30 different reports that we were sending our leaders, so this is a nice, compact way to align everyone's goal to the same tool to manage the business," he adds.

Some companies use a whiteboard that gets updated daily or weekly (and discussed at meetings), and some print charts from spreadsheets and post them on the wall. Still others have dashboard systems, like our Scaling Up Scoreboard, to automatically generate live data. You will succeed only if every team member in your company looks at the information and makes adjustments or decisions based on their KPIs weekly.

The most respected leaders of some of the largest companies do the same. A *Bloomberg Businessweek* article titled "The Happiest Man in Detroit," by Keith Naughton, highlights former Ford Motor CEO Alan Mulally and his weekly 2½-hour Business Plan Reviews with the 15 top Ford executives. In this meeting, Mulally's direct reports were required to "post more than 300 charts, each of them color-coded red, yellow, or green to indicate problems, caution, or progress." There was no hiding from data with Mulally at the helm. As he said: "You can't manage a secret. When you do this every week, you can't hide." Clearly, the charts were telling the truth, and through this rigorous discipline, Mulally and the leadership team drove changes that without a doubt drove profits.

## One Critical Number and 3 to 5 Rocks

Everyone is busy. The magic of the Scaling Up process is getting everyone in the company to accomplish one additional thing that is aligned with the company's focus every 90 days (i.e., *each employee has one Critical Number that aligns with the company's Critical Number for the quarter, illustrating that there is a clear line of sight*). If you have 10 employees, you can get 10 more things accomplished; if you have 1,000 employees, you can get even more done.

And like the company, all employees or teams need to set a handful of priorities (known as rocks) that will help them achieve their Critical Number (i.e., *each individual/team should have three to five rocks that align with those of the company*).

AmRest Holdings SE, an international restaurant company based in Poland, uses a scorecard system across the whole company called its Disciplined Operating System (DOS+). The scorecards are integrated with the company's One-Page Strategic Plan (OPSP), giving everyone insight into exactly how the company is performing against its KPIs, which span financial, people, and customer metrics. DOS starts at the restaurant level by the 2nd of each month and then rolls up to the regional level, district level, brand president, and division president before the scorecards come to co-founder and Chairman Henry McGovern by the 7th of each month.

 **NOTE:** *McGovern, after 25 years at the helm, retired in 2019 after scaling AmRest to more than 49,000 employees working in over 2300 restaurants in 16 countries. And in 2019 AmRest won "Retailer of the Year."*

## Peer Coach

*All executives and team leaders should have a coach (or peer coach) holding them accountable for behavioral changes.* We strongly encourage companies to get an external coach (ideally, a Scaling Up Certified coach) to lead their quarterly and annual planning sessions, and check in monthly to monitor progress.

Everyone should find a peer coach internally at the company, too. Based on your own column 7 of the OPSP and decisions you made on your own One-Page Personal Plan (discussed in "The Leaders" chapter), choose five behaviors or actions you need to start or stop, and then report your progress each day to your peer coach. For more details, search for "Marshall Goldsmith peer coach" on the Web, and you'll find a free document that further details the process. We also have the link on *scalingup.com*.

# Rockefeller Habit #10: Scoreboards Everywhere

**10. The company's plans and performance are visible to everyone.**
- ☐ A "situation room" is established for weekly meetings (physical or virtual).
- ☐ Core Values, Purpose and Priorities are posted throughout the company.
- ☐ Scoreboards are up everywhere displaying current progress on KPIs and Critical Numbers.
- ☐ There is a system in place for tracking and managing the cascading Priorities and KPIs.

We're not big on using sports analogies in business books. In sports, the team gets to practice 90% of the time and perform 10%. In business, it's the opposite: We're lucky if we get 10% of the time to practice through executive training and development.

However, we can all take a page from sport facilities. Even if you're seated in the nosebleed section of a stadium and can barely see the action on the field, you can always see the score. And now that everything has gone mobile, the real-time digital scoreboards available to anyone following her favorite team and sport should be the standards by which we monitor our own company performance.

## Scaling Up

Here's a photo of the digital scoreboard at Australian experience-gifts retailer RedBalloon, one of several visible to everyone in the company and updated in real time. We like how it is made to look like an old-fashioned set of paper charts, though this is all displayed on a large flat-screen monitor.

At a minimum, have your metrics, goals, and plans up big and visible in a place where you host the various weekly meetings (i.e., *establish a "situation room" for weekly meetings, whether they're physical or virtual. In the case of a virtual meeting, the "room" might be a particular conference line*).

Here's what the meeting room looks like at The Miner Corporation, a Texas-based company serving the warehousing and materials-management industries — including a bigger-than-life printout of its OPSP.

Make sure that the *Core Values, Purpose, and Priorities are posted throughout the company*. At Ezypay, Australia's largest direct-debit service provider, Core Values are displayed on walls around the office — in some cases from floor to ceiling, including in the boardroom.

To support daily meetings in its head office, Gung Ho! Pizza created a "situation room" that has all the key elements of its culture, Purpose, and KPIs visible for everyone to see.

Also, highly visible on a wall in the back of each location are these same key elements of the situation room — including the OPSP — distilled down to the store level for frontline teams to see.

Jade Gray and John O'Loghlen, co-founders of Gung Ho! Pizza, are building a franchise model. Making it simple for employees in the stores to see the same information as employees at headquarters is essential to building engagement. "We have numerous locations, and employees don't always have a chance to come to the head office," says Gray. "Everyone from our cleaner to our store manager can look at the wall [in their store] at the start of each daily meeting. This ensures we are aligned. I can walk into a store and speak with a cleaner and nine times out of 10, he or she can tell me what the Purpose of the company is and give me the meaning behind it and why we're in business. How to align the entire team is the biggest thing this methodology has taught me."

## Accountability Management Systems

At some point, when the company is bigger than 50 employees and expanding into multiple locations, keeping track of all the cascading priorities, metrics, and data can become an Excel-spreadsheet nightmare. And as a growing company must continue to upgrade its accounting, CRM, and operational systems, it is important to *have a system in place for tracking and managing the cascading Priorities and KPIs.*

There are several software-as-a-service offerings that give you the capability to update your OPSP online and track all the KPIs and Priorities that arise from a disciplined execution process — and track via your smartphones and tablets. Scaling Up has outstanding offerings, one being *Scaling Up Scoreboard*, which gives you the capability to update your OPSP online and track all the KPI's and Priorities that arise from a disciplined execution process — and track via your smartphones and tablets.

Having a single place to house all of this very important data, not only makes your business run more efficiently, but your team as a whole will have much greater transparency and alignment to the big company objectives that you set.

The end goal is to keep the output from the Growth Tools top-of-mind, like the score of your favorite individual athlete or team.

In the final chapter of the "Execution" section, we outline a set of meeting rhythms that give everyone a routine through which all the input, data, and metrics can be discussed and debated, and decisions can be made.

# 11

# THE MEETING RHYTHM
## The Heartbeat of the Organization

---

**EXECUTIVE SUMMARY:** *To move faster, pulse faster. At the heart of a team's performance is a rhythm of well-run daily, weekly, monthly, quarterly, and annual meetings. These meetings bring focus and alignment, provide an opportunity to solve problems more quickly, and ultimately save time. They also address the #1 challenge people face when they work together: communications. In this chapter, we outline specific agendas and recommendations on who should attend meetings. The monthly meeting is a KEY routine for developing team leaders into mini-CEOs so they are capable of running the business (execution), freeing up senior leaders to focus on strategy. We'll also look at the #1 roadblock to effective meetings: generalities.*

---

Reading *Titan: The Life of John D. Rockefeller, Sr.*, by Ron Chernow, Verne was struck by the magnate's daily luncheon routine. Each day, without fail, he'd sit down with his key people, have lunch, and talk with them. At first, the meetings included only Rockefeller and the four co-founders of Standard Oil. But as the decades wore on and the company grew, the meetings came to include Rockefeller's nine directors. And yes, they continued to meet daily.

A century later, Steve Jobs repeated the same ritual, having lunch almost every day with Apple design genius Jonathan Ive. The late T. Boone Pickens credited a routine of daily strategy meetings, including breakfast each morning with his team, for turning $2.7 million into $4 billion.

Consciously or not, these leaders understood the root meaning of the word *company:* "to share bread." By gathering their team each day for a meal, they strengthened their personal and professional relationships. Fortified for another day, each could go out and do his share to conquer his industry or whatever the current target might be. Did it matter that the meetings occurred daily? No doubt Rockefeller and Jobs would have said an emphatic "Yes!"

And the benefits? "We all know each other very well," said Pickens, commenting about his team in an interview honoring him as *D CEO's* CEO of the Year at age 85. "We shouldn't make many mistakes, and we don't make many." Communicating frequently and breaking bread together assure that this is the case.

## Great Music vs. Noise

Great growth firms are a lot like great jazz bands. While jazz is improvisational and entrepreneurial-like, the discipline underlying it allows even musicians who have never played together before to perform a rocking jam session. This requires four things:

1. **Assembling talented musicians:** They play a variety of instruments, creating a unique sound.

2. **Knowing the rules:** All jazz musicians must master a handful of fundamentals (the Core).

3. **Performing the same song:** This is the equivalent of the One-Page Strategic Plan (OPSP).

4. **Playing to the same beat:** What the drummer communicates to the band, the meeting rhythm does for the organization (alignment).

All of this structure allows for constant and endless improvisation by each player, which is what makes jazz unique and powerful. Imagine if all members of your team could independently and confidently wing it in their roles in a way you knew would be consistent with the company culture and objectives.

Yet playing jazz isn't easy. Great jazz bands just make it look that way. The same goes for great companies. Exceptional firms produce something beautiful, and the rest just make a bunch of noise.

The "People" and "Strategy" sections of this book touch on the jazz band equivalents of the first three factors listed above: including A Players, relying on the Core, and getting everyone on the same page (using the OPSP). This chapter addresses the all-important drumbeat of the organization. And it is a rhythm of communication that drives alignment throughout the organization — a steady day-day-day-day-week, day-day-day-day-week, day-day-day-day-week, day-day-day-day-month. (We'll spare you the entire year!)

Regular meetings act as place holders in everyone's calendar. Because it often takes longer to set up meetings than it does to hold them, pre scheduling reduces hassles in organizing them. Most matters can wait for the daily huddle or the weekly meeting. Bigger issues, which necessitate getting everyone in a room for a few hours, can be addressed during the monthly team leader meeting.

In the best-run global companies, the CEO's calendar is preprogrammed 200+ days of the year. For a glimpse into these meeting rhythm disciplines, read Chapter 11 on meetings in *Managing Up: How to Forge an Effective Relationship With Those Above You*, by Rosanne Badowski. She was Jack Welch's longstanding executive assistant and has written a book that we highly recommend all executive assistants read. Welch, former CEO of General Electric, had his calendar of meetings planned a year in advance, including the one day each month he spent teaching and learning at Crotonville, GE's executive training center.

As the diagram above indicates, this rhythm of meetings shouldn't require more than 10% of a standard 40-, 50-, or 60-hour workweek for the senior leadership; 5% to 7% for team leaders, and 3% for frontline staff. Naturally, there will be other meetings — with customers, suppliers, investors, etc. — but this daily, weekly, monthly, quarterly, and yearly rhythm of meetings is sufficient to manage the business.

## More Frequent Meetings

Many companies have quarterly and annual meetings. In our methodology, the key agenda for these meetings is updating the Growth Tools, including the OPSP.

Having more frequent routines makes it easier to attain goals. This is why the daily, weekly, and monthly meetings are critical. They drive the deliverables outlined in the less frequent meetings, with each meeting building upon the next. Plus, teams need regular, face-to-face huddles to discuss new opportunities, strategic concerns, and bottlenecks as they arise. How many hours is it going to take to hammer out a set of goals for a new year, if the annual meeting is the first time anybody has talked about where the market is going or dealt with the tactical issues that come up weekly?

### Competing on Internet Time

The faster you're growing, the faster your meeting rhythm should pulse. In general, if you're growing less than 15% per year, you can treat each year like a year from a strategic-thinking standpoint. If you're growing 20% to 100% a year, view each *quarter* as if it were a year. That means possibly adjusting your strategy every 90 days. If you're among the elite, more than doubling your revenue each year, you're living the equivalent of "dog years" and need to treat each *month* as if it were a year. For more discussion on this hyperpulsing style of management, read the seminal book *Competing on Internet Time: Lessons From Netscape and Its Battle With Microsoft* by Michael A. Cusumano and David B. Yoffie.

## A Case for More Storytelling

Before digging into the specifics of meeting rhythms, let us make a case for upping the overall talk time in organizations. To do this, we need to go back in time. It's estimated that humans have been around for 200,000 years, the spoken word for 100,000, the written word for just over 5,000 years, and electronic spreadsheets for less than 50!

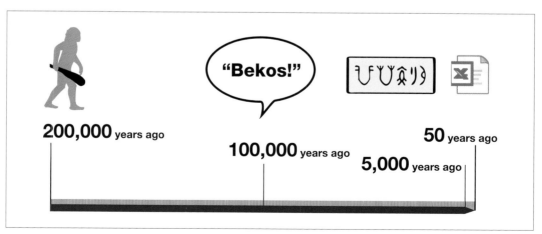

## Scaling Up

Two things have been crucial to humans' survival. One is pattern recognition, the most important cognitive skill connected to extreme success in any field. The other is hearing. You can hear prey long before you can see, touch, or taste it (or it tastes you!). Hearing stories, information, and even numbers connects more deeply to our pattern-recognition capabilities than staring at Excel spreadsheets.

On the flip side, brain-wave scans show that we need to talk out our problems. When we speak, the prefrontal cortex of our brain — the source of executive and cognitive power — lights up like a Christmas tree. It's this power that members of the Young Presidents' Organization, Entrepreneurs' Organization, Vistage, and other CEO organizations experience in their monthly forums (confidential meetings of eight to 10 leaders free to talk about anything). Ninety percent of the benefit is the chance members get to speak about the deeper challenges or bigger opportunities facing them.

### Walk-and-Talks

"Walk-and-talks" became a favorite problem-solving technique of Steve Jobs. Science backs up the power of this simple routine. It's rooted in the same principles that underlie Eye Movement Desensitization and Reprocessing, a new therapy successful in helping people who suffer from trauma, anxiety, panic, disturbing memories, post-traumatic stress and many other emotional problems. It involves the bilateral stimulation of both sides of the brain by moving the eyes left and right repeatedly. (If you catch yourself bouncing your legs when stressed, it's the same mechanism). Walking is found to have a similar calming effect that brings the brain down from an agitated beta state to a more focused and calm alpha state. Combine walking with talking, something Jobs and Rockefeller did a lot of, and you have a powerful cognitive tool at your disposal.

Since the advent of texting, speaking has gone out of style. It is coming back with technologies like Siri and Cortana, that are getting us engaged once again in talking (and hearing) — which our brain loves!

## Three Powerful Advantages to Meeting Regularly

The two main arguments we hear for not meeting regularly, especially for the daily huddle:

1. We don't have the time.
2. We see each other all day anyway.

To address the time issue: If your meetings follow our agendas, they save time. If you need a colleague's input to answer a customer's question, you don't have to tell the caller, "I'll try to find her and get back to you sometime today." You can name the time, because you know you'll have the answer by the end of your daily (or weekly) meeting. Nor will you be going over the same water-cooler conversation three or four times, as is the case when you rely on chance hallway meetings for communication. Because everyone is together in a daily meeting, things get communicated quickly and accurately.

As for the second point: Bumping into each other all day doesn't substitute for tightly focused team discussions. And a lot of that bumping is causing unnecessary interruptions. Casual encounters fail to take advantage of the three most powerful tools a leader has in getting team performance:

1. **Peer pressure**
2. **Collective intelligence**
3. **Clear communication**

By holding one-on-one conversations with their team members in lieu of a weekly meeting, leaders lose these advantages. Unless these individual sessions are for coaching, there can be a lot of private negotiating going on ("You know what I'm up against. ..."), putting the leader in the constant position of being the bad guy.

Meeting as a group, in contrast, takes the heat off the leader and creates peer pressure that increases the rate of deliverables. What a shame to have a high-powered executive or middle-management team that doesn't take even 15 minutes each day or an hour a week to focus its collective intelligence on the opportunities at hand. Last, holding a team meeting means that everyone is hearing the same information. You don't have to repeat the same message three or four times in one-on-ones or casual conversations.

### One-On-Ones

Why do CEOs spend time in one-on-ones with their direct reports each week? Because somewhere along the way they were told to do so. Consuming hours of precious time, these meetings are fraught with all of the issues mentioned above, putting heat on the CEO to hold their individual team members accountable vs. letting peer pressure do the work.

We've yet to find a CEO, who ever went back after replacing their regular one-on-ones with a quick 8-minute daily team huddle. In addition to the 5x – 10x return on time (32 minutes of dailies vs. 4 hours of one-on-ones), the magic of the daily is you're hearing from your team their priorities, data, and constraints daily, and thus you're seeing patterns sooner — and know if you need a quick one-on-one meetup that day vs. later in the week after the issue has expanded or the opportunity has passed.

Lower down in the organization, we're OK with team leads scheduling 20-minute one-on-one coaching sessions every two weeks — where the key question is "What is your goal/priority the next two weeks and what are the constraints in your way — how can I help?" But if any of a CEO's direct reports need coaching, it's better if handled by a professional coach — a role the late "Trillion Dollar Coach" Bill Campbell filled for Apple and our Scaling Up Certified coaches can fill for you.

Let's look more closely at the specific meetings and agendas that drive alignment and communication — Rockefeller Habit #3.

# Rockefeller Habit #3: Meeting Rhythm

> **3. Communication rhythm is established and information moves through organization accurately and quickly.**
> ☐ All employees are in a daily huddle that lasts less than 15 minutes.
> ☐ All teams have a weekly meeting.
> ☐ The executive and middle managers meet for a day of learning, resolving big issues, and DNA transfer each month.
> ☐ Quarterly and annually, the executive and middle managers meet offsite to work on the 4 Decisions.

This rhythm of meetings is designed to support cascading communication around the priorities and metrics-driving strategy. Specifically:

1. **The daily huddle.** A 5- to 15-minute meeting to discuss tactical issues and provide updates. This will help you avoid minor train wrecks and to take quick advantage of unforeseen opportunities. Normally, a daily huddle saves everyone an hour or so of needless email updates and ad hoc interruptions. Issues that emerge drive the main topics for the weekly meeting.

2. **The weekly meeting.** A 60- to 90-minute discussion to review progress on the quarterly priorities and tap the collective brainpower of the team in addressing one or two main topics. This meeting also provides a time to discuss the market intelligence gathered that week from customers, employees, and competitors. Repeated patterns of discussion determine the one or two main issues for the monthly meeting.

3. **The monthly management meeting.** A half- to full-day meeting, in which all senior, middle, and frontline leaders come together to learn and collaboratively address one or two big issues requiring several hours of effort. It's also designed to transfer DNA (knowledge, values, approach) from upper to middle management.

4. **The quarterly and annual planning meetings.** At this one- to three-day offsite meeting, leaders update the Growth Tools and establish the next quarterly and/or annual theme. Once each quarter, the leadership team shares an update of the new plans with all employees in a 45-minute meeting.

 **NOTE:** *Examine the meeting rhythm above in reverse order to see how the more frequent gatherings draw context and continuity from the longer and more strategic planning sessions. Specifically:*

- *The annual sets the strategic direction and priorities for the year and beyond.*

- *The quarterly breaks these longer-term priorities into bite-sized priorities that the company can digest.*

- *The monthly addresses the bigger issues or opportunities that surface around the strategic direction.*

- *The weekly keeps the priorities top-of-mind and drives discussions around input from customers, employees, and competitors, which feeds back into the quarterly and annual planning processes.*

- *The daily huddle tracks progress and brings out sticking points that are blocking execution of the strategic direction.*

Let's take a look at each type of meeting in more depth, examining the structure, timing, and agenda. Equally important, we'll look at why these meetings often fail and discuss how to avoid the pitfalls.

# The Daily Huddle

When Verne labeled the daily huddle an absolute necessity in *Mastering the Rockefeller Habits,* it was because only a few companies were utilizing this important routine. Today, tens of thousands of companies around the world have discovered the freedom and power that comes from implementing this simple rhythm. You even see the daily huddle in best practices like the iterative agile software development framework called Scrum.

In some cultures, issues of saving face make it difficult to share the brutal facts (e.g., the "stucks" mentioned in the daily huddle agenda below). With the help of our coaching partners in Asia and the role modeling of pioneering firms like Ammex Corp. in Shanghai, the daily huddle is now a given in organizations that are serious about making the process of scaling up faster and easier.

*Ammex CEO Fred Crosetto's daily huddle with his senior team.*

## What Kills the Daily — and Most — Meetings?

If the daily huddle is so powerful, why do organizations start and then stop it? In a word, generalities! As teams tell stories and share information, it's critical that they include specifics. We need to hear names, numbers, dates, issues, and concerns if our brain is going to make the kinds of connections that make this process powerful. For instance, if one colleague asks, "What's up tomorrow?" a response like, "I have a meeting with a client" is too vague. More specific and useful is, "I'm meeting with Acme CEO Bob Smith at 10 a.m. to discuss co-hosting a 60-person 'Mastering the Rockefeller Habits' workshop in Cincinnati in the middle of November." These details, which take only a few additional seconds to share, let your team compare this data with information in their own heads:

- Acme is still around and based in Cincinnati — I thought Columbus.
- Bob is still CEO of Acme.
- I might want to participate in the 10 a.m. discussion.
- Is 60 the right number of participants? I thought we agreed on 80.
- Does the middle of November work, given our other commitments?

*Timing* — Set the start of the daily huddle at an odd time, like 8:08 or 16:16. People are more likely to be on time than if you schedule the meeting on the quarter-hour or half-hour. And start the meeting on time, whether everyone is present or not. You don't have a lot of time to waste, and it's important to set that tone from the beginning. It's also important to end on time, not letting the meeting run longer than 15 minutes, or people will drop the habit. We suggest setting a timer for the first few weeks of meetings and ending on time even if the agenda isn't complete. Team members will learn to get to the point and move on to the next item. Plan 1 minute per person, meaning that an eight-person team should expect an eight-minute daily huddle. Time of day? Doesn't matter. Choose whatever time best fits the rhythm of the business.

*Setting* — Meet wherever you want, but stand up or perch on stools. It'll help keep the meeting short. Gathering in the leader's office makes it more convenient for him or her. If some people will dial in regularly, put everyone on a conference call. There's nothing worse than having a few people huddled around a speaker phone every day. We also recommend *against* using videoconferencing, which adds one more level of technology complexity. The exceptions are fixed-based operations that communicate every day. RS Software uses teleconferencing to host its daily standup meeting across 12½ time zones between its offices in Kolkata and Milpitas, California.

*Who Attends* — The general rule is to have more people in fewer meetings, rather than fewer people in more meetings. That's true even if only 10 to 15 participants do most of the sharing. At Microsoft, daily meetings can host up to 60 developers, though only 20 gather in a conference room and the rest attend via the videoconferencing tool NetMeeting when working on a new software release. The Ritz-Carlton gathers about 80 people at headquarters for a 10-minute Daily Line-Up to receive updates from Boston to Bali. Meanwhile, all 40,000+ Ritz-Carlton employees participate in some kind of Daily Line-Up at their local hotels. (A great deal has been written about their Line-Ups. It is worth searching for information online.) In general, frontline employees will be in only one daily huddle, and anyone in management will be in two: one with their direct reports and one with their peers and leader.

 **HINT:** *Daily huddles keep projects between companies/suppliers/customers on time and on budget. Let's say you're working with an IT service provider to install a new CRM system, or with a construction company to build a new facility. Choose someone from your team to interface with a contact on the supplier's team and walk through the same three agenda items listed below. This will keep communication flowing and guarantee your project will get more attention and action.*

 **WARNING:** *We had a client implement daily huddles associated with half a dozen internal projects. The problem: The project teams shared many of the same members, so individuals found themselves in three to five daily huddles, which is unworkable. The solution was to host one daily huddle involving all team members associated with the projects. Only the project leads provide updates (covering six projects in six minutes), and then team members spend the balance of the 15 minutes self-organizing into ad hoc groups to discuss items of interest. This gathering gave everyone a nice 15-minute break from the daily routine and provided the time and place where people could catch up with each other without having to track down and interrupt colleagues the rest of the day.*

*Who Runs the Meeting* — Pick someone who is naturally structured and disciplined (that might not be the CEO) to keep meetings running on time. The leader should use a countdown stopwatch to make sure that no part of the agenda runs away with the meeting. The person running the meeting also has the important job of saying, "Please take it offline" whenever people get off on a tangent that doesn't require everybody's attention.

*The Agenda* — The agenda should be the same every day, and it's just three items long, with five minutes maximum per item:

1. What's up priority (in the next 24 hours)?
2. What are the daily metrics? (All companies should have some.)
3. Where are you stuck (constrained)?

Some teams will mention significant results from the previous day. The Ritz-Carlton and Towne Park, a hotel parking service headquartered in Maryland, review one of their Daily Basics during the daily huddle. Don't pile too much into the daily huddle, or it's going to extend past the 15-minute limit and people will start to resent the meeting.

 **WARNING:** *Avoid checking up on whether someone did something the previous day. Team members will start feeling like they are being micromanaged. In general, looking forward is great management; looking backward is micromanagement.*

Expanding upon the agenda:

**What's up:** In the first five minutes, each attendee spends a few seconds (up to 30) sharing very *specifically* what's up in the next 24 hours (between today's huddle and tomorrow's), particularly their #1 priority. The idea is to let people detect conflicts, crossed agendas, and missed opportunities immediately. These updates should relate to key activities, meetings, decisions, etc., and should NOT be a recitation of someone's daily calendar in 15-minute increments! Team members at Monday's huddle don't need to hear about the sales meeting that happens every Tuesday morning unless there's something unusual or critical coming up.

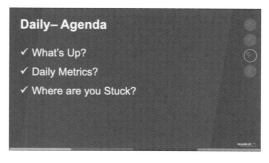

**Daily metrics:** The next five minutes are spent verbalizing the daily metrics that the company monitors: website hits, open positions, proposals submitted, daily sales, cash, workplace accidents, number of consultants deployed, etc. Remember, you're looking for patterns and trends. Since it generally takes six data points to constitute a trend, it's going to take months to see patterns if you look at metrics only every 30 days. If you meet once a day, you'll have a jump on the competition and on your own challenges. We know you may be getting this data in written form. Verbalizing it makes it more visceral for the person sharing, while, in turn, hearing it makes it easier for the team to absorb. The more senses are engaged, the better your team's ability to pick up trends and patterns.

**Stucks/Constraints:** This is the most important agenda item. You want members of the team to bring up constraints and concerns that could prevent them from having a great next 24 hours (i.e., What's the rock in their shoe? What's keeping them awake at night or worrying them? Are they stuck because of another team member?) The brutal facts need to be shared, and the leader needs to see the patterns of "stucks" to understand what underlying issues must be addressed.

There are a couple of reasons why we consider this last part of the agenda crucial. First, there's something powerful in simply verbalizing — for the whole group to hear — your fears, your struggles, and your concerns. It's the first step in solving the problem, because until the mouth starts moving, the brain won't engage. Second, you want to focus your team's energy on breaking through constraints.

 **NOTE:** *Team members should share a "stuck" even if they don't think there's anyone on the team who can help them resolve it. Verbalizing the issue is likely to spur unexpected action to help them.*

 **WARNING:** *Anytime somebody goes two days without reporting a constraint, you can bet there's a bigger problem lurking. Busy, productive people who are doing anything of consequence get stuck pretty regularly. The only people who don't get stuck are those who aren't doing anything or are so stuck that don't know it!! So, challenge the team member who reports, "Everything is fine!"*

 **WARNING:** *Important as they are, conversations about bottlenecks shouldn't be allowed to drift into problem-solving. It's okay if somebody wants to reply to a "stuck" by saying, "Call so-and-so," or, "I'll get on that right away" (if he or she is the "stuck"!), but take anything more than that offline. Remember: The daily meeting needs to be kept short.*

# The Weekly 4D Meeting

If the daily huddles are functioning well, they will lead to immediate action on scores of issues that would otherwise clog up the weekly meeting. You don't want to spend the weekly meeting poring over updates. Everyone should be well-informed via the daily huddles. You also don't want to address the dozens of issues that have accumulated over the week. The idea of the 4D weekly meeting is to keep everyone laser-focused on the #1 priority — and the big rocks supporting that mission. You want to tap the collective intelligence of the team for 30 to 60 minutes on one or two important topics. This affords the group an opportunity to resolve 50 to 100 important things in a year.

The name 4D for the weekly meeting comes from the suggested structure of the meeting, giving you a "4D" look into the business:

Discover: Good News, Metrics & Priorities

Discuss: Issues & brainstorming

Decide: Align & Commit

Delegate: Who What When

The details for each agenda item, and the timing, is described below. As for the name of this meeting, like everything else in your culture, its best if you give it your own unique title.

 **HINT:** *Does your organization spread out its functional meetings throughout the week, thinking that it's best not to take up too much of any one day? If so, let us suggest that you do just the opposite. Pick one morning or afternoon, and host ALL of your functional and project meetings back-to-back. This allows everyone to get in a meeting mindset and flow, and frees senior management to spend the rest of the week out in the marketplace. We picked up this idea from Rick Kay and his team at OTG Software.*

y and three colleagues launched OTG Software in 1992 and grew it through the '90s. k it public in 2000, sold it to Legato Systems for $403 million in 2002, and stayed on until Legato was sold to EMC a year later for $1.4 billion, resulting in a nice double payout to Kay and his team.

Kay's weekly meeting rhythm started Monday morning at 7 a.m., when he hosted a breakfast meeting with the three senior executives who helped him launch the company. This was Kay's "council" meeting. The foursome chalked up significant talk time around the challenges and opportunities facing the growing company.

At 8 a.m., the rest of the senior team, along with Kay's assistant Andy Cleary, joined the meeting for a one-hour meeting of the executive team. At the end, Cleary would summarize "Who's going to do What, When." These were very action-oriented meetings focused on addressing key issues and making decisions, not mind-numbing reviews.

We will illustrate next the real meeting innovation, which we have shared with thousands of other firms. Whereas most companies spread their functional meetings throughout the week, Kay's team concentrated them all in one morning. From 9 a.m. to noon, the entire senior management team of eight stayed for a series of functional meetings. The complete agenda:

7 a.m. - 8 a.m.: Breakfast meeting

8 a.m. - 9 a.m.: Executive team

9 a.m. - 10 a.m.: Sales and marketing

10 a.m. - 11 a.m.: Software development

11 a.m. - 12 p.m.: Accounting and finance

This afforded middle and frontline teams direct access to the entire senior leadership team. (The company had roughly 400 employees around the time Verne was working with it, just before and after its IPO.)

Imagine the power to resolve dozens of issues right on the spot. If a press release needed approval, everyone (including the CFO, the VP of sales, and the software development and marketing chiefs) was there to review and resolve it in minutes. It didn't float around in emails for days, sucking up hours of leadership time. If Sales was having a problem with the CRM system, the head of IT was there. If Development needed to hire additional programmers, the head of HR and the CFO were there to start the process and sign off on the budget.

In fact, Kay had a rule: Do not email big files (or links to websites, as in "When you have time, please look over these updates to the software interface"). Instead, the company gave team members time in the meetings to pull up a website or read through a contract, as Jeff Bezos allows at Amazon's weekly meetings. This gave people time to review and respond in a dynamic, synchronous fashion, with Kay pushing for decisions rather than defaulting to a follow-on meeting. And at the end of each functional meeting, Kay's assistant would summarize the "Who, What, When," so the entire company was clear on the functional priorities for the week.

At noon, everyone headed for lunch and in some cases to the airport, interacting in the market for the balance of the week with no other management meetings (except their daily check-in). This meeting rhythm resulted in more decisions and more real work accomplished in half a day than most senior teams get done in weeks or months. And although OTG's customers were unable to reach senior leaders during those Monday-morning meetings, they found management unusually available the rest of the week. We highly recommend that you adopt this best practice, dedicating several hours a week to get in the flow and work on the business, project by project, function by function. Then you're finished except for a daily, 15-minute touch point.

When it was time for the daylong monthly meeting, OTG held these on Mondays, combining its weekly and monthly activities. The same held true for the quarterly and annual meetings, each of which consumed a Monday as well. Mondays were meeting day, like Fridays are for FedEx and Wal-Mart.

*The Schedule* — Schedule the meeting for the same time, same place each week. Set aside 30 minutes for frontline employees, 60 to 90 minutes for middle and executive teams. Since the Scaling Up team is spread across 11.5 time zones, from Hyderabad, India to Boulder, CO, our several hours of meetings on Mondays are held via conference call. It works.

Let's look at the suggested agenda for a weekly team meeting:

## The 4D Weekly Meeting Agenda

*Five minutes: Good news.* Start each weekly meeting with five minutes of good news, both personal and professional. Sharing professional good news creates a positive start to the meeting and helps generate momentum — good news begets good news. The personal good news keeps the team connected at a human level, lets everyone express gratitude, and normally results in a good belly laugh or two. Laughter releases tension and brings the brain down into a better alpha state, preparing the team to tackle the important issues and decisions for the week. This important routine also serves as a mental health check. If someone has gone a couple of weeks without sharing specific good news, the leader should inquire privately to see if everything is okay.

*10 minutes: Customer and employee feedback.* Spend this time reviewing specific feedback from customers and employees. What issues are cropping up day after day? What are people hearing?

*10 minutes: The priorities.* Review the status of the Red, Green, and Super Green priorities (discussed in "The Priority" chapter) and discuss any gaps in progress. Also review any metrics reported in the daily huddles.

**NOTE:** *Draw a line in your mind. This first 25 minutes warms up the brain and allows you to discover enough internal and external data to help the team see patterns and trends in the performance of the company. The next 35 to 65 minutes are designated for putting the team's collective intelligence to work and making important decisions.*

***30 to 60 minutes: One or two topics (Discuss & Decide).*** Focus the team's undivided attention and collective intelligence on a key topic or two. Base your choice on the patterns and trends from the daily huddles, progress on your priorities/theme, feedback from your employees and customers, and the opportunities and challenges that have surfaced. If a firm wants to discuss a potential partnership, schedule it for this time. If a major event is coming up and you need some decisions made, give it priority. At Scaling Up, Verne sometimes knows the topic well in advance. Other times, he emails an agenda the night before, or the issue surfaces during the meeting. If you have a handful of priorities for the quarter, the weekly meeting affords you an opportunity to review each a couple of times each quarter.

***Who, What, When (WWW) (Delegate).*** Take a couple of minutes to summarize "Who said they are going to do What, and When," and email the notes to everyone.

***One-phrase close.*** End your weekly meeting by asking each attendee to sum up with a word or phrase of reaction. It creates a formal closing for the meeting, ensures that everyone's had a chance to say something, and gives you a window into what people are thinking and feeling. If you find there are lingering issues or conflicts, you can follow up.

 **HINT:** *It's ideal if the series of weekly meetings ends before lunch (like OTG's) or happy hour, so the executives can have a more informal setting in which to discuss issues that surface during the structured part of the meetings. That informal time is often when real decisions are fleshed out.*

 **HINT:** *For those of you who participate in some kind of CEO forum, the weekly meeting is structured a lot like a mini-forum meeting, with a formal check-in, updates, forum topic, and one-phrase close.*

## Critical CEO Routine

Your people want to know what's on your mind on a weekly basis. If you don't share, they will fill the void and that input will likely be negative.

Greg Brenneman, in the famous turnaround of Continental Airlines, recorded a weekly voicemail available to all 40,000 employees; Michael Dell sends out a weekly email; Mark Zuckerberg hosts his weekly "Q&A with Mark" at 5pm PT on Thursdays for all employees to attend on Facetime; the Google boys hosted their infamous TGIF meeting for the same reason. Verne does the same in a weekly Friday email to all the Scaling Up coaching partners around the globe.

Whether it's a quick video, voicemail message, email, or townhall gathering — it's important to keep the entire organization up-to-date on what you're doing, thinking, and prioritizing. Make it less about the numbers (they should be updated daily) and more about being vulnerable. Share your own questions, concerns, doubts and mistakes while continuing to reinforce your vision. This will go a long way to building the foundational trust that creates psychological safety in supporting team performance.

# The Monthly Leadership Meeting

You can tell a great company from a good company by spending just a few minutes inside of the business. In good companies, you'll find the senior team stressed out and overworked from the crush of ever-increasing demands, while the rest of the team seems oblivious to the challenges facing the firm.

In great companies, you find just the opposite: a senior team that's rested and relaxed while the balance of the staff is on fire as they work to capitalize on the ever-increasing opportunities facing the business. We may be exaggerating somewhat, but not by much.

Unless the senior team instills its DNA— namely, the knowledge and values required to make good decisions — in everyone from the team leads on down, the top leaders will find themselves increasingly overwhelmed by the demands of a growing business.

Doing this requires one simple routine: a well-structured, one-day monthly leadership meeting that includes everyone who supervises or leads anyone in the business. It should be a day focused on learning, sharing, and problem-solving vs. a day of mind-numbing reports. Do anything short of hosting this meeting, and the business will ultimately outgrow its middle management. And few things are more painful than seeing a business leave loyal people behind.

## Lessons From India

Nowhere is the need to develop middle management more apparent than in India. And it was a particular challenge for Ashiana Housing Ltd., a 480-employee (and 2,500-contractor) New Delhi-based firm, one of 39 Indian companies named to the *Forbes* list of "Asia's 200 Best Under a Billion". When Verne first met Managing Director Vishal Gupta and his two brothers, who run the construction company founded by their father, they were stressed out over their ever-expanding company, which had five major projects spread throughout northern India. In turn, their middle-management team was relaxed and relatively unaware of the challenges facing the company.

## 7% of Leadership Compensation

To rectify this problem, we strongly recommended that they initiate a monthly leadership meeting, bringing together all 70 leaders from around India for a day of learning and development. Given India's infrastructure and transportation challenges, it was difficult for Gupta to imagine finding a day each month when all the senior and team leads could meet. Plus, how could they pull these leaders out of the field for a day, given the company's growth rate and the crush of work? (Rick Kay had the same concern when Verne pushed OTG Software to do the same for its 40 team leads spread throughout the US.)

There was also a concern about the cost of hosting such a meeting. Figuring on an average of 5% of leadership compensation to host a year of one-day monthly meetings, Ashiana ing ended up spending 7%. Yet the first few monthly meetings generated tangible re- hat paid for the next 10 years of leadership meetings. Three key outcomes the first year:

1. **Revenue tripled.** During the first monthly meeting, the team tackled a huge issue: sales conversions. The market for housing, even in India, had slowed down in 2009, so the company wanted to boost business. The challenge wasn't getting traffic to its developments; it was converting visitors into customers.

   After the 70 leaders discussed the issue for several hours, the big idea that emerged was creating a wow factor at each of its locations, requiring coordination of the construction and maintenance teams. In addition, the team decided to provide customer-service training to guards greeting potential customers and to increase the number of signs directing customers to the sales and rental offices. All activities could be implemented immediately because the entire middle-management team was part of creating the solution.

   The result? Monthly sales tripled by the end of the year and have been high ever since.

2. **Huge time savings**. Ashiana hosts a show-and-tell session during these monthly management meetings in which teams from both construction and maintenance highlight a best practice from the previous month. In one case, the company's new construction team in Pune had created a way to construct a kitchen in six to seven fewer days and for slightly less money.

   Immediately, the construction teams at four other locations implemented these best practices. Cutting down construction time by a week improves cash flow and speeds sales — a big win that provides huge returns from the company's monthly investment.

3. **Breaking down barriers.** Pulling all 70 leaders together forged stronger relationships across functions and business operations. For instance, accounting now understands better some of the challenges maintenance faces. In turn, having all 70 together creates positive peer pressure, as leaders share "their number" at the beginning of the meeting Friday evening. Today, 100% of the 70 leaders have one key performance indicator that definitively measures whether they've had a successful month or not.

   Within the first year, because of the formal and informal training and development that occurred during these meetings, the 70 team leads were able to step up and run the day-to-day operations of the business. That leaves the three brothers more time to focus on the market-facing activities, like land acquisition, that continue to propel Ashiana Housing ahead of its competition.

A decade later (at the time of this book's publication), the monthly meetings are still being held; the team leads act as mini-CEOs in running the business; and the three brothers are more relaxed than they've ever been and are planning for the future. From a performance standpoint, during this same period, Ashiana Housing's stock has risen over 500% while direct competitors' stocks have stagnated.

For your reference, here is Ashiana Housing's monthly leadership meeting agenda:

## Ashiana Housing's Meeting Agenda

### Friday

*6:30 – 8:30 p.m.* After a round of good news from the personal and professional fronts, leaders share "their number." In addition, the owners — the three brothers — review the mission, vision, and values and update the team on key targets for the year.

*8:30 p.m. – ?* Dinner and drinks give the team some important social time. And the personal good news the leaders shared earlier fuels a lot of the conversations, creating bonds among the team members.

### Saturday

*8 a.m. – 10 a.m.* All of the leaders share their issues from the previous month while the senior team looks for patterns and trends. The main benefit, from the owners' perspective, is that this session gives the leaders a chance to vent and verbalize their challenges. Often, other leaders have constructive solutions, which are shared later through private conversations.

*10:30 a.m. – 12:30 p.m.* After a tea break, the team gets two hours of training. Recent topics have included delegation, email etiquette, and executive health. Vishal Gupta, one of the brothers, lost 5 kilograms (11 pounds) as a result.

*1:30 p.m. – 2 p.m.* After lunch, selected leaders make two 15-minute "show-and-tell" presentations, giving them practice with their presentation skills and the opportunity to share best practices.

*2 p.m. – 5 p.m.* The team collectively tackles one or two huge issues, like sales, allowing the senior leaders to tap into the ideas of the team leads and to model their industry knowledge and their approach to decision-making. To wrap up the meeting, they share a round of one-phrase closes, in which each leader reacts to the monthly meeting.

## Monthly Town Hall

In addition to the weekly CEO one-pager, many top leaders also host a monthly town hall meeting, at which they make a few key announcements and give employees an opportunity to ask questions and discuss issues important to them.

 **WARNING:** *One of the biggest mistakes a CEO can make, in the spirit of transparency and openness, is to share important changes and information with all the employees before briefing the team leaders and supervisors. Frontline employees, after hearing about a change, will go to their immediate supervisor for clarification and details, inquiring, "How is this going to specifically affect me?" If the leaders have not been briefed ahead of time, the CEO has put them in an awkward situation. They have no choice but to respond, "I don't know. I'm hearing this for the first time myself." So, brief ALL leaders first, and create a legion of allies for the changes you want to make.*

## Quarterly and Annual Planning Meetings

The main agenda for these one- to three-day offsite planning sessions is to work through and update the Growth Tools. They provide the questions, focus, and agenda for these quarterly and annual planning sessions. Go to the earlier "Strategic Planning" chapter for details.

# SCALING UP
## CASH

# THE CASH INTRODUCTION

**KEY QUESTION:** *Do you have consistent sources of cash, ideally generated internally, to fuel the growth of your business?*

You can get by with decent People, Strategy, and Execution, but not a day without Cash. Cash becomes even more critical as the business scales up, since "growth sucks cash." The key is innovating ways to generate sufficient profit and cash flow internally, so you don't have to turn to banks (or sharks!) to fuel your growth.

Costco Wholesale Corp., the fast-growing warehouse retailer, is a prime example. Co-founder Jim Sinegal made a bold move in charging a membership fee for people to shop at his stores. Today, those fees account for 77% of Costco's profit ($3.88 billion of the $5.01 billion in pretax earnings in 2021), bringing in enough money to finance all new stores.

Great companies, by choice, keep three to 10 times more cash reserves than their competitors, Jim Collins and Morten T. Hansen revealed in their book *Great by Choice: Uncertainty, Chaos, and Luck — Why Some Thrive Despite Them All.* That allows growth firms to weather the storms, and that is why Bill Gates, from the very beginning, mandated that Microsoft always keep a year's worth of operating expenses in the bank. This is a lesson Scaling Up has heeded since running out of cash in the aftermath of 9/11. If you've ever experienced the painful reality of not being able to make payroll, you'll never want to face it again.

## Section Overview

**The first chapter, The Cash,** focuses on improving your cash conversion cycle dramatically. It includes several practical and creative ideas used by firms to generate sufficient cash internally to fuel growth.

**The second chapter, The Power of One,** takes you through the case study of a seemingly healthy $42 million firm that is "growing broke." Co-authored by Alan Miltz and his team, who created the leading software tool for banks to evaluate the financial health of businesses, it walks you through the 7 financial levers that every business leader can control to scale up cash. "The Power of One" refers to the benefit to cash flow if a 1% or one-day change is made to each of the 7 levers that affect it.

**The third chapter, The Exit,** details four keys for maximizing the valuation of your business and shares the pitfalls in the selling process that can strip owners of tens of millions of dollars when it comes time to exit.

Two one-page Cash tools will be covered in this section:

1. **Cash Acceleration Strategies (CASh):** a place to list specific strategies for increasing cash flow

2. **The Power of One:** a way to calculate the impact on cash when making changes to the 7 financial levers

# Cash: Cash Acceleration Strategies (CASh)

**Cash Conversion Cycle (CCC)**

**A** Sales Cycle

**C** Delivery Cycle

**D** Billing & Payment Cycle

**B** Make/Production & Inventory Cycle

| | Shorten Cycle Times | Eliminate Mistakes | Improve Business Model & P/L |
|---|---|---|---|
| **A  Ways to improve your Sales Cycle** | | | |
| 1 | | | |
| 2 | | | |
| 3 | | | |
| 4 | | | |
| 5 | | | |
| **B  Ways to improve your Make/Production & Inventory Cycle** | | | |
| 1 | | | |
| 2 | | | |
| 3 | | | |
| 4 | | | |
| 5 | | | |
| **C  Ways to improve your Delivery Cycle** | | | |
| 1 | | | |
| 2 | | | |
| 3 | | | |
| 4 | | | |
| 5 | | | |
| **D  Ways to improve your Billing & Payment Cycle** | | | |
| 1 | | | |
| 2 | | | |
| 3 | | | |
| 4 | | | |
| 5 | | | |

Download a full-sized copy of this tool at *scalingup.com*

| Your Power of One | Net Cash Flow $ | EBIT $ |
|---|---|---|
| Your Current Position | | |

| Your Power of One | Change you would like to make | Annual Impact on Cash Flow $ | Impact on EBIT $ |
|---|---|---|---|
| Price Increase % | % | | |
| Volume Increase % | % | | |
| COGS Reduction % | % | | |
| Overheads Reduction % | % | | |
| Reduction in Debtors Days | day(s) | | |
| Reduction in Stock Days | day(s) | | |
| Increase in Creditors Days | day(s) | | |

| **Your Power of One Impact** | | | |
|---|---|---|---|

| Your Power of One | Net Cash Flow $ | EBIT $ |
|---|---|---|
| Your **Adjusted** Position | | |

# 12

# THE CASH
## Accelerating Cash Flow

---

**EXECUTIVE SUMMARY:** *Cash is the oxygen that fuels growth. And the cash conversion cycle (CCC) is a key performance indicator (KPI) that measures how long it takes for a dollar spent on anything (rent, utilities, marketing, payroll, etc.) to make its way through your business and back into your pocket. In this chapter, we'll share several ways that companies have dramatically improved their CCC using the one-page Cash Acceleration Strategies (CASh) tool, allowing them to fund growth with internally generated cash and freeing them from the grasp of banks and/or investors. We suggest that you brainstorm ways to improve cash flow at each 90-day planning session and pick a related initiative as one of your handful of priorities each quarter. Constantly improving the cash flow of the company — and better understanding how cash moves through the business — is a powerful driver for improving the firm as a whole.*

---

When Michael Dell was growing his company rapidly, he reached a point in the mid-'90s when he ran out of cash. He was "growing broke," like so many other businesses scaling up quickly. That's when he brought in Tom Meredith as CFO. Meredith calculated Dell Inc.'s cash conversion cycle (CCC) to be 63 days. That meant it took 63 days from the time Dell spent a dollar on anything until it flowed back through the business and onto the balance sheet (into the bank) as cash.

Focusing on one cash improvement strategy/initiative each 90 days, Meredith drove the CCC to negative 21 days by the time he left Dell as CFO a decade later. This meant the company received a dollar 21 days before it had to be spent on anything. As Dell grew faster, it generated cash instead of consuming it. That is why the founder and CEO had sufficient cash to contribute to taking the company private in 2013 (and back public in 2018, netting him $50 billion in what Forbes named the "Deal of the Century" in 2021).

In this chapter, we'll examine strategies for accelerating your cash flow through improvements in your CCC.

## Cash Conversion Cycle (CCC)

Not every business can have a negative CCC, but you can view Dell's example as inspiration to move yours in that direction. It is just a matter of looking for ways to improve it. For instance, Catapult Systems LLC, an Austin-based, Microsoft-focused IT consulting company, used to bill clients on a 30-day cycle. Meanwhile, employees were paid twice a month, leading to what founder and Chairman Sam Goodner calls "a terrible cash-flow story." He simply started billing his clients twice per month, after finding more than 90% were agreeable to the change. This nearly doubled cash flow immediately.

To tackle the cash conversion cycle, start by reading "How Fast Can Your Company Afford to Grow?" a *Harvard Business Review* article by Neil C. Churchill and John W. Mullins. It provides the formulas to help your team calculate the company's overall CCC and discusses many of the financial levers highlighted in the last chapter of this "Cash" section of the book.

 **NOTE:** *John Mullins, serial entrepreneur and London Business School professor, subsequently wrote a book titled* The Customer-Funded Business: Start, Finance, or Grow Your Company with Your Customers' Cash. *The title says it all! Read it for an advanced look at the cash side of your business and for ways to get your customers to fund growth, like Costco did.*

## Cash Acceleration Strategies (CASh)

To help teams brainstorm ways to improve their cash conversion cycles, we created a one-page tool called Cash Acceleration Strategies, or CASh. It breaks down the CCC into four main components:

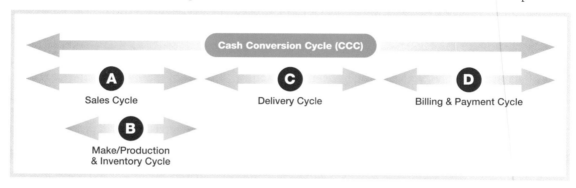

Most businesses will have some aspect of each of these cash cycle components. Even service firms have a form of inventory if they have underutilized staff. What might differ is the sequence of these components, with some cycles overlapping others or occurring in a different order. For instance, if you've structured your business model to collect full payments in advance, like Dell, then the billing and payment cycle occurs after the selling cycle but before the production and delivery cycle. (In other words, Dell arranged to take ownership of inventory only after a computer was sold.)

We encourage management teams to set aside an hour or more each month to brainstorm ways to improve each of these cash cycle components. This is a powerful exercise to do with the broader middle-leadership team at a half- to full-day monthly leadership meeting. It will give everyone a better understanding of how cash flows through the business and how each function can contribute positively.

Some areas of opportunity:

- First, stop saying, "Well, this is just the way it is in our industry."
- Have your available cash reported DAILY, with a short explanation of why it changed in the last 24 hours, and chart it against accounts receivable (AR) and accounts payable (AP) weekly. You'll learn so much more about your business when you see how the cash is flowing on a daily basis. If you want to be paid sooner, ask. Small firms are finding that large companies

(and governments!!) will pay considerably faster or even prepay if you simply ask, ask, ask, ask, and ask some more.

- Give value back to customers who pay on time or in advance.
- Get your invoices out more quickly. Hire one more person in accounting to do nothing but make sure invoicing is timely and follow up on payments.
- Send friendly reminders five days *before* the deadline that payments are due. Many customers are disorganized and will appreciate the reminders, resulting in faster payment.
- If invoices are recurring, obtain recurring credit card authorization from your customers to automate on-time payments.
- Understand why your clients are paying late. They might be unhappy with your product or service. Or perhaps an invoice has recurring mistakes, or it is not structured to flow through the customer's automated invoicing system.
- Understand each customer's payment cycles, and time your billings to coincide.
- Pay many of your own expenses with a credit card so you can play the float. Get your own customers to pay by credit card, so they can pay you quickly even if their cash flow is slow.
- Help your customers improve their cash flow so they can pay you on time. Offer them leasing options, for instance.
- Shorten cycles for delivery of your product or service. All of you have some kind of "work in progress." The faster you complete projects, the faster you get paid.
- Offer a product or service so valuable that you have some leverage with your customers toget them to pay sooner.
- Remember, improving margins and profit improves cash.

 **NOTE:** *Have your CFO or controller give you a cash report every day, like Verne's does. The CFO should summarize the sources and amounts of cash that came in and out of the business during the last 24 hours, along with anticipated cash flow for the coming month. It keeps cash top-of-mind and allows you to react quickly — within days vs. months — if it's heading in the wrong direction. Observing the sources of cash flowing in and out on a daily basis also gives real insight into your business's financial model.*

Almost all of these ideas fall into three general categories where you can make improvements:

1. Shorten cycle times.
2. Eliminate mistakes.
3. Change the business model.

To further stimulate your thinking, here are some ideas in each category that can help you improve cash flow.

## Shorten Cycle Times

Increasing the pace of everything your company does (e.g., decreasing the time it takes to complete a full cycle from customer interest to completed transaction) helps your CCC. This is why we are fans of applying Toyota's Lean process to all aspects of the business. With its focus on eliminating wasted time, it's an ideal tool to improve processes, increase employee productivity, and accelerate cash flow.

Pay particular attention to the sales process. You may be expending enormous amounts of money and time on landing customers. Using negotiation techniques taught by Victoria Medvec (check out her powerful online "High Stakes Negotiation" course at *scalingup.com*), firms like Goldman Sachs have reduced sales cycles from months to weeks and from weeks to days. The quicker you can get a deal in the door, the quicker the cash starts flowing — and you thwart would-be competitors.

On the production side, back when Dell had factories, a production worker could assemble a computer in minutes, and the company held only a few days' worth of inventory. This rapid turn of inventory and the speed of manufacturing contributed hugely to the impressive CCC the company achieved.

Because many accounting departments are short-handed, there are often delays in getting invoices sent out and bills collected. Besides billing twice per month to improve cash flow, Catapult Systems collects faster than most firms. Notes Goodner, the former chairman: "Our collections person in the accounting department works hard to create a personal rapport with our clients' accounts payable teams. She is the most charming, disarming, nonthreatening, likable person you could possibly have. She starts calling the accounting departments of our clients five days before the check is due just to make sure everything is okay, and says that we are doing great on the project. She gives her number just in case anything comes up and says, 'I really look forward to getting that check from you next week.' " And if the check is late, the Catapult Systems' collections specialist places a call to the client the next day. That is another reason to bolster your accounting department resources.

Goodner credits this approach with his company's "unbelievably high" track record of getting paid on time — simply because, he says, "We ask for it."

Meanwhile, a firm in Australia sends inexpensive lottery tickets as thank-yous to its customers' accounts payable clerks when they pay invoices on time. When customers are faced with a stack of bills to pay, this company's invoices seem to magically make it to the top of the pile! And if this might be frowned upon (or deemed illegal) in your industry or locale, a holiday card showing appreciation to the people in accounts payable can achieve the same effect. The point is to have someone pay attention to the accounts payable people!

Also specify a due date (May 31, for example) on the invoice rather than include the standard "due in 30 days." Often, someone higher up in the client organization has to sign off on an invoice before it can be paid, with the 30-day clock starting when this signature is received. If there is a specific due date, even if the signature isn't obtained until the day before, the payables clerk will assume that the sign-off authorizes the payment to occur on the date specified, and will pay the bill immediately.

Examine all of the processes in the organization — sales, production, service delivery, billing, and collections — and find ways to speed up and move cash more quickly through the business.

## Eliminate Mistakes

Nothing infuriates customers more than a mistake. It is the #1 reason they are slow to pay. And incomplete orders, invoicing errors, and missed deadlines are not only costly but also drag down the very processes you want to speed up, snarling cash flow.

Adam Sproule, third generation CEO of Salisbury Landscaping in Alberta, has the company's cash conversion cycle down to a fine art. The approach he has used has helped him optimize the CCC for the past 25+ years. Besides securing deposits up front (with the final payment due immediately upon a project's completion), Salisbury Landscaping has put operating practices in place to finish jobs quickly and in a far less disruptive way than clients usually see in its industry. This, in turn, has given Salisbury a reputation that makes collecting deposits and payments easier.

Tradespeople in landscaping or construction usually work on two to three jobs at the same time, often leaving customers wondering what's happening and why the projects aren't finished yet. "It's a real pet peeve of people we talk to," says Sproule. Instead, Salisbury's crews focus on one job at a time, getting in and out as quickly as possible. "We deal with live plants, so we want to finish quickly," Sproule says. "Not only is it a major disruption to our clients if we don't, but the longer we take, the more likely there will be problems."

As soon as the crew leaves, a member of Sproule's team walks around with the customer to make sure the job is absolutely perfect. "Even if there are just a couple deficiencies, we write them down," says Sproule, who notes that his staff refers to corrections of deficiencies as "adjustments," to avoid any negative perception.

"We then make an adjustment list. Because we're very efficient at what we do, the customer has no reason to doubt us. So a lot of times, they give us the full payment immediately after the walk-around even if there are a few things left to do," notes Sproule. And to close the loop of learning and avoid making the same mistakes on subsequent projects, Salisbury sends out the same crew that generated the deficiencies to handle the adjustments quickly.

PPR Talent Management Group (acquired by Medical Solutions in 2018) freed up a million dollars every month through improved accuracy in its invoicing. Serving the needs of a thousand clients — mostly hospitals, all with different policies and time-sheet protocols — caused considerable complexity in invoicing. As a result, clients delayed paying while PPR sorted out the errors on its invoices. To address this issue, the Florida company hired an additional person not only to build relationships with the payables departments but also to customize invoices to match each specific hospital's billing codes. As former CEO Dwight Cooper notes, "When we changed our process and got it right, the confidence level with our clients came up fast."

Then the latest recession came. As it dragged on into 2009, Cooper says, "We took our eye off the cash ball." It was time to change the entire business model — at least from a cash perspective.

## Change the Business Model

For PPR, collections were not the problem; it was creating the right terms to begin with. To grow the business, PPR needed cash, so it asked customers to pay in advance. "We were pleasantly surprised when many of our customers just said yes," says Cooper.

There are many adjustments you can make to your business model that positively affect your CCC. The two with the biggest results are getting your customers to fund your business, much like Costco does via membership fees, or having suppliers do this, as Dell did through its inventory management.

For sources of cash other than loans or investors, read the *Fortune Small Business* article Verne wrote titled "Finding Money You Didn't Know You Had."

## Improving Profitability

Benetton India also felt the crunch of the economic downturn in 2009, so it embarked on a major cost-saving initiative. Sanjeev Mohanty, CEO of Benetton India Private Ltd., got vendors to bid online for contracts using business-commerce software purchased from Ariba. "Initially, everyone was very skeptical, saying that we would lose quality," he says. Plus, some suppliers had been providing goods to Benetton India for more than a decade, and executives hesitated to disrupt what appeared to be working well.

Mohanty persisted, and the savings have been significant. For instance, Benetton India invited six different suppliers, including the incumbent, to bid on its contract for shopping bags. Suppliers can use Ariba not only to place their bids, but also to see what other companies are bidding. Normally, the whole bidding process can take several hours, but this round closed in 32 minutes, while the executive team watched in real time. Benetton previously paid 52 cents per shopping bag, and the final bid came in at 34 cents — a huge savings. Surprisingly, the incumbent supplier provided the final low bid, so in addition to benefiting from the savings, Benetton India maintained the same-quality bag. Today, company employees must use Ariba to procure any goods or services with a value of more than $10,000. In one recent year, Benetton India saved $1.2 million through this procurement process.

Again, when you improve profitability, it improves cash — as long as you're not funding management waste on the balance sheet, as we'll discuss further in the next two chapters. And for retail companies like MOM's Organic Market and Benetton India, which collect cash or credit card payments for every transaction, the only real internal financial cash lever is on the P&L side of the business.

During the recent financial crisis, fearing credit lines might dry up, MOM's CEO Scott Nash and his team stayed laser-focused on improving profitability (emphasizing pricing, purchasing, etc.). Today, with four times industry average profitability, the metro Washington-based chain has driven up its free operating cash flow to fund its continued expansion. At Catapult Systems, Goodner found cost savings by sitting down with an accounts payable employee every six months to scrutinize what the company is paying for goods and services. Understanding the expenses, one-time charges, and recurring charges leads to savings opportunities that add up. "There's probably tens of thousands of dollars a year I can cut, and the company doesn't feel the difference," Goodner says. For example, when he realized that the company was paying $600 per month for bottled-water service at one office, he decided to purchase a commercial filtration system instead, for one-tenth of the cost. "Recurring charges are the ones that really kill you," says Goodner. "Anything that's a recurring charge forever,I still personally approve before it gets accepted."

# Completing Your
# Cash Acceleration Strategies (CASh) Tool

1. Read the *Harvard Business Review* article by Neil C. Churchill and John W. Mullins titled "How Fast Can Your Company Afford to Grow?"

2. Calculate your existing CCC in days.

3. Calculate the amount of cash required to fund each additional day of CCC.

4. Brainstorm ways to improve your CCC and the 7 financial levers highlighted in the last chapter of this "Cash" section using the one-page CASh tool. Be sure to explore ways in all three general categories — shortening cycle times, eliminating mistakes, and changing the business model — for each segment of the CCC.

5. Choose one cash-improvement initiative every 90 days as one of your quarterly priorities (Rocks).

Imagine you improve your CCC by 30 days (and you run a $30 million business). You now have $2.5 million extra in your bank account, and you can:

1. Pay down your operating credit line.

2. Distribute a dividend to shareholders.

3. Invest in a new project that will support your growth plans.

4. Sit on it until you find the perfect opportunity.

5. Keep it as insurance for when times get rough.

The best part about improving your CCC is that it usually results in your business pulsing faster, which is better for the customer. It will also improve the business savvy of your managers as they become more aware of the impact of their decisions on cash flow. And with more cash in the bank, everyone will sleep better as you scale up the business. This is one routine that will really set you free and give you sticking power in the market.

The key to improving cash flow and profitability is investing more in the accounting side of the business. It's hard to make intelligent decisions without data.

## Accounting: Underappreciated

If the #1 weakness of growth firms is marketing, the #2 problem is accounting. Accounting is often underappreciated. It is seen as a necessary evil to keep the tax collectors at bay; invoice, collect, and pay bills; and provide monthly accounting statements — which often receive at most a cursory glance at the bottom line of the P&L.

Accounting is often underfunded as a result. Most entrepreneurs, if they have an extra dollar of profit to spend, invest it in either making or selling stuff. Those are good uses of the money. However, we've seen profits and cash double within a year when businesspeople also devote just a little more attention and resources to accounting

*"The #2 weakness of growth firms is accounting."*

(remember, John D. Rockefeller was an accountant by train-ing). Hiring just one additional person to either support the CFO or carry some of this executive's workload enables him or her to provide the following:

1. Better cash and cash-flow management
2. Waterfall graphs, which we will explain shortly, to share more granular accounting data for better decision-making
3. Trend analysis and early-warning systems to support better prediction
4. Two sets of books — for the right reasons!

## Waterfall Graphs

A key accounting activity is to slice and dice a company's financial data as granularly as possible. This lets the leadership team view the gross margin, profit, and cash flow by categories, such as individual customer, location, product line, salesperson, etc. Accountants do this by creating a series of waterfall graphs (see the diagram below).

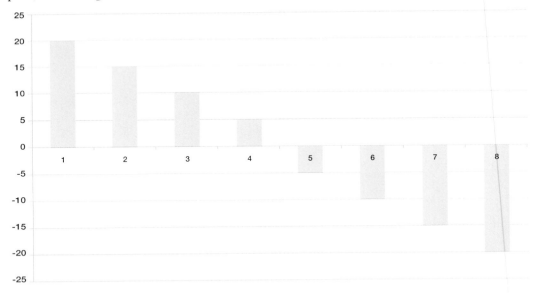

 **NOTE:** *The vertical axis might measure gross margin or profit percentage, while the horizontal axis might enumerate specific customers, locations, salespeople, product lines, or SKUs.*

The leadership team soon discovers from these waterfall graphs that the company is making a bunch of money from a limited part of the business and losing some or a lot in other parts, resulting in a gross margin or profitability that is mediocre. It's the less profitable parts of the business that tend to suck up most of management's time and attention. It was a series of waterfall graphs that Dell CFO Tom Meredith presented to Michael Dell and the leadership team to convince them to change their business model and move out of 40% of the product lines and distribution channels they were in.

Turnaround specialists like Greg Brenneman, the Houston-based chairman of private equity firm TurnWorks Inc., also rely on this kind of data to eliminate consistently unprofitable routes, as he did at Continental Airlines, and menu items, as he did at the Quiznos restaurant chain.

So why do we continue to hold on to these losers? "For strategic reasons" is the excuse! Yet what is strategic about losing lots of money over a long period of time? Apple could have easily argued that selling its money-losing handheld computers was a strategic

> *"What is strategic about losing lots of money?"*

move, but Steve Jobs eliminated the product line when he came back to run the firm a second time. Any loss leaders you might need — and these should be kept to a minimum — should be treated as a marketing expense in your accounting. For more insight into this common strategic mistake, read Brenneman's *Harvard Business Review* case study on the turnaround of Continental Airlines.

## Trend Analysis

A fundamental responsibility of leaders is prediction, and they need both frequent quantitative data and qualitative feedback from the market to make the right calls. As we've mentioned, any data more than a week old is history and is not useful for making the fast decisions necessitated by our highly connected global economy.

The accounting function is critical in this regard. It should provide the kinds of reports and graphs that help the leadership team see into the near future. For example, we helped the CFO of a distributor of electrical supplies to set up a series of weekly bar charts (rather than eye-straining Excel spreadsheets) that monitored major customers' purchases of various product lines. Sales to these accounts constituted 80% of the firm's revenue.

After a few months, the company could see that one of the customers was slowly reducing its relative order size. That was an early warning that something was amiss and alerted the account manager to follow up more quickly than normal. The company was also quicker to notice and act on other trends, like the change in popularity of certain product lines, now that leaders were seeing this visual data weekly, rather than monthly or quarterly.

### Mapping Software

Where are all the maps with pushpins you used to see populating sales and marketing offices — and the offices of CEOs? We wish companies used them more. Seeing data mapped out this way helps you visualize patterns you wouldn't otherwise discern. For instance, we mapped a database of scaleups against cities where we have coaching partners and could immediately see where we had gaps in our coverage.

Barrett Ersek used a series of maps and Microsoft's powerful MapPoint software (replaced by Bing Maps in 2015) to see patterns in where he was making sales (based on close ratios) and getting callbacks within his lawn care business.

See how many Excel spreadsheets you can replace using mapping software, and encourage your accounting team to create more maps.

## Two Sets of Books

One set of accounting books is needed to satisfy the rules of the Financial Accounting Standards Board (FASB) and the tax authorities. However, rarely should you make business decisions based solely on these regulations. For instance, computer hardware and software can be amortized over several years for tax purposes. However, Michael Dell wanted business units to implement only solutions that had a quick payoff. So, for internal purposes, Dell treated all technology costs as an expense against a division's P&L within 12 months.

For more on this topic, we encourage all CFOs to read Thomas A. Stewart's classic book *Intellectual Capital: The New Wealth of Organizations*. Pay particular attention to the extensive appendix, where he suggests specific accounting rules that better align with an information-based economy than with a manufacturing-type economy, which generated many of the FASB rules we follow today. For example, whereas you can amortize software over several years, you must expense employee training and development in the quarter in which it's provided. Stewart argues strongly that if any expense could legitimately be amortized over a longer period of time, it is education. The ideas your team learns today will continue to have an impact for many years.

The key is to decide on the practices and rules by which you want the company to run, and have accounting align your internal books in support. Use Stewart's book as your guide to grow a 21st-century-focused organization.

## Gross Margin Dollars

Revenue is vanity (and the weakest number) when it comes to your P&L. Focus instead on a redefined version of gross margin to be revenue minus all NONLABOR direct costs. This definition of gross margin gives you the true economic top line of the business.

Understanding this is especially important for businesses that utilize subcontractors, have high materials costs, or operate as distributors with low margins. There is no way that a $4 million distributor that gets a 10% commission on all its sales or a custom home builder with high costs for materials and subcontractors compares to a $4 million service firm. In essence, nonlabor direct costs, which are paid out of revenue, are simply pass-throughs. You definitely want to get them at the best price, but you usually cannot move the price enough to make up for any profit deficiency in your business model. The same holds true at employment agencies and professional employee organizations, where revenue is the total payroll that passes through the organization. The net dollars they have to operate their businesses are a fraction of this amount.

In most service-companies, gross margin dollars becomes the new top-linefocus, instead of revenue. This guides the business to seek opportunities that result in the highestgross margin per labor dollar. This is a key step in going from breakeven to 10% profitability and beyond.

Instead of obsessing about revenue, shift the internal discussions to generating gross margin, the real top line of the business. (Talk about revenue with outsiders if you want.) And note: The focus is more on gross margin dollars than gross margin as a percentage.

## 4X Industry Average GM$/Employee

Andy Bailey took this advice to heart at his firm NationLink Wireless, a chain of telecommunication retail stores. When he started implementing Scaling Up his gross margin dollars per employee was $75,000. By focusing each quarter on ways to improve this KPI, seven years later he drove that number to $275,000 gross margin dollars per employee, 4x industry average. This allowed him to exit for an outsized valuation.

Please start tracking this critical KPI, which has a tendency to drop as the company scales (because we "throw people at the problems").

### The Power of Gross Margin

Gross margin doesn't get enough respect. It's bad enough that it's stuck in the middle of the P&L and often gets glossed over. It's actually THE most powerful indicator of an effective sales team, a differentiated strategy, and real growth. As a company scales up, the market demands better pricing (e.g., your largest customers now ask for discounts). When this is combined with the complexities and increasing costs that come with being a larger company, we often see gross margins shrink by 3% to 4% — from, say, 55.4% to 51.8%. At the $10 million or $100 million level, such a dip results in $300,000 to $3 million becoming unavailable to fund infrastructure, pay a key executive, or fuel profitability.

There are two options to improve your gross margins. The first is to refine your strategy to maintain enough differentiation and uniqueness in your offering that you can hold your line on pricing (see "The 7 Strata of Strategy" chapter). This requires both salespeople who can sell this differentiation and a marketing function that keeps them armed and focused on the right customers. In these cases, you can actually see gross margins increase a few percentage points with growth. This is why hyperspecialization is powerful.

Of course, there are some markets that are just brutal — especially for lower-margin products and services. In these cases, if you get too focused on the gross margin percentage, you may miss an opportunity to grow, and your only option is to simply drive up overall gross margin dollars. That last gross margin dollar shouldn't cost you as much as the first one, so bring in as much cash as you can, factoring in how you might have to ramp up fixed costs.

If the market tells you the price that customers are willing to pay, you have to make your costs fit and still turn a profit. This is called a cost-led pricing strategy.

 **WARNING:** *Since gross margin dollars more accurately measure sales performance, you should never base sales compensation on revenue unless your cost of goods sold does not vary from sale to sale. You will be paying commissions on revenue while allowing your salespeople to set the price!*

# 13

# THE POWER OF ONE
## 7 Key Financial Levers

**EXECUTIVE SUMMARY:** *Revenue is Vanity, Profit is Sanity, Cash is King. The major financial challenges facing businesses today are inflation and supply chain disruptions. This results in margins dropping, overheads increasing, suppliers demanding faster payments and rising inventory levels. Never before has Cash been more important to a business. There are only 4 actions that any business can implement to improve Profit; increase prices, sell more, reduce cost of goods/direct costs and reduce overheads. To improve Cash Flow, 3 additional actions can be implemented; collecting faster, paying slower and reducing inventory or invoicing your work sooner. we call these the 7 Power of One Levers. Co-Authored with the team at Cash Flow Story, Alan Miltz and Joss Milner, have dedicated their lives to making the numbers simple. Alan and Joss have created an online software tool www.cashflowstory.com to enable everyone in your team to understand your Power of One, embrace your numbers and drive improvement in Profit Cash and Value. By implementing the Power of One in your business, the financial DNA of your company will change forever.*

## The Power of One

Over the last 25 years Alan Miltz and Joss Milner have established themselves as the global thought leaders in improving Profit, Cash and Value. They have spoken to thousands of businesses around the world, they always get asked "What is the number one thing we need to do to improve our Cash Flow?" The answer is simple, make the Power of One part of the DNA of your business, ensure that every major decision made by your management team is filtered by your Power of One. By understanding your Power of One, you will make better decisions resulting in improvement in Profit Cash and Value.

The Power of One consists of 7 Levers. There are 4 Profit & Loss and 3 Balance Sheet Levers:

1. **Price**: You can increase your prices.
2. **Volume**: You can sell more.
3. **Cost of goods sold (COGS)/Direct Costs**: You can reduce the price you pay for your inventory or direct labor.
4. **Operating expenses**: You can reduce your operating costs.
5. **Accounts receivable**: You can collect faster.
6. **Inventory/work in progress**: You can reduce the amount of Inventory you have on hand or bill your work sooner.
7. **Accounts payable**: You can pay slower.

## Scaling Up

Decisions are being made in your company every day without understanding the financial impact. Does your company know your price, volume sensitivity to Profit and Cash? How have you mitigated the impact of supply chain disruptions on Cash Flow? How will inflation impact your Margins and Cash Flow? Is increased sales volume detrimental to Cash Flow?

## The Power of one will change how you look at your business

Here are some real examples:

### Company A — A successful manufacturer

Turnover — $35 million and steady

Profit — $7 million and rising

Cash Flow — $7 million and rising strongly

### The Code of Your Business
Impact of a 1% or 1-day improvement

|  | Cash Flow | Profit |
|---|---|---|
| Price | +329,740 | +369,135 |
| Volume | +32,058 | +118,865 |
| Cost of Goods | +297,681 | +250,269 |
| Overheads | +41,069 | +41,069 |
| Recievables | +101,133 | |
| Inventory | +68,567 | |
| Payables | +68,567 | |

What the company learned from their Power of One:
- Price impacts Cash Flow 10 times more than Volume
- Receivables had blown out by 10 days, negatively impacting Cash Flow by a Million

What the company did:
- Stopped all discounting, reeducated the sales team about pricing and collections
- Implemented tighter collection processes

**Company B — Importer Distributor, financially stable.
However, impacted by Inflation and supply chain issues**

Turnover — $50 million and rising

Profit — $8 million and dropping, margins dropping as well

Cash Flow — $1 million negative, inventory rising, suppliers demanding faster payments

The impact of inflation and supply chain can be seen below, with a $1.5 mill reduction in Profit and $6.7 Million negative Cash Flow.

**Power of One**

| | Improvement | Cash Flow | Profit |
|---|---|---|---|
| Price | – 0% + | 0 | 0 |
| Volume | – 0% + | 0 | 0 |
| Cost of Goods | – -6% + | -1,898,708 | -1,528,202 |
| Overheads | – 0% + | 0 | 0 |
| Receivables | – 0d + | 0 | |
| Inventory | – -46d + | -3,209,923 | |
| Payables | – -23d + | -1,604,961 | |
| | | **-6,713,592** | **-1,528,202** |

What the company did:

- Ran a Power of One Workshop with the senior management team
- The following changes were agreed

**Power of One**

| | Improvement | Cash Flow | Profit |
|---|---|---|---|
| Price | – 5% + | 1,974,533 | 2,703,490 |
| Volume | – 10% + | 784,550 | 2,859,976 |
| Cost of Goods | – 0% + | 0 | 0 |
| Overheads | – 0% + | 0 | 0 |
| Receivables | – 15d + | 2,222,047 | |
| Inventory | – 0d + | 0 | |
| Payables | – 0d + | 0 | |
| | | **4,981,130** | **5,563,466** |

The company could not completely eliminate the negative Cash Flow impact of inflation and supply chain issues. However, the mitigation strategy kept the company within its funding obligations whist increasing their Profit substantially.

## Company C — A fast growing IT services Company, burning Cash

Turnover — $100 million and growing fast, chasing Revenue

Profit — $8 million loss

Cash Flow — $9 million negative

### The Code of Your Business
Impact of a 1% or 1-day improvement

|  | Cash Flow | Profit |
|---|---|---|
| Price | +1.157,534 | +1.300,000 |
| Volume | +199,451 | +312,000 |
| Cost of Goods | +958,083 | +988,000 |
| Overheads | +392,000 | +392,000 |
| Recievables | +356,164 |  |
| Inventory | +356,164 |  |
| Payables | +270,685 |  |

What the company learned from their Power of One:

- Price impacts Cash Flow 6 times more than Volume
- Volume increase is the least sensitive item
- Each day of unbilled work is $356k

What the company did:

- Invoiced their customers 2 weeks earlier
- Put up prices by 5%
- Focused on improving people utilization

# How to implement the Power of One in your business

The Power of One can be implemented by any business, the concept of improving the 7 Levers of your company will result in improved financial performance.

- To get started run a Power of One Workshop with your senior management team:
- List the 7 Levers on a whiteboard and workshop lever by lever
- For each lever rank from most to least important
- At the end of the meeting choose 4 or 5 ideas that can be implemented.
- Create a who; what; when action plan for each idea

The meeting should be attended by Sales, Marketing, Operations and Finance. We recommend you run quarterly Power of One meetings to entrench a culture of driving continuous financial improvement

The Cashflowstory software will show you your Power of One, enabling you to understand your story, your sensitivity, your bang for bucks and alter preconceptions in your business. Running a Power of One workshop on your numbers enables everyone in your management team to understand the impact of changes on Profit and Cash Flow.

| Price | Idea 1 | Idea 2 | Idea 3 |
|---|---|---|---|
| Volume | Idea 1 | Idea 2 | |
| COGS | Idea 1 | Idea 2 | Idea 3 |
| Overheads | Idea 1 | Idea 2 | Idea 3 |
| Accounts Receivable | Idea 1 | Idea 2 | |
| Inventory | Idea 1 | Idea 2 | Idea 3 |
| Accounts Payable | Idea 1 | Idea 2 | |

The Power of One is a disruptor, it is very easy for businesses to justify current performance with statements like "our customers won't…" "we can't increase prices because…" "our market doesn't..". Management thinks their business operates in a paradigm where change is extremely difficult. By knowing the impact that the small 1% or 1 day changes to the 7 Levers will have on Profit and Cash Flow, management perceptions change.

# The Story of Your Business

Your Power of One is driving improvement in your Profit, Cash Flow and Valuation. This is the most important exercise you can do in your business. However, you also need to understand the financial story of your business. A story of numbers is told over 4 Chapters, Chapter One of your story is Profit. The result of your story in Chapter 4 is your Cash Flow. You will never understand your story unless you read your whole book, Chapter 2 and 3 is your Balance Sheet. Most companies look at their Profitability and don't measure or understand their Cash Flow or their Balance Sheet.

The 4 Chapters is a unique methodology that will provide you with a structured storytelling approach that can be understood by anyone. Imagine if your management team all understood your story in a consistent way and used the Power of One to drive improvement.

**The following Case Study will outline the 4 Chapters:**

## Gary's Furniture

Established in 2001, Gary's Furniture imports and manufactures high-end furniture. Over nearly 20 years of operation, the business has grown from a start-up to a well-established firm, with revenue of $42 million. Its customer base continues to grow, as does its geographical reach. The business has grown profits for the last 10 years. Gary is a member of a local CEO forum group. When asked by the group to score his satisfaction with his business performance, he consistently scores his business 10 out of 10!

Gary had no concerns when his bank called a meeting one day at its head office, shortly after he submitted his recent financials. But what Gary didn't know was that he was "growing broke." (Read that again!)

## Profit vs Cash

What is more important, Profit or Cash? If you're a growing business, it's Cash. This is why Amazon has continued to thrive while at near breakeven or, frequently, while posting losses. Amazon's business model generates significant Cash Flow — $35.3 billion in 2019 — which, in turn, fuels its rapid growth

The following case study shows how a healthy Profit and Loss statement can mask pending Cash Flow issues that will only get worse as the business continues to scale. Gary didn't know it, but he was outgrowing his ability to fund the business — growing broke — because he didn't understand the supreme importance of Cash.

In such a situation, unless you continue to raise emotional money (that is, Cash from people who love you), the smart money will flee, which only speeds up the demise of the business.

*"Gary didn't know he was 'growing broke.'"*

It's imperative that you understand your business from the perspective of bankers and Investors, so you're not frustrated by their apparent lack of appreciation for the company you're scaling up. Cashflowstory software has been developed for Business Leaders and Advisors to enable them to improve Profit, Cash Flow and Value and understand the story of the business. Hang in there through this case study, and you'll learn the story of a business and how the 7 Levers will improve Cash Flow dramatically and sleep better at night

## The Dreaded "Hospital Division"

When we left off, Gary was heading to the Bank. He could just as easily have been going to a meeting with an Angel Investor, a Private Equity Firm, or a potential acquirer who would be looking at the business through the same financial lens that Gary's bankers used.

When Gary was ushered into the meeting room, in front of him were not only his relationship manager and her assistant, but also the district manager and two other people dressed in suits. Gary was introduced to the two new parties, who were from the Bank's Special Credit Division.

The duo explained to Gary that their division was charged with managing clients deemed by the bank to be high-risk. Every Bank has a group like this. It may go by different descriptions, depending on the bank, among them "asset management," "credit restructuring," and "special business services." We call it the Hospital Division.

These people have the hardest job in the bank. They are responsible for determining rapidly whether a client is providing the best return on the bank's capital assets, relative to the risk of loss. If not, it is their job to maximize the recovery of capital as quickly as possible. Because these bankers did not write the original deal and have a very distant relationship with the business owner, they are well-positioned to make hard decisions, but they face limited personal career consequences if the bank incurs a loss when exiting from the relationship.

*"These bankers were idiots and didn't understand his business."*

Gary was absolutely shocked. How could his bank see him as high-risk? Had the bankers not read the recent financials? At this point, Gary could think only one thing: These bankers were idiots, and they clearly didn't understand his business. Gary tuned out from the meeting as his mind whirred through his potential next steps. He missed most of the conversation as the bankers explained how they would increase his interest rates and restrict his access to further increases in funding. He was livid.

Immediately after the meeting, Gary rang his accountant, who called us. We arrived at Gary's office the next day to find him still in denial, cursing and swearing about his bank's audacity in increasing his rates.

We use a phrase in our business when we first meet most clients: "Business speaks Spanish, and Banks (and Investors) speak Portuguese. To the uninitiated, they sound like the same language, but they are actually totally different." This was exactly Gary's situation: He and the bankers were speaking two different languages, but he couldn't tell the difference.

## The Numbers

Gary provided us with a copy of his last two years of financials, as summarized to the right.

At a glance, the business looks healthy. However, it faced a problem that's present in 80% to 90% of all companies that we visit: inadequate Cash Flow. Businesses are Profit focused. In Gary's case, he was looking at Revenue and Profit that were growing significantly, and he was feeling great.

However, there is an old saying: "Revenue is vanity, Profit is sanity, and Cash Flow is King." You do not pay bills or distributions with Profit. You can buy your spouse that holiday house or nice car only when you have sufficient monthly Cash. Until businesses become serious about measuring and growing Cash, in addition to Profit, they often run short.

## What Is Cash Flow?

The only indisputable facts in any set of financials are the numbers that relate to Cash. Your Profit is an opinion, and data can be manipulated to provide a specific outcome. Your Balance Sheet is for the most part also an opinion; you can adjust numbers such as Inventory value, to produce a desired result. Only your Cash and Debt balances are facts. Banks recognize this and use these numbers to determine your performance.

Our first question for Gary was simple: "What was your Cash Flow in 2021?" Gary could not answer this. (Look back over the financials. Can you calculate the answer quickly?) Every day, business leaders produce their financials and share the results with their management teams, and yet very few of them can readily answer such questions.

| Profit & Loss | 2020 | 2021 |
|---|---|---|
| Revenue | 35,000,000 | 42,000,000 |
| Gross margin | 10,500,000 | 13,020,000 |
| Overheads | 6,751,140 | 8,401,150 |
| Operating profit | 3,748,860 | 4,618,850 |
| Interest | 1,165,900 | 1,363,480 |
| Tax | 930,280 | 1,172,348 |
| Net profit | 1,652,680 | 2,083,022 |

| Balance Sheet | 2020 | 2021 |
|---|---|---|
| Accounts receivable | 6,712,330 | 8,630,137 |
| Inventory | 10,336,960 | 14,291,507 |
| Current assets | 17,049,290 | 22,921,644 |
| Fixed assets | 8,500,000 | 9,500,000 |
| Total assets | 25,549,290 | 32,421,644 |
| Accounts payable | 4,028,550 | 5,557,808 |
| Short-term debt | 5,019,740 | 7,279,813 |
| Current liabilities | 9,048,290 | 12,837,621 |
| Long-term debt | 9,000,000 | 10,000,000 |
| Total liabilities | 18,048,290 | 22,837,621 |
| Share capital | 2,001,000 | 2,001,000 |
| Retained earnings | 5,500,000 | 7,583,022 |
| Total liabilities and equity | 25,549,290 | 32,421,643 |

*"Only your cash and debt balances are facts."*

Cash Flow is an expression that is used in businesses every day: "I have good Cash Flow." "I need more Cash Flow." "We need to improve our Cash Flow." Most businesspeople use the term to describe a general availability of Cash. It refers to an almost intangible quality of a business. However, to a Banker, Cash Flow has a specific meaning. It is a number that indicates management competence. And that competence starts with you, the business leader, understanding the information that follows.

If you don't, the money people will always have an advantage over you. In the sections to come, we will give you a high-level overview of what you need to understand to stay in control of your business.

# Two Uses of Cash

Whether you're sitting on a pile of Cash or a mountain of Debt, keep reading. The lessons apply to you in either case.

Cash Flow is the change in Cash and Debt balances across a given period. Because Gary operated using an overdraft account, labeled on the Balance Sheet as "Short Term Debt," there is no specific 'Cash' line item (i.e., he had no Cash of his own in the bank). His Short Term Debt increased in 2020 from $5 million to $7.3 million, and his Long Term Debt increased from $9 million to $10 million. The company's Cash Flow for 2021 was minus $3.3 million. Gary had gone backward in Cash.

This information, presented in this way, was new for Gary and surprised him a little

Owners like Gary choose to spend money every day to grow their businesses. However, sometimes they are spending their hard-earned money to cover management influenced waste (read that again). Did Gary actually need to spend $3.3 million of new money from the Bank to increase his Revenue from $35 million to $42 million and to raise his Profit from $1.7 million to $2.1 million — or was this increase in borrowing used simply to fund poor management practices?

This question highlights the only two uses for Cash Flow:

1. Cash is used to fund growth
2. Cash is used to fund management influenced waste

| Opening net debt | |
|---|---|
| Short-term debt | 5,019,740 |
| Long-term debt | 9,000,000 |
| | 14,019,740 |
| **Closing net debt** | |
| Short-term debt | 7,279,813 |
| Long-term debt | 10,000,000 |
| | 17,279,813 |
| **Net cash flow** | **-3,260,073** |

And yet too few growing businesses are able to visualize their Cash burn in this simple framework!

## Your Balance Sheet

Balance Sheets are perceived to be very complex. In fact it should be very easy to understand because it is really just an equation that will always balance.

**Funding  =  Operations**

Equity + Net Debt  =  Working Capital + Other Capital

## Scaling Up

### Working Capital

There are only 3 key items that your management team is responsible for:

- Accounts Receivable, also known as Trade Debtors
- Inventory or Unbilled Work in Progress
- Accounts Payable, also known as Trade Creditors

### Other Capital

If you know your Debt, your Equity and your Working Capital, Other Capital is the balancing item i.e., Fixed Assets plus the rest of the Balance Sheet.

### Gary's Equation

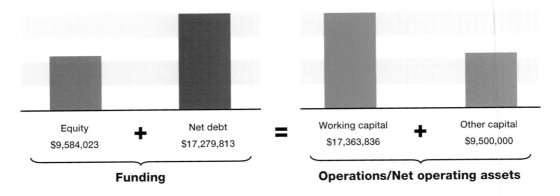

| Equity | | Net debt | | Working capital | | Other capital |
|---|---|---|---|---|---|---|
| $9,584,023 | **+** | $17,279,813 | **=** | $17,363,836 | **+** | $9,500,000 |
| **Funding** | | | | **Operations/Net operating assets** | | |

This Equation highlights the fact that the Bank has put approximately $2 into this business for every $1 invested by Shareholders.

Anyone in the Company should be able to understand the Balance Sheet Equation.

What does this Equation tell us about Gary's business:

- The Bank has funded $2 for each $1 invested by the Shareholders
- The management team is responsible for $17.3 million of Working Capital

The Balance Sheet is at a point in time, if you understand your current Balance Sheet and compare it to the previous period, the movement is the story of the business

| **This year** | | | | | |
|---|---|---|---|---|---|
| Equity | + | Net Debt | = | Working Capital + | Other Capital |
| 9,584,023 | | 17,279,813 | | 17,363,836 | 9,500,000 |

| **Last year** | | | | | |
|---|---|---|---|---|---|
| Equity | + | Net Debt | = | Working Capital + | Other Capital |
| 7,501,000 | | 14,019,740 | | 13,020,740 | 8,500,000 |

| **Change** | | | | | |
|---|---|---|---|---|---|
| Equity | + | Net Debt | = | Working Capital + | Other Capital |
| 2,083,023 | | 3,260,073 | | 4,343,096 | 1,000,000 |

What does this tell us about Gary's business?

- Gary made a Profit of over $2.08 million
- Gary's Borrowings increased by $3.26 million
- Gary's Funding increased by $5.34 million
- This was used to grow Working Capital by $4.34 million and buy $1 million of Fixed Assets

By understanding the Balance Sheet Equation and movement, you now know why Gary made a Profit but needed to borrow money from his Bank. By implementing The Power of One you will be able to drive improvement in Profit and Cash Flow.

# The 4 Chapters

The story of numbers consists of 4 Chapters

Chapter 1 Profit

Chapter 2 Working Capital

Chapter 3 Other Capital

Chapter 4 Funding

Just like any murder mystery book, no matter how many times you read Chapter 1, you will never know whodunnit unless you read the whole book. The exact same thing is happening in business around the world. If you only read your Profit Chapter, you will never understand your Cash Flow.

## Chapter 1 Profit

Most Companies are focused on Revenue, Margins and Profit and generally understand their Profitability. Gary believes he is doing a good job.

## Scaling Up

To add value to P&L analysis the following 3 graphs will help to gain a better understanding of how the business is performing. The Graphs should be read together.

| Profitability | 2020 | 2021 | Change |
|---|---|---|---|
| Revenue | 35,000,000 | 42,000,000 | +7,000,000 |
| Revenue growth % | 11.11 | 20.00 | +8.89 |
| Gross margin % | 30.00 | 31.00 | +1.00 |
| Overheads % | 19.29 | 20.00 | +0.71 |
| Operating profit % | 10.71 | 11.00 | +0.29 |
| Operating Profit | 3,748,860 | 4,618,850 | +869,990 |
| Net profit % | 4.72 | 4.96 | +0.24 |

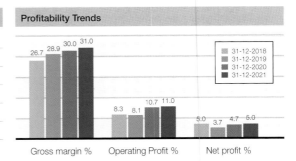

From the Profitability trends graph we can see that Gary's Gross Marin % is increasing but his Operating and Net Profit as a % are flat.

Looking at the Revenue Growth vs Overheads Growth graph it is clear to see that although Gary's Revenue grew by 20% his Overheads grew by 24%. Approximately half the companies we see have the same problem even though the company will always say our Overheads are fixed. By ensuring your company has an accountable person for each key P&L line item you can help mitigate this issue.

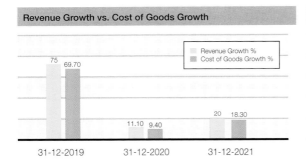

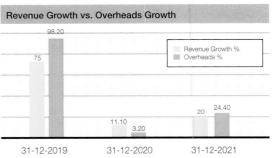

Most people understand their Profit & Loss but don't understand the critical relationships between the numbers such as Price vs Volume and their impact on Cash Flow. We recommend that everyone in your management team understands the impact that the 4 Power of One Profit drivers have on Profit and Cash Flow. Gary has a fast growth problem; volume growth is detrimental to Cash Flow. By looking at Chapter 1 in isolation you could come to the wrong conclusion as to what is best for the company.

## The Code of Your Business
Impact of a 1% or 1-day improvement

|  | Cash Flow | Profit |
|---|---|---|
| Price | +333.699 | +420.000 |
| Volume | -43.438 | +130.200 |
| Cost of Goods | +377.137 | +289.800 |
| Overheads | +84.012 | +84.012 |

## Chapter 2 Working Capital

We define Working Capital as the 3 critical numbers that your management team are responsible for in the Balance Sheet:

- Accounts Receivable (AR)
- Inventory or Unbilled Work in Progress (INV or WIP)
- Accounts Payable (AP)

Working Capital = AR + INV or WIP – AP

| Working Capital Management | 2020 | 2021 | Change |
|---|---|---|---|
| Accounts receivable days | 70.00 | 75.00 | +5.00 |
| Inventory days | 154.00 | 180.00 | +26.00 |
| Accounts payable days | 60.02 | 70.00 | +9.98 |
| Working capital days | 163.98 | 185.00 | +21.02 |
| Working capital % | 37.20 | 41.34 | +4.14 |
| Marginal cash flow | -7.20 | -10.34 | -3.14 |

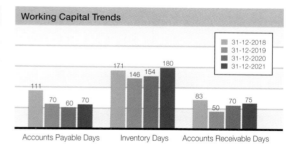

The most effective way to understand your Working Capital is in days

Working Capital days are connected, its vitally important that your management team understands the linkages. In Gary's Furniture:

- Inventory arrives on day zero
- The inventory is paid for 70 days later
- On average his inventory is held for 180 days before being sold
- 75 days later his customers pay which is on day 255

Gary needs to fund the Gap between paying suppliers and banking the money from his customers which is 185 Days. As we can see from the graphic below last year was 164 days.

This increase in his gap of 21 days has cost the business over $1.84 million. To explain this another way, if the business had achieved this year's Revenue on last year's Working Capital cycle they would have banked an additional $1.84 million.

## Working Capital Timeline

12 months ending 31-12-2021

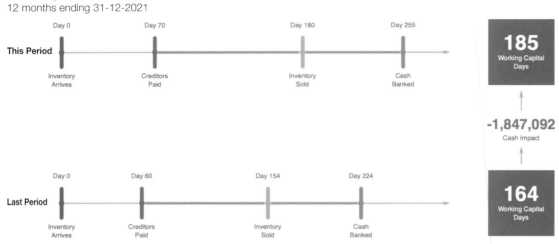

Your management team is equally responsible for managing Profit and Working Capital. Most companies struggle to explain the difference between profit and cash if they are purely profit focused.

## Marginal Cash Flow

If you ask most companies what happens when you sell $1 more of your product or services, the answer is almost always "we make extra Gross Margin". This is only half of the story, the impact of the Working Capital cannot be ignored. The impact of Revenue growth on Receivables, Inventory and Payables must be taken into account.

Marginal Cash Flow is the Cash flow generated or absorbed if you sell $1 more of your product or services. This measure calculates the amount of Cash retained by the business's Working Capital Machine and compares it to the amount of Profit the business produces at the Gross Margin level.

If we look at Gary's business, we see that it produced a Gross Margin of $13 million from $42 million in Revenue that the business achieved in 2021. By dividing Working Capital by Revenue, we can determine how much Working Capital is required for each $1 of Revenue. Gary requires $17.4 million of Working Capital.

### Marginal Cash Flow for the Next $1 of Sales

| Gross margin | | 13,020,000/42,000,000 | 31% |
|---|---|---|---|
| *Less* | | | |
| Accounts receivable | 8,630,137 | | |
| Inventory | 14,291,507 | | |
| Accounts payable | (5,557,808) | | |
| **Working capital** | | **17,363,836/42,000,000** | **41%** |

As we can see if Gary grows his Revenue by $1 he generates 31 cents of Gross Margin, but invests 41 cents in Working Capital. Gary's Marginal Cash Flow is -10 cents, this means that the more he sells the worse his Cash Flow will be!

Profitability and Working Capital management are equally important. By using the Power of One, Gary's management team should now workshop the 1% and 1 day improvements in order to address the problem.

Marginal Cash Flow can be applied to segments of a business, you should know which segments of your business are generating or absorbing Cash. You should focus growth on segments that you are generating Cash and reengineer poorly performing Cash Flow segments.

## Color Coding your business

To create visibility in Profitability and Working Capital Management color coding your business is very useful. The first two tables below were constructed, with the right-hand columns representing good, average, and bad results.

| 1 – Profitability | Ideal Profile | G | A | B |
|---|---|---|---|---|
| Revenue % | 100 | | | |
| Gross margin % | 30 | >30 | 28-30 | <28 |
| Overheads % | 20 | <20 | 20-22 | >22 |
| Operating Profit % | 10 | >10 | 8-10 | <8 |

| 2 – Working Capital | Ideal Profile | G | A | B |
|---|---|---|---|---|
| AR days | 60 | <60 | 60-70 | >70 |
| Inventory/WIP days | 90 | <90 | 90-100 | >100 |
| AP days* | 60 | — | — | — |
| Working capital % | 22 | <22 | 22-25 | >25 |

*Your good, average, and bad results will depend on your relationships with your suppliers.

| 3 – Profitability | Ideal Profile | G | A | B |
|---|---|---|---|---|
| Revenue % | 100 | | | |
| Gross margin % | 30 | 31 | | |
| Overheads % | 20 | | 20 | |
| Operating Profit % | 10 | 11 | | |

| 4 – Working Capital | Ideal Profile | G | A | B |
|---|---|---|---|---|
| AR days | 60 | | | 75 |
| Inventory/WIP days | 90 | | | 180 |
| AP days | 60 | | (70) | |
| Working capital % | 22 | | | 41 |

The ideal profile was constructed to guide management and provide a means for simple comparison against actual results. Ranges were set so that Gary's management was able to construct a monthly results table, which demonstrated in simple colors how the company was performing.

Gary's results are shown in tables 3 and 4, by color coding the results in green (for good), yellow (for average), or red (for bad), the team could get a very quick visual assessment of its performance. The goal is to teach the company how to operate in color code green so that everyone knows the parameters for success and the progress the company is making. The Sales team was focused on the Revenue and Gross Margin results, since they had responsibility for product discounting. The Buying team looked for products that would enhance Gross Margins. The Finance and HR units kept an eye on Overheads. Both the Sales team and Finance monitored Receivables (AR). Meanwhile,

# Scaling Up

the Warehouse group monitored and reduced Inventory, and Finance focused on when the company paid Suppliers (AP).

Please note that color coding your business is not Benchmarking. Your ideal profile is typically your budget numbers for next year. The goal is to review you're your color coding every quarter and to drive continuous improvement. If every measure is green, consider whether you are challenging your business sufficiently.

## Chapter 3 Other Capital

As discussed previously funding equals operations.

| Net Debt | + | Equity | = | Working Capital | + | Other Capital |
|----------|---|--------|---|-----------------|---|---------------|
| 17.3 | | 9.6 | | 17.4 | | 9,5 |
| | Funding | | = | | Operating Assets | |

The management team is responsible for Operations which is $26.9 million. How can we tell if they are doing a good job? Is the company generating sufficient Operating Profit from their Operating Assets? The best measure to determine this is Return on Capital Employed (ROCE).

$$\text{Operating Profit} / \text{Operating Assets} = \text{Return on Capital Employed}$$

The ratio can be further broken down into:

$$\frac{\text{Operating Profit}}{\text{Revenue}} \quad \times \quad \frac{\text{Revenue}}{\text{Operating Assets}} \quad = \text{Return on Capital Employed}$$

This is a very powerful ratio for measuring management effectiveness. Your management team are equally responsible for the management of your Profitability as well as your Balance Sheet Efficiency

The Operating Profit / Revenue measures P&L efficiency (i.e., how much Profit is produced from every $1 of Revenue). This tells you how efficiently you're operating and whether you are squeezing the most Profit from every dollar of Revenue.

In turn, the Revenue/Net Operating Assets measures Balance Sheet effectiveness known as Asset Turnover. It also is a key indicator of Revenue effectiveness — telling you how much Revenue the business can generate from the least amount of Assets or Investment.

The calculations show that Gary's business produced a Return on Capital of 17.19% in 2021. This falls below our expectations of good business performance. By breaking down the performance into

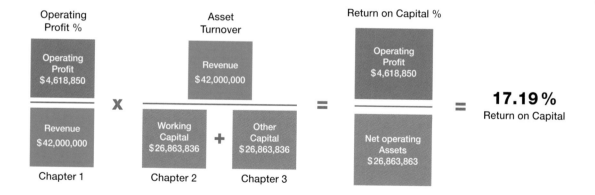

| Operating Profit % | | Asset Turnover | | | Return on Capital % | | |
|---|---|---|---|---|---|---|---|
| Operating Profit $4,618,850 | X | Revenue $42,000,000 | | = | Operating Profit $4,618,850 | = | **17.19%** Return on Capital |
| Revenue $42,000,000 | | Working Capital $26,863,836 | + Other Capital $26,863,836 | | Net operating Assets $26,863,863 | | |
| Chapter 1 | | Chapter 2 | Chapter 3 | | | | |

Profitability (Chapter 1) and Asset Turnover (Chapter 2 and 3) we can see that Gary is producing strong Profits. However, Gary' is not performing in Balance Sheet efficiency. Gary is producing only $1.56 of Revenue for each $1 invested. His Balance Sheet is carrying too much unproductive Capital as we learned in the analysis of Chapter 2. Gary is running his Working Capital in colour code red. A company should strive to optimize their Return, which will be achieved by running your Profitability and Working Capital in colour code green.

## What is a minimum Return on Capital Employed?

The answer is a relative one, as it will depend on the alternative investment choices available to investors. To keep it simple, however, midsize businesses should target at minimum a 30% Return on Capital. If you are not achieving this, you need to consider whether the Profit you are producing from the Revenue generated is sufficient, or whether the business is producing enough Profit for the Operating Assets. If not, your investors (that includes the owners!) might be better off investing their money elsewhere.

**Return on Capital Employed**

*"Midsize businesses should target at minimum a 30% return on net assets."*

As a business owner, you should also remember that your Equity is the most expensive source of funding and that it is can often be cheaper to source Debt financing. Either way, to improve Return on Capital it is mission-critical over time that management grow Operating Profit faster than the investment in Operating Assets.

## The Bank

Through our analysis, we were able to highlight a number of points that were hurting the banking relationship, to Gary's surprise:

1. The Bank had $2 in the business for every $1 invested by shareholders.

2. In Gary's case, Revenue Growth is detrimental to Cash flow. The more Gary sold, the worse his Cash Flow got (his Gross Margin was 31 cents, while his Working Capital investment was 41 cents).

3. Gary didn't have the Cash capacity to repay the Bank.

Working together, with clear definitions of success — and using Cashflowstory the inexpensive online software tool at www.cashflowstory.com — Gary's team turned around their Cash Flow very quickly. The company has now moved to a much more favorable position with its bankers, who were astounded by the business's rapid turnaround and significant Debt reduction. Today, Gary has a standard reporting format that he uses to inform his board.

# In Conclusion

To Scale Up your Profit, Cash and Value you should implement the following:

- Run an initial Power of One Workshop with your team (Repeat Quarterly)
- Review your most recent annual results to ensure you understand your Cash Flow
- Prepare a 4 Chapter summary of your company (Repeat Quarterly)
- Color code your business and review quarterly
- Review your next quarter's budget and use the Power of one to uplift performance

All growth firms hit bumps in the road (or craters!). Having sufficient Cash is key to surviving another day. We hope the ideas, tools, and techniques covered in this section help you through the rough times and fuel your good times as you Scale Up your Business.

Remember You can get by with decent People, Strategy, and Execution, but if you run out of Cash it is game over.

# 14

# THE EXIT
## 4 Keys to Maximizing Valuation

*EXECUTIVE SUMMARY: Scaling to sell, using the Scaling Up tools/techniques, maximizes the value of your business whether you plan to exit or not. The first half of this chapter highlights four keys to driving a significant increase in valuation: Become redundant, gain control of an industry constraint, achieve a 10x internal advantage, and generate consistent growth. The second half details the pitfalls to avoid in selling your business. Buyers' calculated (devious?) moves can cost you tens of millions in cash if you're not careful.*

Stephen Adele and his four co-founders at QuickBox Fulfillment, a Denver-based firm that does e-commerce fulfillment, grew the company to 500 employees and $57.3 million in annual revenue in two years. They sold an 80% controlling interest in the firm, founded in 2017, to Pike Street Capital in 2019 in an eight-figure deal.

How did they pull off this quick exit? The Scaling Up platform helped them achieve their goal of building the company to sell. "I wasn't even sure some of the practices would work but found them to not only work but be incredibly powerful in scaling the business," says Adele, who led the company as CEO and is now a member of the board of directors.

If you are planning to exit in the next six to 36 months, using the Scaling Up platform can help you to do what Adele and countless other founders and CEOs have done: maximize the valuation you receive, often to two to three times an industry standard multiple. This puts tens of millions of dollars more into your pockets as business owner(s). In the meantime, the platform makes it easier to scale while driving industry-leading topline and bottom-line results

### Additional $100 Million

Greg Slamowitz's journey was a bit longer than Adele's. As he describes it, his life was exhausting as he launched and ran Ambrose Employer Group, a professional employer organization (PEO). After eight tough years he managed to get to 35 employees and $2.5 million in earnings — and was stuck.

He then discovered Scaling Up, hired a Scaling Up coach who facilitated quarterly planning sessions for eight years, and attended our annual Scaling Up Summits with 12 of his leaders without fail. He figures he spent roughly $300,000 on coaching and learning. The result? He was able to scale to $20 million in earnings "with ease and loving life." After exiting to General Atlantic, he credits Scaling Up with generating a $100 million of the $200 million all cash offer he received — more than a 3,000% return on his investment. Here's a link to a video where he explains the process and results.

*https://vimeo.com/689465085*

## Billion-Dollar Promise Kept

Four of the five companies from the first London cohort of our 20,000 Scaleups initiative launched in 2018, have already seen exits, with a combined value near $920 million:

- Exponea, a leading customer experience and data platform, was acquired in 2021 by Bloomreach, a leader in the ecommerce experience, and received a $150 million investment by Sixth Street Growth.
- LegalX, which was the UK division of the Australian tech firm GlobalX, was acquired by Dye & Durham for AUD 170 million in 2021.
- Carousel Logistics, after merging with another European logistics carrier, DANX, was acquired by the private equity firm Axcel in March 2022.
- Point A Hotels, with 1,520 rooms across 10 hotels, was acquired by Tristan Fund and Queensway, for £420m in April 2022

With plans to launch in 150 cities around the globe, one of our promises to supporting cities is that the 20,000 Scaleups initiative will help several of their local firms exit for a combined $1 billion. We delivered on this promise within 48 months of our launch in London. This matters because these companies and their owners tend to reinvest a portion of their exit funds back into their cities (charities, angel funds, etc.).

Additional case studies of firms crediting the Scaling Up tools/techniques for driving eight, nine, and 10 figure exits can be found on our media site *www.scaleups.com*.

Following are the four competitive advantages, which many owners credit with driving up the valuations of their businesses. These four align with our Scaling Up Performance Platform framework: People, Strategy, Execution and Cash, which are covered throughout the book. How many of these valuation-enhancing attributes does your company possess? It's worth a final review as this book comes to a close.

## People: The CEO Is Redundant

When the owner is critical to a company's success, it is much riskier for someone to purchase the business. It's best for future business owners, and you, if the business can both survive and thrive without you.

Think Apple. Many people thought Steve Jobs' baby would never survive after his passing in 2011. Yet a decade later, the company achieved a valuation almost 10x what it was when he passed. Just like in parenting, the measure of your success is how your "children" behave when you're not around!

The Scaling Up Performance Platform helps you do just this. It reduces by 80% the time it takes for an owner to manage the business. And after 36 months, with the support of a coach, most CEOs are able to spend as little as a few days a quarter primarily driving strategy. And this gives owners time to be actively involved in the process of exiting their business. Warning: Keep it a secret that you're spending almost no time "in" the business.

Working 100-hour weeks? Put more of the business on autopilot with a well-functioning senior team implementing Scaling Up and see your valuation (and life!) soar.

## Strategy: Control an Industry Constraint

Giving CEOs more time to focus on strategy, the Scaling Up Performance Platform next provides the tools and techniques they need to identify the key constraint in an industry. Gain control of this and you'll be better able to control your destiny.

In my second book, *The Greatest Business Decisions of All Time*, I detail how the late Robert Taylor "blackmailed" Colgate-Palmolive into purchasing his firm for a gazillion dollars ($75 million, a lot of money in the Eighties). He recognized that the key component of his Softsoap liquid soap offering was the spring pump. Given there was only one manufacturer of those pumps at the time, he purchased the entire annual production of the manufacturing firm (100 million units at a price of $.12 per unit), guaranteeing Colgate, P&G, and others couldn't compete with him — and forcing Colgate's hand in eventually purchasing the company.

Virtual Technology Corp (VTC) did the same, locking up all the unique talent in its military simulation niche. Raytheon later came along and purchased VTC for a gazillion dollars (we can't divulge the amount) to keep the competition from having access to this critical source of talent.

Is there a key constraint in your industry? Gain control and your valuation will soar.

## Execution: Insider 10x Advantage

After you've won control of a key external constraint, the Scaling Up Performance Platform will help you identify the equivalent in your business model. Labeled an X Factor, it's an internal 10x advantage over the competition. This advantage helps strengthen the moat around your business and signals to a strategic buyer what they could achieve, given their much larger resources.

The late Wayne Huizenga was able to negotiate a price for the videos Blockbuster rented that was 1/11th the price competitors paid. John Ratliff's Appletree Answers call-center firm had 10x better employee retention than the industry average (18% vs. 200%). Barrett Ersek's firm Happy Lawns landed customers in 5 minutes vs. an industry average of 5 weeks. Steven Adele's firm figured out how to generate 5x the revenue per delivered package than many of the company's rivals. And all four exited for outsized valuations.

This internal advantage is like a buyer knowing there is a "Rembrandt in the attic" of a home they're buying. Buyers are going to be much more willing to offer considerably above asking price to secure this outsized internal advantage.

Is there an aspect of the business where you outperform the competition by a factor of 5 - 10? Nail this and your valuation will soar.

## Cash: Steady Growth

Achieving a 10x advantage that addresses a widespread internal issue in the industry is also key to bringing stability to growth. Your valuation will be much greater if you've had consistent growth in revenue, profitability and, especially, gross margin dollars, than if your growth has been erratic. Disciplined and steady performance, which the tools/techniques of Scaling Up help to provide, proves the company can create and deliver consistent results in a chaotic environment.

Greg Alexander achieved a $162 million exit from his management consulting firm, Sales Benchmark Index, which specialized in sales effectiveness in the B2B space, by using the Scaling Up Performance Platform to deliver consistent results in that industry — compounding an annual and steady growth rate of 30% for a decade.

Is your growth rate consistent and lacking drama? Demonstrate you have control of your business, even in periods of economic chaos, and your valuation soars.

## Conclusion: Master All Four

Become redundant in your business, gain control of an industry constraint, achieve a 10x internal advantage, and generate consistent growth — and scaling your firm will be easier and more fun. And if you exit, you'll receive an outsized valuation.

The Scaling Up Performance Platform has helped thousands of founders and owners master each of these advantages. Again, our media site *www.scaleups.com* details many success stories, including those that eventually exited.

The most exciting two days in many founders' lives are the day they start their business and the day they sell it. Putting the right systems in place can help you ensure that you enjoy the journey in-between and that your exit is as rewarding as it can be. This will pave the way to new opportunities to achieve an impact in the next chapter of your life.

The challenge, if you decide to sell the business, is navigating the exiting process to assure you get top dollar for all the years of blood, sweat, and tears.

# The Games Buyers Play

Business owners work years building up the value in their company, only to give a big chunk of it away when it comes time to sell. Why? Savvy corporate acquisition and private equity teams wear down the most seasoned and savvy owners using a well-practiced method, backing them into a corner where they have to sell for a steep discount.

Here are some of their questionable, (and sometimes dirty) tricks.

## Promises, Promises

The first step is counterintuitive, which is why it's so effective. The buyer — typically a significantly larger corporation — offers the owner an insanely high price for the business and suggests the deal can close in weeks.

The price, almost always expressed indirectly as some multiple of earnings before interest, taxes, depreciation and amortization (EBITDA), will be a price that is 25% to 100% more than what the business owner even thinks the business is worth. At this point the owners think they've landed the deal of the century — while the reference to earnings sensitizes the seller to reduce expenses (more on this later).

Why would the buyer do this? To get sellers to drop their guard. Nothing builds a temporary relationship faster (look, the CEO is not likely to stick around after the sale) than offering a premium price for the business.

It also gets the owners and their spouses dreaming about the life they will lead after the sale — the houses, boats, and vacations — once they have a boatload of money. The potential buyer will often take them to dinner and discuss these precise topics to help them imagine their future. But when buyers casually ask about vacation homes and boats the seller might buy, it is never casual. It is a big red flag!

The buyers are also offering a price they don't plan to pay to entice sellers to sign an exclusivity agreement that prevents the owners from talking with other potential buyers for a few months (there goes the competition for your firm), while the buyers do their due diligence — which they promise will go quickly.

The sellers will usually sign on the exclusivity dotted line, relieved that they are going to get a great price and not have to deal with other buyers, which is extremely time consuming. The trap has been set.

## Psychological Warfare

Once the document is signed, the buyer now drags out due diligence for months, while promising all along the way that everything will be wrapped up shortly. If I had a nickel for every time a seller heard "It's just a couple weeks more," we could all retire.

Because the buyer implies all along the selling price is tied to some multiple of EBIDTA, the sellers start putting off key expenditures they would otherwise make to keep the business humming — a key hire, marketing spend or training/planning session.

To make matters worse, the buyer, early on, asks about anniversary dates, planned vacations, industry tradeshows and other key plans and then starts disrupting the seller's rhythms and life through the infamous "emergency meeting." The evening before the seller departs for a family vacation or major trade show, the M&A team will call to say that there's been a problem with the deal and demand that he or she show up for a meeting the next day to straighten things out.

Afraid to derail the deal, the frazzled seller will cancel the departure. Now the family and business team start pushing to get the deal done. The pressure continues to mount.

## Diminished Performance

With the owner mentally checked out of the business, cutting back on critical expenditures to pump up EBITDA and worn out from missing vacations and the grind of due diligence, the business typically suffers a temporary slump. It's all part of the buyers' game plan. The buyers want the company's performance to suffer a little so they can use it as a giant sledgehammer to drive down the price at the 59th minute of the eleventh hour.

They might seize upon something they have deliberately left open to negotiation in the Letter of Intent (LOI). One classic example is the "working capital peg." Companies are often sold "cash free, debt free" which means the seller takes out the net cash to pay off debt, with some reasonable working capital left in to operate the firm. In one classic late renegotiating tactic, buyers will pressure the seller to leave a more "reasonable" amount of working capital in the business than expected.

Beat up by the entire process, the seller begrudgingly gives in to this or other kinds of last-minute demands and concessions, and ultimately lowers the price — to a fraction of what was originally offered. The buyer wins big, and the seller leaves millions on the table.

## Bidding Wars

How do you avoid this scenario—and still sell your business? Always enlist an outstanding sell-side advisor experienced in M&A work (this is no time for amateur hour). All professional athletes and entertainers have agents for a reason. It's impossible to represent yourself without getting dirty. You need a "bad cop" in the deal when things get dicey, and they always do.

The primary job of the sell-side advisor is to seek out strategic vs. financial buyers — and to help uncover/discover the "Rembrandts in the attic" (described earlier in the chapter) that will drive your strategic value in the marketplace. Then they'll set up an auction for you. Don't let a single potential buyer call the shots. One friend's sell-side advisor identified 23 strategic buyers of which seven came to the table to bid for the business.

*"...the best practice is to run a full "reverse due diligence" on your company long before a buyer does.."*

If a serious prospect wants an exclusivity agreement, only after your sell-side advisor has run a soft-auction (never before), limit it to 30 days. This puts pressure on the buyer to complete due diligence quickly. And have "the box" of materials prepared in advance so you are bulletproof during due diligence. In fact, the best practice is to run a full "reverse due diligence" on your company long before a buyer does. It can help identify key issues before hand. Surprises in diligence have killed many deals.

## Due Diligence Warning

During due diligence, emphasize that this is NOT a time to renegotiate the deal but to verify what has been negotiated in getting to the LOI. This is where your sell-side advisor is key. Make it clear early that any attempt at an unreasonable re-negotiation is a cause to terminate exclusivity and will not be tolerated.

Last, as best you can, insulate yourself from the transaction. Have your CFO or another trusted executive work with your sell-side advisor to act as a go-between with the buyer, so you don't get distracted from leading your team. Push back against last-minute demands for meetings. You want to be calm and think clearly every time you negotiate—and not fresh out of a fight with your spouse about cancelling the family vacation.

Overall, keep your head in the game and continue running the business as if the deal isn't going to happen up until the moment you cash the final check!! Your willingness to walk away from the deal is the ultimate competing buyer. That mindset will put you in your strongest negotiating position, as will lining up other buyers who understand how they can multiply your strategic value in the marketplace.

By finding the right strategic buyers you can create a group that doesn't just "want" to buy your company, but "needs" to acquire it to further their strategy. This shifts the balance of power entirely to your side. Having two or more bidders on fire to buy you is an entirely different experience than negotiating with a sole-sourced buyer acting like they are doing you a huge favor.

## Public Company Multiples

Whenever a business owner has mentioned they want to sell their business, we steer them to certain sell-side only advisors and advocates. The first time was a close friend who had almost signed with a major accounting firm to sell his firm. The allure was its global reach and that it had brokered many firms in a similar space with significant contacts in my friend's industry.

Though purporting to represent the seller, these large accounting and M&A firms have much closer relationships with the buyers, likely helping to facilitate dozens of transactions for them. In turn, they are likely to do only this one transaction with you. To whom are they more loyal?

Worse, if the M&A firm has done a lot of transactions in your industry, they can't afford to get you a much higher valuation as a multiple of earnings than they did the previous dozen transactions, to protect their reputation. You will be stuck in a financially driven formula that ultimately gets you three to seven times earnings, depending on the standard in the industry.

To these larger brokerage firms, you are just another transaction. Additionally, they may do other work for buyers around quality of earnings, valuation, etc., so they can be conflicted. In contrast, the right sell-side advisor focuses on maximizing your return.

## Unique Strategic Advantage

You've spent years, if not decades, scaling the business. Most of your net worth is likely tied up in all this effort. Our approach is to discover your unique strategic advantage — one you are so close to you don't even see it (it takes a fresh set of eyes to uncover it) — and then to identify a potential pool of up to 200 buyers.

And it's important to bring to the table international buyers who are willing to pay much higher valuations for firms simply to enter the seller's market(s). Ultimately, the right sell side advisor creates a soft auction among a handful of buyers until it gets two or three firms fiercely competing to buy your business.

This is a much lengthier process and usually the fees increase as a percentage of the sale if it gets you considerably more for the business (isn't this how it should be). Luckily, my friend engaged the right sell-side advisor, which sold his firm for 3x the number in his mind (on the high end of multiple of earnings in his industry), and 5x the number in his spouse's mind. The extra tens of millions matter.

Many of Scaling Up's clients have achieved exit multiples of 15, 20, 30, or more of earnings. To be fair, most of these firms have used our Scaling Up tools/techniques to scale their businesses, making them much more attractive to larger companies. Public companies especially appreciate the quarterly discipline and meeting rhythms Rockefeller Habits 2.0 instills within organizations. These larger firms often note that our clients operate better than they do! This is why several of the CEOs we coach have gone on to become CEOs or senior executives inside global 500 firms.

## Golf or Tennis Pro

If you're within six to 36 months of wanting to exit your firm, please reach out to me at *verne@ scalingup.com* and we'll arrange for a complimentary consultation on what the valuation would be for your business from strategic international buyers.

Selling (or scaling) a business for the first time is like the first time picking up a golf club or tennis racquet. You can be an outstanding athlete, but you will be no match for a seasoned player. Worse, you are often up against world class players in the market and M&A space.

It is millions you're risking and likely one of the most important transactions you'll make in your life. Make the very best of it so you can keep scaling your impact for generations to come!

# NEXT STEPS
## 5 Things to Do Now

---

*Implementing the meeting rhythms and quarterly themes/goals has improved our productivity drastically. It's actually hard to believe how well it is working!*

David Lee, COO World Embrace, Uganda

---

Thank you for reading *Scaling Up*. To jump-start implementation and benefit immediately from the ideas in this book, here are five things to do now:

1. **Have your entire leadership team (and employees) read or listen to the book.** And Verne's entire 2.5 day Scaling Up course is online at *www.ScaleUpU.com*. This will give everyone a common language and context for implementation. Then complete a complimentary 4 Decisions Assessment and decide which of the four — People, Strategy, Execution, or Cash — to pursue first. Go to that section of the book and focus on reading and implementing one chapter per month for the next quarter. The assessment, list of public (or private) workshops, and bulk discounts on books are available at *scalingup.com*.

2. **Form a weekly "council."** In addition to organizing a weekly management meeting, assemble a few key leaders to discuss strategies and the bigger opportunities and challenges facing the company. Go to Pages 110 to review the details of this crucial weekly "talk time" routine. Focus on completing the 7 Strata of Strategy worksheet; assembling a list of influencers; and working through the 4Ps or 4Es of marketing.

3. **Launch a Quarterly Theme.** Choose a measurable goal that addresses some choke point in the business (something keeping you awake at night), and focus the entire company on achieving it in the next few weeks. There's no need for a fancy theme if you're short on time, but give it a name. Put up a whiteboard in a common area of the company and start tracking progress via the daily huddle. Then host a celebration at the end. Pick a goal that's challenging but doable, so the team tastes success quickly.

4. **Start the daily huddle.** Begin by holding a daily huddle for the executive team. Then, when these leaders are comfortable with the routine, let them implement it with their respective teams, cascading this crucial communication rhythm down through the organization. Share specifics, but don't fall into the trap of problem-solving, and keep these initial huddles to 15 minutes or less.

5. **Plan your first quarterly or annual offsite (with a coach).** Set the dates for your next strategic planning session and start preparations — employee and customer survey, completion of the SWOT by middle management and completion of the SWT by the top leadership team. Once

at the offsite, start filling in the boxes of the various one-page Growth Tools. Focus initially on the basic decisions represented on the Vision Summary worksheet (Core Values, Purpose, Brand Promises, BHAG®, and Priorities) and choose a couple of habits from the Rockefeller Habits Checklist to implement next.

Most important, relax with the process. Thousands of companies have successfully implemented the Rockefeller Habits 2.0.

## One Step at a Time

Whatever you do, avoid doing everything all at once. Our 4D Framework is a process of working on one aspect of the business at a time so no one gets overwhelmed. It generally takes two to three years for all the tools, techniques, and habits to become part of the company's DNA, and another two to three years to truly master the use of them.

It is critical to pick someone to drive overall implementation of the Rockefeller Habits. For many founders, it might be best to give this accountability to your #2 in command. Verne wrote a column specifically for entrepreneurs on how to "Hire the Right #2." Go to *scalingup.com* to download a copy.

## You're Not Alone — Coaching, Learning, and Technology

To support and speed up your implementation of our tools and make the process more enjoyable, we've built a team on six continents offering a variety of services, including:

**Coaching:** No one has ever achieved peak performance without a coach. If you need help implementing these tools, we can give you access to our elite team of certified coaching partners spanning the globe. Utilizing a coach fast-tracks implementation and takes a load off the leadership team, so you're generating significant revenue and profits much sooner. Book a complimentary 30-minute call for a debriefing of your 4 Decisions Assessment.

**Learning:** Book your team into a one-day public or private Scaling Up workshop. Take the idea further, and have a member of your team earn a Scaling Up Master Practitioner Certification through our online learning and coaching program. This person can support implementation internally.

In addition, we can offer you an extensive online array of accredited short courses through our Growth Institute, taught by top business thought leaders, to provide you and your management team with the kind of continuing business education in leadership, marketing, sales, hiring, etc., that keeps you ahead of the competition. You can access all of this from the comfort of your desk or home — *www.growthinstitute.com*.

**Technology:** We offer an online software-as-a-service (SaaS) management accountability system called Scaling Up Scoreboard, which has more than 10,000 users. It's the CEO's (or COO's) tool for managing the cascading priorities, key performance indicators, and accountabilities that can become an Excel-spreadsheet nightmare when you grow beyond a handful of employees, especially when your teams are spread across multiple locations. *www.scalingup.com/software/*

These support systems typically provide a 10x return on your investment. Information is available at *scalingup.com*.

## Who Will Succeed

In 2002, the year *Mastering the Rockefeller Habits* was first published, Verne hosted the 10-year reunion for the executive program he founded and chaired on the campus of MIT (called EMP today). This program was the genesis of what you've learned in this book.

During the Q and A session, one of the alumni asked him a key question: *"Over the years, you have seen many business leaders succeed and fail. Have you noticed anything specific about those who made it to greatness?"*

Verne's answer to that question is the same today. Success belongs to those who have these two attributes:

- An insatiable desire to learn
- An unquenchable bias for action

Those who win are constantly looking for better ways to do things and to improve. They don't sit back and let others pass them by. They use their tools and resources to address constraints and make things happen.

Want to succeed with this book and your business? Keep on **learning** and **acting** as you scale up.

# 3 SUGGESTED PRIORITIES
## FOR SCALING YOUR BUSINESS

**1.** Sign up for Verne Harnish's **"Weekly Insights"** to receive the latest in ideas, tools, and techniques for growing your business.

**2.** Download copies of the **One-Page Strategic Plan** and other One-Page tools.

**3.** Access, on *scalingup.com*, short **"Growth Guy"** articles offering practical tips on setting up advisory boards, daily huddles for sales people, and 75 other topics.

## Go to **www.ScalingUp.com**

**SCALING UP**
A GAZELLES COMPANY

---

## SCALE UP to 2X FASTER

Companies using the software typically see a 2x increase in number of priorities completed after 12 months.

 **Run Daily and Weekly Huddles**

 **Your hub for your One Page Strategic Plan and other Growth Tools**

 **Cascade priorities and track KPI progress**

 **Power of One and Cash Acceleration Strategies**

## SCOREBOARD
SCALING UP

### The Official Software for Implementing Scaling Up
Powered by align

Request a demo at scalingup.com/software
or call 888-315-4049

# Implement Scaling Up faster and with fewer challenges.

- Get professional feedback, peer motivation, accountability, and a seasoned external perspective.

- A Scaling Up Coach provides highly-qualified guidance and support.

- Get matched with a Coach who's been expertly trained in People, Strategy, Execution, and Cash decisions and fits your unique business needs!

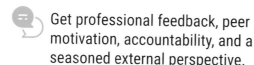

## SCALING UP
### COACHES

*We worked with a Scaling Up Coach at a turning point in the business. In the next 12 months, we smashed it. Revenue went up by 156% and order intake increased by 136% (with fewer people), and we engendered an amazing culture!"*

— Ryan Mee, Eco2Solar

**Discover what a Scaling Up Certified Coach™ can do for you today.**

To get started, email us at:
*coaching@ScalingUp.com*

---

# Transform your organization into a **SCALING UP** MACHINE!

Be a part of the next online class of **75 selected leaders** who, within 3 months, will remodel their company's operations with the guidance of **Verne Harnish & Scaling Up Coaches.**

Join the next class at
## growthinstitute.com/scale

GROWTH INSTITUTE
SCALE IMPACT & REDUCE DRAMA

# Appendix
## Top 12 Business Books

Master these dozen books and you'll have the most practical MBA in the world. And for a complete list of all the books, articles, and other resources mentioned in the book, go to *www.scalingup.com* and click on the "Free Chapters and Resources" link next to the picture of the book in the banner.

*The Goal: A Process of Ongoing Improvement* by Eli Goldratt

If you only read one book, this is it — the #1 business book of all time. Eli, RIP, taught us two things: 1) don't smoke (he died of lung cancer way too soon), and 2) the most powerful concept in business: "The Constraint!" Spending time or money focused on anything but the immediate constraint, in your company or market, is a waste. This concept serves as the foundation for the tools/techniques in Scaling Up.

 **People**

*Care to Dare: Unleashing Astonishing Potential Through Secure Base Leadership* by George Kohlrieser

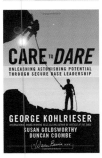

A world class former hostage negotiator, George teaches at IMD and leads the #1 leadership workshop in the world — attend if you can! In the end, leadership is about caring for your people. If they feel cared for, then they will care for your customers, your company, and you!

*Bringing Out the Best in People: How to Apply the Astonishing Power of Positive Reinforcement* by Aubrey Daniels

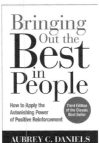

The top human behaviorist in the world and an adjunct professor at Harvard University, Aubrey explains why children and team members act up, despite our best efforts at reinforcing the right behaviors, and what you can specifically do to change their actions in a positive way.

*Influence: The Psychology of Persuasion* by Robert Cialdini

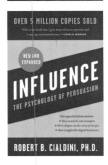

Unarguably, the #1 talent needed to scale is the ability to influence –the market, investors, employees, etc. Considered the "godfather" of influence, Bob details the seven ways, ethically, you can influence individuals and the masses. After Influence, read his book Pre-suasion to learn what to do before attempting to influence someone to set yourself up for success.

## Strategy

*Uncommon Service: How to Win by Putting Customers at the Core of Your Business* by Frances Frei

A leading Harvard strategy professor, Frances has written a book that is less about customer service and more about tradeoffs and the willingness to "piss off" (her words) 93% of the market so you can create raving fans for the 7% of the market that has all the cash (my words)! Trying to be everything to everybody is the quickest way to becoming a commodity. Avoid it at all costs.

*Hidden Champions of the Twenty-First Century: The Success Strategies of Unknown World Market Leaders* by Hermann Simon

Dubbed the Peter Drucker of Europe, Hermann is the only person to have thoroughly researched the mere mortals of the business world — privately held, family-owned businesses. He details the 7 keys to dominating global niches, generating insane gross and net profits. Hint: look for his SlideShare PPT — 73 slides of brilliance.

## Cash

*The Customer-Funded Business: Start, Finance, or Grow Your Company with Your Customers' Cash* by John Mullins

Serial entrepreneur turned top London Business School professor, John is the only guy who has written on this important topic. The cheapest cash you can obtain is from customers!! Get the cash flow part of your business model correct (Michael Dell finally did) and you'll age slower and sleep better!!

*Confessions of the Pricing Man: How Price Affects Everything* by Hermann Simon

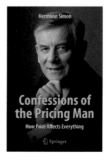

Yes, it's Hermann again and the reason I'm such a fan and proud to call him a dear friend and mentor. The #1 lever on our Power of One one-page Growth Tool is "price," yet leadership teams spend woefully too little time on their pricing strategy. And because we're selling to people, who are not logical but psychological, re-study Influence in combination with this book, get pricing right, and watch top and bottom-lines (and cash!) increase by hundreds of percent.

## 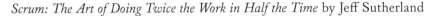 Execution

*Great by Choice: Uncertainty, Chaos and Luck — Why Some Thrive Despite Them All*
by Jim Collins

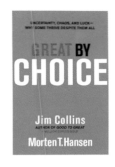

This is Jim's absolute best book and should be more popular among scaleups because it's the one where he details how to go from startup to greatness. Start with his chapter on Return on Luck (ROL) — and then read the rest of this insightful book and spend time on his informative website www.jimcollins.com. It's full of short videos you won't want to miss, including one detailing ROL. Then grab a copy of his quick read Turning the Flywheel to put what you learned into action.

*Scrum: The Art of Doing Twice the Work in Half the Time* by Jeff Sutherland

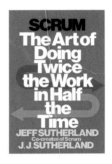

You don't have to read this book — written by the co-founder of Scrum — as much as stare at the cover for the rest of your business life! There really is this much slop inside scaleups — and like hallway closets and garages, it's better to do some spring cleaning than build bigger ones. The key metric is gross margin dollars per employee — drive hard on this number!

## 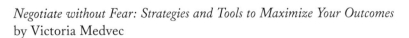 Personal

*What's in It for Them?: 9 Genius Networking Principles to Get What You Want by Helping Others Get What They Want* by Joe Polish

This quintessential networker has written the modern-day version of the 1936 classic How to Win Friends and Influence People. As Joe notes in the beginning "The secret to success in life and in business is learn¬ing how to connect and form relationships with other people — and most people don't know how to do that." This book details how and emphasizes you must give value in the relationship first with no expectation of return.

*Negotiate without Fear: Strategies and Tools to Maximize Your Outcomes*
by Victoria Medvec

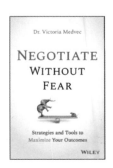

Most negotiating techniques work best when you never have to see the other party again. But playing hardball can backfire when you're negotiating with people you hope to have a long-term relationship with: customers, suppliers, key staff and investors, to name a few. Victoria, a professor at Northwestern University's Kellogg School of Management, will show you how to maximize your outcomes while strengthening relationships. I've made and saved more money from Victoria's advice than any other thought leader. Now you can do the same.